Hillary's Turn

Inside Her Improbable, Victorious Senate Campaign

MICHAEL TOMASKY

THE FREE PRESS
NEW YORK   LONDON   TORONTO   SYDNEY   SINGAPORE

*f*P

THE FREE PRESS
A Division of Simon & Schuster Inc.
1230 Avenue of the Americas
New York, NY 10020

Copyright © 2001 by Michael Tomasky
All rights reserved,
including the right of reproduction
in whole or in part in any form.
THE FREE PRESS and colophon are trademarks
of Simon & Schuster Inc.
Manufactured in the United States of America

10   9   8   7   6   5   4   3   2   1

Library of Congress Cataloging-in-Publication Data Is Available

ISBN: 0-684-87302-8

For Sarah

Contents

Hillary's Turn

Prologue:
The Do-Gooder

I HADN'T TOLD MANY of my colleagues at the magazine that Hillary Clinton would be stopping by for an interview on the afternoon of Friday, March 2, 2000. I wanted to keep the circus to a minimum. But we don't get many Secret Service men coming around, so the one who appeared about two hours before her arrival gave away the game. He was—quite unlike those taciturn, reflector-shaded robots in the movies—easygoing and polite as he asked to trace her expected route from the elevator, down the hallway, and into the room where the interview would take place. He wanted to know where the doors in that room led. With special care, and in a discreetly lowered voice, he asked about the location of the nearest ladies' room, and wanted to know how many female employees had access to it (the answer, for that afternoon, was none).

Suffice it to say that word got out. By the time she arrived, small groups were huddled here and there, people waving tentative and nervous hellos (arms in tight to the chests, shoulders hunched, fingers wagging), or just gawking, not sure what to do in that blurry half-second when you first behold in the flesh someone you've seen eighteen thousand times on television.

Hillary, at this point, had eight months' experience on the New York campaign trail. She'd had a disastrous autumn with one mistake after another, a not-so-great winter, and, finally, a moderately improved spring. Through it all she'd managed to stay close to Mayor Rudy Giuliani in the polls. And, through it all, she'd rolled out positions and made speeches and taken reporters' questions—always two or three fewer than it felt like she should have taken—at hasty press availabilities. "I may be new to the neighborhood," she'd say, which was as close as she could bring herself to acknowledging the issue that maddened even many of her supporters, "but I'm not new to New Yorkers' concerns." She had gone through the motions of being a candidate, but she'd never said a single illuminating thing. Now, finally, she was sitting for a small number of one-on-one interviews.

Her unflappable press secretary, Howard Wolfson, and I had set the date about three weeks before. In February she had already sat down with the chief political reporters at four or five of the state's major dailies, and the results, through no fault of the reporters, had been less than enlightening. A wise friend who had done one of those interviews warned me off asking any policy questions. "It's death," he told me; she'll answer for twenty minutes, it'll be dry as dust, and you'll be sitting there sweating out every minute and looking at your watch. I wasn't very interested in hearing her talk about Medicare reimbursements anyway. She had done plenty of that already. And I wasn't all that curious about the White House travel office or the billing records or her feelings about Monica. I knew—from talking to her aides, and from watching how she'd dealt with such questions along the trail—that she would assert she'd complied with the law, offer up some quick boilerplate about how that was the past and she was certain that people were really more interested in the future, and stare at me as if to say, "Next."

She'd talked about issues. She'd explained, in her rigid and vague way, why she was running in New York. And, while she was hardly anxious to speak about the scandals, she had come to accept that she had to endure inquiry about them. What she had never, ever talked about was herself. Which, I decided, was the only thing I was really curious about: Just who *was* this woman?

She arrived a little before three o'clock, wearing the black pantsuit that was her city uniform (upstate, she tended toward pastels). People who enter rooms with retinues understand that all heads will turn their way when they arrive, and Hillary knew how to walk into a room and take charge, leaving no risk of awkward silences. She knew how to shake hands firmly, make eye contact, and lead the six seconds' worth of small talk that would help untie the tongue of whomever she was meeting. After she shook a few hands, she and Wolfson and I retreated to the conference room and got down to business.

I wanted to know if she had any interests in life outside politics and policy. She skipped a beat, surprised. Sure, she said, and, with more spontaneity than she'd ever shown on the stump, went off on a random and cheerful string of associations. For starters, she had a thing for archaeology and ancient civilizations. She said a high point of her time in the White House had been walking the Olduvai Gorge in Africa, where the Leakeys had made their discoveries, and talking with palaeoanthropologists and archaeologists about "the transition to *Homo sapiens* and then to man." She spent nearly three minutes recalling a visit to Australia, where an aboriginal guide told her that boiling the bark of a certain tree cured gangrene. "Think how many generations it took," she said, "to figure out what you boiled and put in the sun to cure a dread disease." She tossed in the Peloponnesian Wars and Pericles's funeral oration. She fast-forwarded to modern art, speaking of her delight in adding an O'Keeffe to the White House collection.

By the time she got around to mentioning Dostoyevsky and Hardy, I was thinking: Is this a put-on? How can it be that I've read thousands of words about this woman and didn't know any of this? Is she just trying to sound well-rounded and, for my magazine's demographic, arty? I've asked many politicians such questions, and if they didn't come up totally blank, as they often did, they stuck to the safe and unassailable ground of Shakespeare or Churchill's history of World War II. One might have expected Hillary—given the particular voting bloc that New York candidates feel obliged to woo above all others—to expound on a not-previously-voiced fondness for Philip Roth or Marc Chagall or the folk tales of Sholom Aleichem. The political utility of archaeology, by contrast, was slim indeed.

This was more interesting than her rehearsed monologues about saving Social Security. Having heard about her refined interests, I became curious about her guilty pleasures. A truly well-rounded person, after all, has room for bad taste, too. I acknowledged a weakness for *The Flintstones.* This elicited from her a long story about her father hating *The Flintstones* theme song; and about how, when Hugh Rodham was in a coma and near death, she and her brothers gathered around him in the intensive-care unit and sang it in one last vain attempt to get a rise out of him. After that she rhapsodized about the Three Stooges, at one point leaning close to me and, with a clearly practiced expertise, snapping her fingers and rapping her knuckles in my face, exactly as Curly does to Moe. Wolfson's face turned red and his jaw hit the table. To tether the enterprise to earth, I did ask about her failed health-care reform and why that episode should recommend her to us as a legislator, how she expected to get anything done in a Senate run by Trent Lott, why she was so cautious with every syllable she uttered on the stump, and a few other questions from the usual menu. On cue, she immediately reverted to dull mode.

I knew many people would find my questions odd and beside the point, or judge the interview soft. But I was fascinated. Not because she was so fascinating; rather, I was fascinated by the very fact of her normalness. Here before me was the most polarizing woman in America. That title had been bestowed on her in some respects unfairly, by a howling opposition that saw evil in everything she did. On the other hand, she had certainly done her part to earn the designation. Yet what struck me most from our eighty minutes together was how regular she was. She wasn't enigmatic or brittle; she had enthusiasms and a playful side.

But who thinks of Hillary Clinton as enthusing about boiled bark and Moe Howard? No one. It was information that fit with nothing known about her. And it shed light on her basic problem in this election. As she said her goodbyes and headed down the elevator, I thought: She has seven months to go until election day. The question of whether she can win will hinge not merely on how well she learns the state or talks about the issues. It will depend, also, on whether she can defeat people's fiercely held preconceptions and compel them to think of her in a new and more complex way. Most candidates don't have to demonstrate to people that they're human beings. But most candidates aren't Hillary.

Hillary Clinton has existed primarily as a symbol, both to those who admire her and to those who detest her. She was either a role model for a new kind of first lady and a touchstone for feminism's triumph, or she was an unreconstructed flower child and a threat to the social order.

The warring interpretations of her have been described and debated in various biographies and countless magazine articles, and on even more countless televised screaming matches. There is no need to restate those well-worn arguments in detail here. But there are two points worth making about those arguments, points that bear more directly on the subject matter of this book, which is her journey from cosseted first lady to flesh-and-bone candidate for office. The first is that she has been misinterpreted ideologically; the second, that she has been mis-characterized personally.

With respect to ideology, both those who praise her and those who damn her see her entirely through the mist of the 1960s. It's un-derstandable that people came to analyze her in that context; she is, after all, a daughter of that decade. The biographical details that are now so familiar—the story of her famous Wellesley graduation speech, when she tore up her script, upbraided the commencement speaker, Massachusetts Senator Edward Brooke, and announced her genera-tion's search for "more immediate, ecstatic, and penetrating modes of living"—give us someone who was very much a part of the liberal-left movement of students who wanted to change society in fundamental ways. And all the arguments about her have been, in some sense, an ar-gument about that decade's legacy. It is a legacy we've been debating through almost every cultural and political venue that exists in this country since the decade ended. When Bill and Hillary moved into the White House, the debate grew even more frantic. Liberal Baby Boomers—though not genuinely radical ones, who saw the Clintons as having sold out the values of the 1960s on their march to power—saw Bill's victory as their own, a validation of their mores. Conserva-tives saw his victory as a descent into turpitude, and as something of a cheat, since he won with less than 50 percent of the vote. To them, it was a victory without honor, just the sort you'd expect out of the gen-eration of spoiled kids who cost us Vietnam. Arguments over the Clin-tons may nominally have been "about" whether Hillary lied about her work on Whitewater, or Bill had sexual relations with "that woman." But at bottom, they were all about the 1960s, and the rise to power of the first Baby Boomer president and his bossy "co-president" wife.

Hillary does come from the 1960s. But the arguments over Hillary-as-sixties-avatar aren't quite right. Certainly the Hillary Clin-ton who spent sixteen months campaigning across New York was scarcely the gladiatorial tigress of her reputation. Nor was she some throwback liberal. She was an extremely—at times, maddeningly—cautious candidate who spent her time talking about things like utility rates and upstate technology corridors. She stuck to these issues in part as a matter of strategy—to soften her sharp edges and base this improbable campaign of hers on safe and uncontroversial issues. But over time it became evident to all but the most cynical that she actually cared about utility rates. If this was 1960s radicalism, it was awfully well disguised.

By temperament, she seems to belong not to the 1960s but to another American political tradition: that of the nineteenth-century woman's-movement reformer. To read about the great women leaders of the nineteenth century, like Susan B. Anthony and Elizabeth Cady Stanton and Julia Ward Howe and Lucy Stone and Frances Willard, is to trip constantly across the many striking similarities between many of those women and Hillary Clinton. A good number of them were Midwestern, or from the western parts of upstate New York, which, culturally, amounts to pretty much the same thing. They were deeply religious for the most part, and their reform impulses were rooted firmly in Scripture. They were courageous personally, but often cautious and pragmatic politically. They believed fervently in the righteousness of their cause. It was the cause that was important, not the individual. Individuals were merely vessels for enlightenment and for God's will. All this should sound familiar to the close Hillary watcher.

Frances Willard, especially, is Hillary's antetype. Willard was born outside Rochester, New York, in 1839, but she spent her formative adult years in Evanston, Illinois—a stone's throw from Hillary's hometown of Park Ridge. Her parents were nearly perfect matches for Hillary's—her father a starchy and disapproving conservative, her mother, quietly more liberal. Like Hillary, Willard was a devout Methodist. She was the first president of Northwestern Ladies' College, later merged into Northwestern University, but she left pedagogy and, in 1877, attached herself to the woman's movement, becoming the president of the Woman's Christian Temperance Union. Willard was not a firebrand. Rather, in the words of her biographer Ruth Bordin, she consistently "used conservative values to promote radical ends."

Temperance, in the 1870s, meant banning alcohol, but it meant doing so for a specific political purpose: to give women more power in the home. Temperance activists believed in suffrage, partly for its own sake but, more important, because if women had the franchise, more dry candidates would win office, the cause of temperance would be advanced (there were *lots* of drunken husbands in America in the nineteenth century), and women would have greater control over their destinies. When Willard started her temperance proselytizing in 1873, the title of her lecture was "Everybody's War." She decided that came across as rather threatening and harsh—like the Washington Hillary who came on like gangbusters in 1993?—and changed the title to "Home Protection." Thus did a conservative-sounding catchphrase become the rallying cry for a progressive goal. Very much like the way "children and families" is the rhetorical basis of Hillary's arguments for expanding the federal government's role in health care and education.

That's what Hillary Clinton most profoundly is: the "home protection" neo-progressive. She embraced many aspects of the 1960s revolution, but she was never a radical. The Wellesley speech won her national attention as a student leader, but compared to the other rhetoric that was flying around America's elite campuses at the time, hers was fairly tame, emphasizing more the awakening of individual human potential than any collective blows to be struck against the power structure. Home from college during the summer of 1968, she and a girlfriend watched the Chicago police have at the student demonstrators during the Democratic Convention; she did not feel moved to participate. She admired the radical Chicago organizer Saul Alinksy, but she broke with Alinsky during law school, spurning a job offer and making it clear to Alinsky that she expected to be, not fight, the power.

She is, instead, a do-gooder, in the style fashioned by nineteenth-century Midwestern women. The religio-reformist tradition of women like Stone and Willard has deep roots in Hillary's native Midwest that those of us on the noisier coasts often don't care to understand. But that is exactly the tradition she comes from. These were strong-willed, smart, and not overtly sexual women. (Victoria Woodhull, a Willard contemporary who advocated free love and wanted to outlaw marriage was more sexually aggressive, and, perhaps not surprisingly, she was a New Yorker.) Women whom men tended to regard as unapproachable and a little scary. Male dread of these women sprang up in the culture in ways large and small, from the intense opposition the suffrage movement faced from men to even the *New Yorker* cartoons of Midwesterner James Thurber, whose hefty and hectoring housewives always seemed to be lunging across the furniture toward their backpedaling husbands. That male dread came to new life when our contemporary women's movement started, and, with respect to Hillary—actually, with respect to many powerful women—it exists today.

This fear of women like Hillary is not merely ideological. It is psychological and emotional and, sometimes, personal. Such intensity of feeling can make for some pretty wanton attacks; and wanton attacks, in turn, can make for wanton defenses. And so Hillary Clinton has not only been misjudged on ideological terms, but she has also been mischaracterized on personal ones, with both her friends and foes ascribing to her traits she just doesn't possess.

Her admirers see her as their courageous field general in the values war. Her detractors see in her a madly ambitious woman who lusts for personal power. The Hillary Clinton who campaigned in New York was neither of those things. In the sense that leading an army requires exhibiting the personal qualities that people should emulate and admire, Hillary showed little desire to put herself forward as anybody's field general. In the entire campaign, she had exactly one truly inspiring moment, at a black church in Harlem in March, and one runner-up, right when she needed it the most, the weekend before the election. The rest of the time, she stuck cautiously and relentlessly to a carefully selected set of middle-class issues. This was the chosen strategy of her chief advisers because it polled well for her; as we shall see, there were, throughout the spring and into the summer, intense fights within her campaign over the question of whether she should stay with this approach or try to open up about herself and deal with some voters' negative emotional reactions to her. She ended up trying to ignore the latter, partly on the advice of her experts. But mostly she stuck with this approach because it was her nature. She never asked anyone to vote for her because of her smile. To Hillary, your smile and your personality and whether people really liked you were beside the point. They were distractions. "You make a mistake," she told me in that interview, "if you let any campaign become about you." Campaigns were about issues, period.

And with regard to ambition, Hillary was ambitious, all right, but not in quite the way her conservative critics say. To be sure she was not afraid to seek power, a trait that many men and not a few women found it impossible to come to terms with. But she was ambitious in the way that do-gooders are—for her cause, for her vision of the just society and how to get there. This is not as benign as it sounds at first blush. Reformers like Hillary tend to see the world in stark good-and-evil terms. They are often capable of accomplishing much good. Often they're equally capable of imputing evil to all who disagree with them. Her well-known suspicion of the press and her political enemies may or may not have been grounded in the fact that she had horrible secrets to hide. More likely, she couldn't comprehend how her opponents could fail to recognize that she was trying to make the world a better place, and she saw their criticisms as declarations of war that had to be answered in kind. Ken Starr wants documents? Stonewall him. Republicans want to change the health-care bill? Steamroll them.

Perhaps she learned from those episodes, because the woman who campaigned in New York was, day after day, nothing so much as a reformer, unveiling the latest iteration of the improvement crusade she had waged since college. She had not, by all accounts, taken the proposition of running in New York seriously when it was first broached to her. But the more she thought about serving in the Senate, the more she liked the idea. She wanted to run for the Senate, people close to her told me, for an almost naive reason: she concluded, surveying her post-White House options, that she could do more to advance the causes she believed in as a senator than as a lecturer or as the head of a foundation.

Of course, to *be* in the Senate, you have to get there first. And winning elections is a talent reformers don't often possess. So it shouldn't have been surprising that, for several months, she was a lousy candidate. Republicans hated her, of course, and Democrats, surveying her comedy of errors, began to wonder just what they'd gotten themselves into. Women, who had rallied to her when she was a cuckolded spouse, now saw her as someone who was, in the name of gender solidarity, asking altogether too much of them. Jewish voters soured on her. The number of liberals who spent months saying things like "I could *never* vote for her" was, from her perspective, dangerously high.

Each group had reasons for its skepticism, but in the end the skepticism came down to the fact that even people who wanted to like her could not, after all these years and all that exposure, define her; she wouldn't let them *know* her in the way people want to know politicians. That opacity, combined with her exalted position in the world, produced the most fantastic arguments and discussions. Manhattan women spent $165 an hour talking to their therapists about her. Judith Shulevitz, writing in *The New York Times Magazine* two months before the election, reported that she found herself arguing with a friend over which of two female characters in Henry James's *Portrait of a Lady* Hillary more closely resembled. "Can anyone imagine," Shulevitz asked, "Rick Lazio inspiring that kind of debate?" (I see certain parallels with Dorothea Brooke in George Eliot's *Middlemarch*. Miss Brooke married a shriveled up old prune of a scholar—hardly Bill Clinton. But she was a woman—"very naive with all her alleged cleverness"—who did not fear invading "the provinces of masculine knowledge" and who even, uncannily, immersed herself in health-care reform.) These kinds of discussions and reflections were made possible because from the moment she became a public person, Hillary had been so reluctant to fill in the blank spaces of her life that people filled them in for her, according to the few clues she dropped along the path, and according to their own ideals and neuroses.

In short, she was not a politician. Successful politicians emote. Successful politicians never let themselves get too attached to one view of the world. They certainly don't concern themselves with a bunch of folderol about good and evil. And the very best politicians are roaring egomaniacs. They think far more about themselves than they do about the world. Last summer, while Hillary was stuck at 45 percent in the polls and still struggling to overcome New Yorkers' resistance to her candidacy, I got a book in the mail, *To the Best of My Ability,* a collection of essays about the presidents edited by the historian James M. McPherson. *Newsweek*'s Evan Thomas wrote the Bill Clinton entry, and in his first sentence, he attributed to Bill the following qualities, which made Clinton "a natural-born politician": he was "warm, physical, commanding, exuberant, soulful, tirelessly empathetic." Hillary is none of those things. She has many positive qualities: in addition to her genuine passion for the ideals she believes in, she is intelligent and studious, actively considerate of those who work for her, tough as reinforced steel, and has a will to succeed that is the strongest I've ever seen up close in an aspirant for office. But she was not born a pol.

It was hard to imagine, given all the above, why she wanted to do this—why she wanted to join a club whose leadership seemed to hate her, where she would probably find herself in the minority, and where the majority would be in no mood to alter the world according to her designs. It was hard to imagine why she'd want to become someone who had to engage in the sort of back-slapping bonhomie with the enemy that senators must—not to mention why she'd want to spend her weekends flying to town-hall meetings in remote Adirondack villages. And it was harder still to imagine why she wanted to come to New York, of all places, to earn the right to go back to Washington.

People have always come to New York either to lose themselves or to find themselves. To lose themselves in the place's endless, and comforting, anonymity. Or to announce their potential to the world on its most conspicuous, and treacherous, stage. Hillary had been on such a stage in Washington, of course, but only as a supporting player. First ladydom encases its occupant in a protective carapace; for all the passions she stirred in people as first lady, the office, if we are to call it an office, is still something of a dollhouse, within whose state dinners and ceremonial functions she could always linger during the difficult stretches.

New York is the world's biggest anti-dollhouse. It's a vast screwball comedy of a place. The city is at war with the suburbs, which are at war with the countryside, which is at war with the city. Its various corners are as remote from one another, psychologically and physically, as they could possibly be. (More miles separate New York City from Buffalo than from Virginia Beach.) The whites and blacks and Italians and Irish and Jews and Puerto Ricans and Caribbeans and Arabs all have their piece to say. Newspaper headlines come barreling at you in print larger than the top line of an eye chart. The political alliances and fallings-out, and the grudges nursed, are not easily learned by the newcomer, even one who grew up watching the gears grind in Cook County.

It's not an environment that has much patience with its politicians, or anyone else, standing on ceremony. A New York candidate has to talk about a thousand things—race relations, the police, Israel, the papacy, gay rights, Northern Ireland, milk prices, Mohawk land claims, lyrics to Billy Joel songs, the design of bridges to Canada, et cetera—and talk about them confidently and knowledgeably. A candidate in New York will be seen and touched and felt by millions of people; she will be accosted by strangers, confronted by critics, booed in parades, catcalled at rallies, bloodied in the papers, hammered at by people she didn't even know existed, and, in Mrs. Clinton's case, greeted with "Go Home!" signs and small but hostile bands of protesters everywhere she went. Say this for Hillary, and it's no small thing: almost anything else she might have done with her life would have been easier.

Another thing about New York: though still more Democratic than the country at large, it's hardly the liberal playground of its national reputation. Like an ancient wall that collapses with the removal of one or two bricks, the liberalism that held sway in New York for decades crumbled with the back-to-back elections, in 1993 and 1994, of the two Republican chief executives, Mayor Giuliani and Governor George Pataki. This decline and fall is a useful context in which to ponder just what Mrs. Clinton got herself into with this race. While it's true that New York is one of the few states that would have welcomed this outsider, things had changed enough in New York during the last decade that a Democrat seeking statewide office could not win using the playbook of elections past.

They are weird things, these New York elections. Hillary wanted to debate issues, but precious little coverage of New York elections is devoted to issues. New York elections are obstacle courses. A candidate who hopes to win a high-profile election in New York has to be acceptable on the issues, but mostly, that candidate has to jump and crawl and tunnel and rope-climb her way through the course's various elements and come out looking a little less roughed up than the other guy. The elements of the course will have distinct characters and test different talents. They will come at the candidate suddenly and unexpectedly, and she will have to make a snap decision, and the decision will be interpreted and reinterpreted and made to stand as the proof of her poise or ineptitude.

The candidate never knows when those moments of decision will come. Could Rudy Giuliani have known that a gossip columnist would walk in on a dinner he was having with his "very good friend"? Should Rick Lazio have remembered that the White House might be sitting on that picture of him glad-handing Yasir Arafat? Could Hillary have anticipated that Suha Arafat was going to give a speech about the Israelis poisoning Palestinian children? (The Arafats loomed large in this race, as one might have predicted; one could not, however, have foretold that E. B. White would have his day, too.) A dinner with a girl-friend, a handshake, a kiss, a too-aggressive march across a stage to the other candidate's podium. These are the questions on which New York elections turn.

But let's not carry New York exceptionalism too far, as New Yorkers are wont to do. Those character-defining moments shape all elections to one extent or another (Al Gore's heavy, condescending sighs during the first debate, for example). This race's dramatic moments were, to be sure, New York-centric. But the fact that these moments attract so much attention reflects the overheated media atmosphere of our age. With the media so pervasive and cacophonous, any high-profile campaign has to consider virtually every word or image it sends out against the possibility that it can be misinterpreted. This was more true of Hillary's campaign than most, as closely covered as it was for such a long period of time. More column inches in the New York papers were devoted to analyzing her *posters* than were devoted to covering most of the state's congressional races. That's how it goes; she knew all this, or should have, going in. But it only served to make her even more cautious. She avoided the cable talk shows. When she at last appeared on two morning shows in the campaign's final week, she didn't even *pretend* to answer the questions put to her. And that face! Once in a while, her features would jump to life. But a lot of the time, on television especially, her face was so fixed in an emotion-less glower that she looked like some wax figure of herself. She gave the media less access and satisfaction than any candidate I've ever seen, and the story of her candidacy is in no small part the story of that constant and at times all-consuming conflict.

As we know, she overcame these hurdles. She persuaded people, at least 55 percent of them, to see her anew. In a year in which the contentious presidential election was decided in December by a few hundred votes, that was no small achievement. And she became a pol—not a great one, but enough of one. This happened on the morning of Sunday, October 8, at her second debate with Rick Lazio, when she was so fluent and casually effective that her bearing virtually sang: "I'm comfortable doing this now." She had transformed herself.

What she gained and lost in the transformation can't yet be measured. Candidate Hillary was, or tried to be, quite unlike the Hillary

Clinton she had put forward to the world previously. As a young woman, blazing her trails at Wellesley and at Yale Law, Hillary was fond of saying that she liked to define politics as "the art making the impossible possible." She said this occasionally on the stump in New York. But she said it with decreasing frequency as the campaign wore on, until eventually it disappeared from her speechifying altogether—the utopian language of the reformer edited out in favor of the more earthbound rhetoric of the vote-seeker.

If that sounds unspectacular, well, it often was. But her campaign met with pretty spectacular results. No one, not even her own pollster, expected her to win by the margin she did. So something interesting must have happened along the way. True, the other team lost its starting quarterback about midway through the second quarter, and the backup quarterback wasn't up to the job. Those facts didn't hurt her chances. But it wasn't only that the other side lost the election. She won it, and she won it precisely because she ignored all the craziness— the media carnival and the Hillary-haters and all the rest—and presented herself to voters, especially in upstate New York, as their earnest problem solver who had traded in her once-grand crusades for more modest, and, as far as the voters were concerned, more useful ones. That is not the Hillary Clinton of her reputation. Whether it's the real Hillary Clinton still remains to be seen. But it is the Hillary around whom New York voters rallied. In late 1999, she had been distrusted even on the Upper West Side—Ground Zero of New York liberalism. A year later, at an appearance on West End Avenue just four days before the election, she received an ovation so warm and sustained that it surprised even her. A transformation had taken place.

This book is about that transformation, but it's also about the turbulent big city, the placid state with which it coexists so strangely, and the singular characters who populate both. It is only here that this preposterous, true drama could have unfolded.

CHAPTER 1

The Set-Up

"If You Don't Want to Do This, Don't Mouse Around With It!"

THE LIFE SPAN of political events is governed by the public's ability to remain amused. And as 1999 dawned the great amusement of 1998, the Monica Lewinsky affair, was looking shopworn. The House of Representatives, before the holidays, had voted four articles of impeachment against President Bill Clinton. Now the matter was moving to trial in the senate. It was meant to be, and sometimes was, a sad and sobering episode for the American people. But America was less than transfixed. The upcoming Senate trial was purely academic, and the possibility that two-thirds of the senators would vote to remove Clinton from office merely theoretical.

But of course it was *the story,* and Washington had invested quite a lot in making it that. So impeachment was the main topic of discussion on the chat shows on Sunday, January 3. On *Meet the Press,* Tim Russert gathered six senators to mount their partisan horses. But perhaps the showman in Russert understood that a new amusement was needed, so, after he dispensed with that subject, he threw a little curve ball. He brought out Gail Sheehy and David Maraniss, two of the punditocracy's inveterate Clinton watchers, to consider the future of

Hillary Clinton. At the time, Hillary was the object of considerable sympathy for the dignified way in which she had carried herself through a most undignified season. Her decision to stay with and defend her husband was by no means universally admired, and it would face harsh reinterpretation in the coming months; but in January 1999 the dissenters were relatively few, and the revisionism distant. For now, she was enjoying something of a cultural apotheosis. She, perhaps alone among all the impeachment saga's dramatis personae, was emerging with her reputation not only intact, but enhanced. The press was full of speculation about what Hillary would do next. A couple of minutes into the segment, Russert hit his guests with this:

> Here's a little mini-bombshell. Senator Robert Torricelli of New Jersey, who heads the Democratic Senate Campaign Committee, told me before the program that if he had to guess, he believes that Hillary Rodham Clinton will run for the United States Senate seat from New York being opened by the retirement of Daniel Patrick Moynihan, which means Mrs. Clinton would have to establish residency in New York before the end of the president's term. Gail Sheehy, would that surprise you?

It would not surprise her at all, Sheehy averred; Maraniss agreed. Hillary, Sheehy said, "is determined to shape her own identity" like her hero Eleanor Roosevelt. The conversation explored the unprecedented nature of such a run—that if she did this, she would be seeking office while her husband was still president. The segment ended, and the show came back from break with the usual flashback, often a clip of the show's former host, Lawrence Spivak, with Henry Cabot Lodge or some other golden oldie. With impeachment in the air, one might have put money on Peter Rodino or Sam Ervin. But on this day, *Meet the Press* obliged Sheehy's comparison by showing a clip it had readied of Mrs. Roosevelt from 1956. It was almost a public-relations segment. It was certainly a new amusement.

Like a few million of her fellow Americans, Hillary Clinton watched *Meet the Press* that Sunday. So did Harold Ickes. A political operative with some thirty years' history in New York politics, Ickes had a reputation as America's toughest liberal. He had known the Clintons intimately since the early 1970s, back when he was the boyfriend of Hillary's close friend Susan Thomases. He was the one who had introduced Bill and Hillary around New York's liberal circles in preparation for Bill's first presidential run. He had stage-managed the 1992 convention at Madison Square Garden, making sure it was a tightly organized (words that did not normally describe Democratic conventions) Clinton lovefest. When various partisan fires—Whitewater, Travelgate—started crackling during Clinton's first term, the president brought Ickes in as the deputy chief of staff to tamp them down. He became, inevitably, a focus of controversy himself—a kind of surrogate to the Republicans in Congress for the president they could never quite catch. The reward for his efforts was to be cast out of the White House by Bill rather summarily after the 1996 election; the president passed him over for chief of staff—without mustering the nerve to tell him directly—and chose Erskine Bowles. Ickes managed to keep his real feelings to himself and his relationship with Hillary, at least, intact.

When his telephone rang that Sunday morning in January 1999, he picked it up and heard Hillary Clinton's voice on the other end. "Well, did you see that?" she asked. He had. She wondered what he thought. He assumed she'd found it entertaining and flattering, but little more. "Well, Hillary," he told her, "if you don't want to do this, don't mouse around with it. Issue a Shermanesque statement, and that'll be the end of it." But he heard something from the other end of the phone that he hadn't expected. "She said," he told me later, " 'Well . . . that's not where I am with this.' "

Ickes was taken aback. Was she really considering doing this? Okay, then. Immediately, he started thinking it through a little more seriously. And, immediately, his mind raced to the hurdles. A sitting first lady, running for office while her husband was still president. In a state where she'd never lived. How could she establish credibility in New York and learn the ins and outs of so large and diverse a state in less than two years' time? Still, he was intrigued. She was his old and close friend, after all. And New York was his state. And the two of them had just watched three card-carrying members of the chattering classes refrain from laughing the notion out of the park and in fact give it their tacit stamp of approval. Furthermore, there was one historical irony in particular that helped him warm to the idea. His father, Harold Ickes, Sr., FDR's great Interior Secretary, had tried to persuade Mrs. Roosevelt to run for the Senate in New York in 1946. Eleanor had demurred. But maybe it was up to him, and Hillary, to pick up the ball where his father and her heroine had laid it down. He decided, for now, to let her lead the dance, and he said nothing either to encourage or discourage her.

It had not been Hillary's idea, this strange notion. It had emanated from New York State Democratic leaders. Months on, even as the election approached in November 2000, one would hear voters complain, in effect, "Who does she think she is, barging into our state and demanding this seat like some sort of queen?" But that's not what happened. New York Democrats begged her to run. She seized on the opportunity. But she did not choose New York. New York chose her.

Since New York started this, let's consider why New York was interested. Why would the leaders of one of the country's wealthiest and largest state Democratic parties, with roughly five million enrolled members and not a few respectable members of the House of Representatives to choose among, need as their candidate someone who wasn't from their state and didn't share their history? New York Democrats, like all politicians, are concerned in the first place about their own survival. And just lately—no, let's make that for the previous generation or two—things hadn't been going all that swimmingly for New York Democrats. They were inheritors of a proud tradition that, by the 1990s, was a vestige of its old self: The mayoralty of New York City and the governorship of the state had gone to Republicans, and in 1995 the party had been in so much debt that it didn't even have the money to rent an office. The party's leaders needed, or felt they needed, someone with the stature of Hillary Clinton to revivify them. To understand fully where they hoped she would carry them, we should understand something of where they'd been, and where they stood as 1999 opened.

The Collapse of the One-Party State

On a chilly morning in March 1997, New York Democrats gathered at the National Arts Club, a lovely if somewhat baroque mansion facing Manhattan's Gramercy Park. The press had been summoned to watch

David Dinkins, the former mayor, endorse Ruth Messinger, the Manhattan borough president running against incumbent mayor Rudy Giuliani. The event exuded all the confidence of a pep rally at a small college the day before the game against Nebraska.

I looked around at all the familiar faces, arrayed next to one another below the heavy draperies and nineteenth-century oils, that could not bring themselves this day to muster the compulsory cheer common to such occasions. The West Side pols. The lawyers and public-relations people who'd shuffled in and out of various Democratic administrations. And Messinger herself—a politician who had at one time enjoyed near-universal admiration as an intelligent and utterly incorruptible public servant; by 1997 she was a museum piece, running for mayor eight or twelve years past the time when her very liberal politics might have won a mayoral election.

Decent people, one and all. But looking at them that day aroused nothing but intense feelings of depression, even disgust. It struck me that morning with a force that it hadn't quite before: This is the end. These were the people on whose watch New York liberalism had turned into a corpse.

It was once a mighty thing, New York liberalism. It was liberals, of one shade or another, who were in charge as New York grew into the world's greatest city, bursting with industry and creative genius. And their influence echoed far beyond the five boroughs. Such was the prominence of New York, and the vision of its political leadership, that New Yorkers changed the state, the nation, and, at least as far as the Roosevelts were concerned, the world.

New York liberalism provided America's first and best model for an activist government that could address problems, often heroically and ingeniously, and respond to pressing civic needs. It's no mere coincidence that Franklin Roosevelt, who created modern liberalism in America, rose to power with the support of Tammany Hall, the old urban machine that ran the city's political life dating back to the early nineteenth century. What most people know of Tammany Hall today has to do with corruption, patronage, and graft. But Tammany has a more sinister reputation than it deserves. It made generations of immigrants, arriving from places where the right to vote was barely a theory, into functioning citizens. Of course it told these new arrivals exactly *how* to vote, but it also responded to the needs of this constituency it had created. In the 1920s, at the tail end of the great wave of immigration, it finally became a matter of civic agreement that someone ought to educate the children of all these immigrants. That someone was the city, which throughout the decade of the 1920s built a new school building, on average, every three weeks. For ten years running!

Tammany produced or supported most of New York's famous leaders from the early part of the century into the 1960s. Al Smith, the governor in the 1920s and the first Roman Catholic candidate for president. Frances Perkins, the first woman to hold a major cabinet post in America as Franklin Roosevelt's secretary of labor. Roosevelt himself, who succeeded Smith as governor before he became president. Robert Wagner, FDR's contemporary, the New York senator who gave his name to what is still the century's most important piece of pro-labor legislation. Adam Clayton Powell, Jr., an eventual victim of his own hubris and taste for long idylls in Bimini, but before that a key figure in Congress in enacting the civil-rights and voting-rights laws of the 1960s. Bobby Kennedy, who had grown up just north of the city, moved to Massachusetts, returned to New York to become its senator—with the support, though people don't often like to say it these days, of the back-room bosses.

Tammany yielded to Fiorello La Guardia, the mayor during the 1930s. Though a Republican, La Guardia was a liberal and an ardent New Dealer. He oversaw the great transformation of New York—the construction of most of the major bridges and tunnels, the first airport, the expansion of the subway, the vast expansion of the City University system (then tuition-free!), Rockefeller Center, the landmark 1939 World's Fair. Tammany lingered on after La Guardia, and returned to power under the leadership of Carmine DeSapio, the last of the New York bosses. But after World War II, a new political class, more highly educated and assimilated than the immigrants of days past, arose, with demands for a more open and honest government. Thus was born New York's reform movement, which sought to take the party out of the bosses' control—to open up the primary process and let candidates actually contest elections; to improve the quality of the congressional delegation and the bench; to institute civil service. The "reformers" (WASPs and Jews, white-collar, Manhattanites) and the "regulars" (mostly Irish and Italian, blue-collar, from the outer boroughs) fought a civil war that hummed along throughout the 1950s and early 1960s.

Eleanor Roosevelt, by the time of that 1956 *Meet the Press* appearance, had returned to New York and become the movement's figurehead and spiritual leader.

By 1961, the reformers controlled Manhattan, if not the whole city. Patronage was curtailed. And it was the time of civil rights, Vietnam, and the liberalization of abortion and divorce laws. Reformers— who included New Yorkers who went on to national fame, like Bella Abzug, and two young West Siders named Harold Ickes and Dick Morris—brought the party's priorities up to the present, and nationalized, even internationalized, them. (City Council nominations could turn on the question of where the candidates stood on Vietnam.) The reformers helped John Lindsay, a liberal Republican, win reelection as mayor in 1969. But by the 1970s, they began to lose the larger vision of what they were fighting for. They grew more concerned with purity, procedural and ideological. The chief reform Democratic organization, the one that vetted the movement's nominees to go up against the regulars for major offices, was called the New Democratic Coalition; the joke was that N.D.C. really stood for "November Doesn't Count." At the same time, the city was smacked in the face with social maladies that liberalism had neither the ingenuity nor in some cases the desire to cure. There was crime, the drug trade, the welfare explosion. Finally, the fiscal crisis hit: The city went broke, lost its credit rating, and couldn't float bonds. There was no money even to pay teachers, let alone solve erupting social problems. And while New York City may have suffered the most, Buffalo and Rochester and Utica and the other industrial centers of upstate New York were hemorrhaging.

Some things got better through the 1980s and 1990s, some worse. But nothing really *changed,* and the problem was this: New York, throughout the 1970s and the 1980s, was a one-party state. The Democrats. "And in one-party states," as New York labor activist Ed Ott once put it to me, "ideas are seditious." So people quit offering ideas. It was business as usual. The politicians had no incentive to change a thing, because, hey, they were in office, their friends all had jobs, the lobbyists and PR people they knew all had nice contracts, and the lawyers all had good client lists (how like the old bosses they had become!). Each of the new agencies the city invented to address this malady or that may not have been able to solve the problems assigned it, but each developed a clientele, which usually consisted of politicians' friends or friends of friends. Who could change all that, even if they wanted to?

New York liberalism built, furnished, and then finally neglected its home. By 1993, the victories—the completion, in less than two years, of the glorious George Washington Bridge in 1931—were as remote as Washington's triumph at Saratoga. By 1993, in a city whose citizens could once assume that their government would build it or do it and it would be the best, residents knew all too well that if their city did it, chances were it wouldn't work. By 1993, crime—including 1,995 homicides that year—was *the* civic preoccupation, and few had confidence in liberalism to sort it out. By 1993, New Yorkers were ready for change.

A Man Not of His Time

Liberalism's collapse created an opening for someone to come in and throw industrial-strength cleanser over the whole place. It would take a person with a strong will to do it.

It so happened that there was one.

Rudy Giuliani was born in Brooklyn, the only child, improbably enough, of Catholic parents. He went to parochial schools—and as a youngster, in the borough where the fortunes of the Dodgers were followed perhaps less solemnly than the rituals of Easter and Passover but not much else, put on a little Yankees uniform, parading his defiant preference in his playmates' faces. As a grown man, he reflected tellingly on this set-piece, saying, "It made me feel like a martyr."

He was a man not of his time. Like most young Catholic men of his age, he admired John Kennedy—he was sixteen when JFK was running for president—which is the main reason he became, at first, a Democrat. But any taste he might have developed for the new world the 1960s were making stopped there. There exists no account that Dylan or the Beatles or French New Wave cinema or the culture of protest and rebellion ever held the slightest interest for him; in 1960, while a junior in high school, he started an opera club. From all the hundreds of news articles and magazine profiles devoted to explaining him, one gleans that his passions today seem to be exactly what they were when he was fifteen, or even five: The Yankees; the opera; Italian food; martyrdom.

He spent the 1960s at Manhattan College (which is in the Bronx, naturally) and at New York University School of Law. He became an assistant U.S. Attorney in Manhattan, and his role in the successful prosecution of on-the-take cops made him the model for the protagonist of Sidney Lumet's 1981 film *Prince of the City*. His politics changed. McGovernism held no allure for him, so he became first an independent and later a Republican. He went to work in Ronald Reagan's Department of Justice, where he had regular meetings with a colleague named Ken Starr. Then, in 1983, he got the job he'd hungered for, the golden ring of the federal justice system—Reagan named him the United States Attorney for the Southern District of New York.

It was there, of course, that he made his reputation. He won convictions of mobsters and corrupt politicians. Magazines profiled him. Newspaper columnists wrote paeans to him. He luxuriated in praise from conservatives and liberals alike, who saw him as some sort of god, smiting his hammer of righteousness across a benighted landscape. If there were occasional early-warning signs of Giuliani's overzealousness—to nail a judge accused of corrupting the bench, Giuliani had her clinically depressed daughter wear a wire against the judge, her own mother!—they were largely forgiven.

When he left the U.S. Attorney's office in 1989, it was with the express intent of running for mayor. He lost a close and contentious race to David Dinkins, by about 45,000 votes out of around two million cast. Giuliani left that race, people in his circle have told me, persuaded that he would have beaten a white man with Dinkins's record; and that race—that is, black racial solidarity—was an irrational and corrosive force. But the loss also humbled him. He once surprised me over lunch by telling me, in essence: You know, looking back, I don't think I deserved to be mayor in 1989. I really didn't know enough about the city—the budget, the various agencies, and so on. Dinkins actually knew more than I did about these things. And so what I'm doing now is having these weekly meetings with experts on transportation, on health and hospitals. Learning. I'm going to be much better prepared in 1993.

He was, and he ran a much better race. A tough race—he was staunchly pro-cop, and he whacked Dinkins over the 1991 Crown

Heights riots repeatedly. But he was a smarter candidate. And, to his credit, he didn't tailor what he said for this audience or that. His reaction to the politics of racial solidarity came out in the slogan "One City, One Standard." It had its nasty side in its obvious implication that Dinkins favored blacks (or, apropos Crown Heights, that he wouldn't crack down on lawless blacks). But it had its hopeful side, too; our rights, the challenger would repeat, are derived not from the fact that we're black or white or whatever but from the fact that we're human beings, Americans, New Yorkers. This credo gave Giuliani's 1993 campaign a grounding in a political philosophy, something of a rarity in municipal elections.

He won, by 55,000 votes. Over the next four years, he did something few politicians prove themselves capable of doing: He created a realignment.

Consider the results of three mayoral elections from the 67th Assembly District, which takes in parts of Greenwich Village (liberal, gay) and Chelsea (more liberal, gayer), and the heart of the Upper West Side up to 95th Street. In 1989, Dinkins beat Giuliani there, 58 percent to 42 percent. In 1993, Dinkins held on, but with a slimmer margin: 53 percent to 47 percent. Then, finally, in 1997, when Giuliani was running against Ruth Messinger, he carried the 67th with 62 percent of the vote.

Something happened in those three elections that transformed New York—the city, but, because the city is the state's economic and symbolic core, the state as well—more profoundly than anything else that has happened politically in the fifteen years I've lived here. There arose a new breed of voter: Giuliani Democrats. These were not Reagan Democrats. Reagan Democrats were functional Republicans—on race, on cultural questions—who'd never bothered to change their registration, out of laziness or vestigial loyalty to the Kennedys or, in New York City, because of the fact that many elections are decided not in November generals but in Democratic primaries. No, Giuliani Democrats were a new type, theretofore undefined and unnamed, either in New York or for that matter in America.

Giuliani Democrats were liberals. White, mostly Jewish liberals. People who supported abortion rights, gay rights, all the usual liberal causes. People who had never voted Republican before. People who loathed the national Republican Party, Newt Gingrich, Trent Lott, Ken

Starr, the National Rifle Association, and, as a matter of fact, Ronald Reagan. Couldn't stand him. People like the woman *Newsday* found, on Election Day 1993, buying books (what else?) on the Upper West Side, wearing an "I Believe Anita Hill" button, a teacher from a Democratic family who refused to give the paper her name out of shame that she'd voted for Giuliani. "I feel very guilty," she told the paper. "It was a slightly sinking feeling, a little like, 'What have I done?' "

It's not that Giuliani Democrats ever liked Giuliani. They didn't. They felt bad—a little guilty—about the way he treated blacks. But they didn't feel *that* bad. They wanted to feel good again about the city they lived in. They hadn't been able to for years. I remember once, before I moved to New York, watching an episode of *Family Feud*. The civil war in Lebanon was raging at the time. Horror scenes from Beirut were on the news almost nightly, and the place had become a punchline for Carson jokes. Richard Dawson asked his contestants to name a dangerous city to visit. "New York!" the woman barked, and the audience applauded; I knew it at home, too, in Morgantown, West Virginia, and of course it was the number-one answer, with something like seventy-five responses. Beirut was second with, I still remember, fourteen. That was New York.

No more. *Time, Newsweek, U.S. News & World Report* covers all screamed: *New York Is Back!* Streets safe. Hotels booked to capacity (Giuliani cut the hotel tax). Hollywood starting to do location shoots in the city again (Giuliani got tough with the unions). Even changes that had nothing to do with government, like the *Today* show's move to its street-level studio, seemed like bold symbols of Giuliani's triumph—it would have been unthinkable a few years before to show America the sidewalks of New York. Such was the extent of Rudy's realignment that it spread beyond the boundaries of the city itself: to the rest of America, through the media, and, crucially, to the city's suburbs, whose denizens could come in to see a play on a Saturday night and marvel at how clean and decent New York had become.

A Path out of the Darkness After All

Dark days for the New York Democratic Party. Not only did Democrats lose Gracie Mansion in 1993, but the next year saw Mario

Cuomo, the liberal tiger, lose to Republican George Pataki, a state senator from exurban Putnam County, who said only three things: One, he'd lower taxes; two, he'd reinstate the death penalty; and three, whatever he was, one thing he was not was Mario Cuomo.

The night Pataki beat Cuomo was the same night the Republicans regained control of the House of Representatives, picking up a stunning fifty-four seats. I was at the New York Hilton, the scene of Cuomo's election-night shindig. New York being the most intensely parochial city in America, I had trouble finding anyone who shared my passion to find out what had happened in the congressional races. Finally, I saw a member of Congress I knew hanging up a pay phone. What about the Congress, I asked. "Bad." "How bad?" "I hear it could be as high as fifty seats."

The speaker was Brooklyn Congressman Chuck Schumer. No one could know it that night, but four years later it would fall to Chuck Schumer to revitalize the party.

In 1998, Al D'Amato, with eighteen years of history as "Senator Pothole" behind him, was seeking a fourth term. If the movie *The Manchurian Candidate* had been made in, say, 1988, the shady and buffoonish senator who is Angela Lansbury's husband would surely have been based on him. Nevertheless, he was, and is, a total political genius. A survivor. Invariably, three years before reelection, with ethics questions and stories about his brother Armand's law practice swirling around him, his approval rating would be 29 percent. Equally invariably, it would rise, by election time, to 50 percent, because he had done something for Holocaust survivors, or because he had announced his support for some surprising liberal thing, like gay rights (New York is a state where support for gay rights is an electoral plus). Invariably, he would win.

D'Amato could handle pretty much anything. But he was not ready for Chuck Schumer. In 1974, Schumer first won a seat in the New York State Assembly. The most striking memory his former colleagues have of him is this: Albany is three hours from the city—three-and-a-half from southern Brooklyn, where Chuck grew up and which he represented. When the legislature was in session, most members spent the week in Albany and drove back to the city on weekends. Chuck, the better to catch both the legislative sessions during the day and the constituent meetings at night, would sometimes travel back and forth every day.

Along with his nonstop capacity for work, Schumer managed to create, by New York standards, a moderate image for himself. He had a very liberal voting record as a member of Congress, scoring 85 percent or better on the tally sheets prepared by the unions and the abortion-rights groups. He passed the Brady Bill on background checks for gun sales; it simply wouldn't have happened without him. So he'd done enough work on Capitol Hill to get his liberal ticket stamped back home. But he was never part of the New York City liberal establishment. He'd never quite been either reformer or regular. He'd never affiliated himself with David Dinkins, or with the Rainbow Coalition style of politics that Dinkins represented. Some people urged him, privately, to run for mayor against Giuliani in 1997; privately, he told them that, personality aside, the mayor wasn't really doing much wrong. The self-marginalizing decline of New York liberalism, and the rise that this had given to the Giuliani Democrats, was a development Schumer understood keenly, and he wanted no part of it.

In 1998, Schumer decided to challenge D'Amato. That first meant challenging, in the Democratic primary, former representative Geraldine Ferraro and City Public Advocate Mark Green. Ferraro, the Democratic vice-presidential candidate in 1984 and still an icon to many New York women, was the obvious front-runner. In January, when she announced her candidacy, the event was carried live on CNN, and she was miles ahead in the polls. Green, a citywide elected official and a former Nader's Raider, was considered the type of person Democratic primary voters might go for—that is to say, the most liberal of the three. Those February polls had the race roughly: Ferraro 50, Green 25, Schumer 12.

The primary was September 15. The result: Schumer 51 percent, Ferraro 26, Green 19. Ferraro just ran a miserable campaign, and with respect to Green, voters decided that November Did Count after all. But mostly, it was Chuck. He had the money: $13 million, smartly husbanded over years of service on the more remunerative House committees. He had a long record of accomplishments. He was a steamroller.

But there was something else at work, too: New York Democrats were tired of losing. So they put aside some of their doubts—Schumer was for the death penalty, which a majority of Democrats were not—and backed the guy who could win. In fact, Democrats elected the most centrist nominees possible on the whole 1998 slate. It was an admission—finally, at least a decade after liberals elsewhere in America had conceded the point—that liberalism's salad days in New York were over.

On the day that Schumer won the primary, his media consultant, Hank Morris, was already in the studio, cutting commercials against D'Amato that carried the unusually harsh tag line, "Too many lies for too long." D'Amato and his longtime media adviser, Arthur Finkelstein, started with their standard line of attack: "Liberal Chuck Schumer. Wrong on taxes. Wrong on welfare. Wrong on crime. Wrong for us." But he couldn't really nail Schumer as too liberal. D'Amato then thought he'd found gold in the fact that, while campaigning, Schumer had missed 100 votes in Congress. He pounded at it relentlessly, every day. He called Schumer "the Phantom." In a debate held in Schenectady on October 24, he brought every question back to it. Every commercial was based on it. Then, on October 27, Wayne Barrett reported in *The Village Voice* that D'Amato, as presiding supervisor of the Hempstead, Long Island, town meetings when he first ran for the Senate, missed five of six meetings as he campaigned in mid- to late 1980. And, since town boards vote on so many little things, the number of votes D'Amato had missed was nine or ten times the number of votes Schumer had missed. D'Amato's whole line of attack was shut down.

On election day, by five o'clock, insiders knew from exit polls that Schumer had won by around ten points, far more than expected. His office sent out word that he was shaking hands with voters at a subway station at 72nd Street and Broadway—Giuliani Democrat country—so I went to have a look. It was a little surreal—for appearance's sake, he had to urge people to make sure they got to the polls, even though he knew already that he had won handily. Into the bargain, Eliot Spitzer, the centrist Manhattan attorney, had won the attorney general's office, and the Democratic incumbent comptroller, Carl McCall, had won, giving Democrats three of the four major state offices up for grabs that day.

All the victories were significant, Schumer's especially. First, it was something for a Brooklyn Jew to win statewide office. None ever had. Second, there is a generally accepted mathematical formula by which a

New York Democrat can win a statewide election: two-thirds of the city vote, maybe 40 percent in the six counties that constitute the suburbs, and one-third of the vote in the upstate counties. Schumer had met or exceeded those percentages in every category. He even came within a cat's whisker of beating D'Amato in Nassau County, Long Island, which was one of America's most Republican jurisdictions and D'Amato's home base to boot. And third, he won the Giuliani Democrats overwhelmingly. Schumer's attributes—he was aggressively liberal on most of the high-profile issues, but intent on broadening liberalism's appeal in the suburbs and upstate—could form the basis of a new phase of New York liberalism. Maybe there was a path out of the darkness after all.

One other force was credited with helping Schumer achieve victory. Someone who visited the state four times on his behalf. Someone who shared with him the goal of reconnecting the Democratic Party to suburban and swing voters. Someone who, at this particular point in time, was regarded as a savior, a visiting angel, the best thing the Democratic Party had going for it. "Certainly Matthew Shepard's murder and Dr. Barnett Slepian's murder, just in the last few days, have shocked the nation and made clear once again that there is no room for intolerance in our country," the savior said, referring to the slain young gay man in Wyoming and the Buffalo-area doctor who'd been killed by a zealous pro-lifer. Yes, insiders agreed, Chuck Schumer had won this race with his own wiles and money and skill, and with a Democratic (especially African-American) turnout sympathetic to President Clinton. But if there was any Democrat to whom he owed a debt, any Democrat who had rallied voters to his cause, it was the woman who made those four whistle-stops. It was the woman New York voters seemed to listen to above anyone else. It was Hillary Rodham Clinton.

CHAPTER **2**

Early 1999:
The Notion

The Field Clears

CHUCK SCHUMER BEAT Al D'Amato on Tuesday, November 3. Three days later, Pat Moynihan was scheduled to tape an appearance on *News4orum,* a WNBC-TV public-affairs show hosted by Gabe Pressman. Moynihan had done the show, a central whistle-stop on the local television circuit, many times over the years. This time he had something up his sleeve. He and his wife, Liz, who had managed each of his campaigns, had been discussing it for some time, and, now that New York had elected a fellow Democrat to the Senate, he felt ready to say it. He was going to announce that, when his current term ended in 2000, he would retire.

It was an extraordinary thing for a politician to say so soon after an election. Usually, a pol will let speculation build over months, watch his putative successors jostle one another, then finally strike a deal with one of them. But Moynihan had never been much for the game of politics. His cerebral approach, his practice of politics as an art in the mold of some sort of latter-day Metternich or Burke, always ensured his distance from the fixers. Besides, he'd passed 70 now and had served four six-year terms. He'd decided, and that was that. Pat's and Liz's hope was that Pressman would sit tight on the news.

But the political world is not the best place to keep secrets. According to his biographer, Godfrey Hodgson, Moynihan was in a "down" elevator in the NBC building at Rockefeller Center, having just finished taping the show, when a stranger startled him by speaking of his retirement. And New York 1, the local all-news cable channel, had gotten wind of the taping. So, by late morning, the news of Moynihan's retirement began its predictable march: the announcement; the tributes; the speculation about possible successors.

Carl McCall, the state comptroller, was first on all the lists. McCall was centrist, African-American, a Dartmouth man, a proven statewide vote-getter. Second was Andrew Cuomo, Bill Clinton's HUD secretary and the son of the former governor, who seemed to have inherited his father's profound intelligence and even more profound prickliness (and who sounded so like his father that it could give one dreams—or, depending on the listener, nightmares). Next came Robert Kennedy, Jr., Bobby's son and Andrew Cuomo's brother-in-law. Kennedy was an environmental lawyer and an especially intriguing choice, since the seat Moynihan was vacating had been held by his father from 1964 until his assassination in 1968. You had only to look at the younger Kennedy's eyes, exactly like his father's, to imagine voters falling for the son-claims-father's-inheritance story line in an instant. There was Mark Green, the city's Public Advocate (a kind of citywide ombudsman), who had run in 1998 and lost, but whose command of national as well as local issues always landed him on these lists. After those four came the obligatory list of fanciful choices: John F. Kennedy, Jr., whom Judith Hope, the chairwoman of the state party, had asked in 1997 to consider challenging D'Amato, but who at the time was editing *George* magazine and who told Hope, in essence, not yet (and "yet," alas, never came); George Stephanopoulos, who had moved back to his native New York after leaving the Clinton White House. Finally, there were three congresswomen: Nita Lowey of Westchester County, Carolyn Maloney from the Upper East Side, and Louise Slaughter of Syracuse. To varying degrees, all were plausible second-rank choices if the big names dropped.

That same day, New York 1's David Lewis went over the list with a source, who suggested that he toss one more name into the mix. So when Lewis went on the air that night, he ran down the above names and then threw in, almost as a joke, "And did someone say Hillary Clinton?"

Several people had, starting with Judith Hope. The notion first came to her, Hope says, at the White House Christmas party in 1997, when she was talking with the president about his, and his wife's, unstoppable popularity in New York. That night, Hope says, she mentioned to the president that "maybe Hillary has a future in New York." Shortly afterward, she relayed the gist of the conversation to Frederic Dicker, the New York Post's pitbullish Albany bureau chief. On December 8, Dicker ran the first news item speculating that Hillary might run for the Senate from New York at the top of his usual Monday column. The idea, at that early date, seemed so remote from reality that it didn't even generate much gossip. A source close to Hope remembers calling the first lady's press secretary, Marsha Berry, to say the remark had been blown out of proportion. "Stuff like this always gets blown up," Berry said. "Don't worry about it. But don't keep pushing it."

In the summer of 1998, during the heat of the Lewinsky scandal, the Clintons, on the prowl for places where they could safely show their faces together, hit the Hamptons for two fund-raisers. At both shindigs, Hope recalls, applause for Bill was warm; for Hillary, ecstatic. During the applause at one of these events, at the home of Alec Baldwin and Kim Basinger, Bill turned to Hope and whispered, "Wow, they really love her here, don't they?"

"Mr. President," Hope replied, "Hillary *owns* New York."

"Maybe," Clinton answered, "she should run for office from here."

That September, Hillary led a group of legislators on an expedition to the Dominican Republic, which had just been devastated by Hurricane Mitch. Charlie Rangel, the Harlem congressman, was part of the entourage. One night, Rangel started talking about New York politics, about the impending Schumer-D'Amato senatorial election, and about the possibility that Moynihan would retire. The state had not seen an open Senate seat since 1958. Rangel told Hillary that he knew someone who could come to New York and win that seat. Hillary asked who. "You," he responded.

"She wasn't offended, let me put it that way," he told me later. "And she didn't say it was impossible." Reporters on the junket began asking a few questions. Oh, don't tell me Charlie's gotten to you, too, she joked with them.

Thus began the notion. Three idle, half-joking conversations. Then came a chain of events that moved the notion out of idle and into gear. The front-line Democratic contenders started dropping out. The first was Kennedy. He told the *New York Post* on November 18 that "everyone has asked me [to run] except the one person who counts, my wife." Kennedy's announcement came as a disappointment to many Democrats—he possessed a formidable combination of intelligence and charm, and had a strong record as an environmental lawyer. But he had always been ambivalent about elected office. He had five children, the youngest just a year old. He didn't want it.

Next came McCall. Around Christmas, many insiders still thought he would run. The first African-American to win statewide office in New York, he had name recognition and a base of contributors, and he had just been reelected by a huge margin. But McCall, too, had always shown ambivalence about higher office, and a reluctance to risk what he already had, at least if he didn't think the prize worth the risk. At a meeting with his staff just before Christmas, he told his people he was not running. "Rationale," says an aide, "is something Carl's always been a big believer in." And McCall, whom voters had returned to the comptroller's office just weeks before, didn't see his for a Senate race. He waited until the week between Christmas and New Year's, when his office leaked to Adam Nagourney of *The New York Times* that he was bowing out, citing distaste at the thought of "hav(ing) to raise $25,000 on every business day between now and the start of the campaign to raise the $10 million he would need to run."

McCall's reluctance to rattle the cup before donors was real enough. But he might have felt differently had the prize not been a mere Senate seat. It was the governorship he was after. Ditto Andrew Cuomo. He didn't announce his decision until mid-January, two weeks after the *Meet the Press* episode set off the Hillary frenzy. But in fact, he had pretty much decided not to run in the second week of December, when his kitchen cabinet met in the Manhattan apartment of Dan Klores, one of the most connected public-relations men in the city. Cuomo was sitting on pretty favorable polls, but the advice he got that night was mixed: You like your job; you'd prefer being governor; there's a sporting chance you could be chief of staff to a President Gore. Why enter a tough, expensive race for a job you're not even dying to have? "From that point on," my source says, "he was headed in the direction of not running."

By New Year's, Hillary Clinton could see from her perch in Washington that the field was clearing. Why? It's an observable, and amusing, truth of politics in New York that, at bottom, no one really wants to go to Washington. A seat in Congress is thought respectable enough; a nice little gewgaw for the occasional state legislator who has demonstrated actual intelligence and initiative, as Schumer had, or as Manhattan's Jerry Nadler did later. But in general, once a New York pol reaches a certain exalted level, the only thing he wants to be is governor. The governorship means jobs, contracts, money, power. The governor is the boss. The governor points at the map and says, "There—spend the money there."

A senator? He has influence with the governor—maybe—but little more. Exceptions are made for the rarities like Moynihan, who, with his erudition on topics ranging from the International Monetary Fund to *Federalist* No. 10 to the financing for the Triborough Bridge, gratified New Yorkers' intellectual vanity. For the most part, however, New Yorkers don't bother very much with Washington. They notice it only in moments of crisis like war or scandal. Every so often a news article will bemoan New York's declining influence in the capital. Several explanations are bruited, but never the real one, which is that New Yorkers do not want to have to spend time in Washington—endure its mores, eat in its restaurants. Even Albany is considered preferable; at least it doesn't try to pretend that it's more important than New York. And Albany is where McCall and Cuomo wanted to be.

But even though most New York pols may not want to move to Washington themselves, they yearn for someone important to take the plunge. And while it's true that New York has produced its share of mediocrities and hacks, it does have a history of sending outsized men—statesmen—to the Senate. The aforementioned Wagner. Herbert Lehman, who marched alongside Eleanor Roosevelt as a leader of the reform movement. Jacob Javits, the liberal Republican who wrote the War Powers Act. Bobby Kennedy. And Moynihan. No one has ever gone broke overestimating New Yorkers' opinions of themselves, and for the Senate, New Yorkers want someone they see as worthy of their own high place in the world. Someone of stature.

A Collision of Fortuities

Hillary Clinton's desire for stature had been clear ever since she told Saul Alinsky that she wanted to be, not fight, the power. Her success in attaining it had been somewhat more mixed. The great irony of her life is that she achieved her highest stature, reached her apogee as a public person, not because of widespread admiration for something she had done, but because of public sympathy over something that was done to her.

Certainly when she did things, it usually brought her, to use a word she would surely learn while campaigning in New York, tsouris. When she and Bill began advertising her as the co-president in early 1992, it worked for those who were Clinton supporters already ("Hillary, Mrs. President," some signs read). But it didn't go down so well with most people: In April of that year, 67 percent of respondents told a Gallup Poll they did not like the idea of her having a "major position" in her husband's administration. During the health-care debacle, she and Ira Magaziner made a complete mess of things with their closed meetings and unwillingness to negotiate with Republicans. Her popularity collapsed—nearly as low as Nixon's during Watergate, or Truman's during the Korean War.

She withdrew. Her hard-wired distrust of the right, and the press, and anyone who questioned her motives, intensified. Everything went wrong. In March 1994, the commodities-trading story broke, revealing that she had made $100,000 on a $1,000 investment over nine months. A month later, she held the infamous "pretty in pink" press conference about Whitewater and Travelgate, her first unscripted reckoning with reporters, who circled her like vultures around dying prey. Whitewater figure Jim McDougal appeared on *Nightline,* vouching for the president's credibility but refusing to do the same for Hillary's. Vince Foster, her old Rose Law Firm confidant, killed himself in July 1995. In January 1996, Ken Starr refused to depose her at the White House or some other neutral site, forcing her to walk the media gauntlet in front of Washington's federal courthouse. In the press, the sometimes sympathetic accounts of 1992 had dwindled to rarities, and even the nonpolitical press joined the pile-on. *Spy,* the satirical magazine, depicted her on its cover with male genitalia peeking out from under her skirt. "I don't get this whole image-creation thing," she said in 1995. As first lady, she was reduced to chores like lending her imprimatur to a book of children's letters to Socks and Buddy, the first pets, and campaigning to save historic sites like Edith Wharton's home in Lenox, Massachusetts. There her picture and a framed letter bearing her signature are respectfully mounted near the grand staircase—an encomium of the sort not accorded to a policy expert or copresident, but to a traditional, and in her case severely humbled, first lady.

Her public fortunes began to change after January 21, 1998, when the Lewinsky story broke. After a rocky start (the whole "vast right-wing conspiracy" business), Hillary spent the rest of the year sewing the tattered pieces of her image back together. In a Washington of wobbly morality—her philandering husband, the Pecksniffian prosecutor, the distempered commentariat, the hypocritical Mr. Gingrich—she seemed to be the only person who hadn't completely lost her marbles. Her public appearances with her husband over the course of the year were relatively few, but when she made them, she managed to convey a graceful balance of political solidarity and personal disapproval. She praised her husband's economic stewardship, but she stopped there, at the water's edge of the personal. She talked about the saga in terms of "saving the Constitution," not saving Bill Clinton. He would give her a little peck on the cheek, and she would not return it. Chelsea, whenever possible, was the physical buffer between the two. You could well imagine her, after they had left the stage or clambered into the helicopter, turning to him and snapping, "You'd better be grateful for this, asshole," and you *hoped* she did just that, as he hung his head in shame. In response to her husband's unreliability, she seemed to act all the more reliably; even her hairstyle stayed the same.

Politically, too, she flourished for the first time. Her appearances for Chuck Schumer were only part of a massive political offensive she launched in the fall of 1998 on behalf of Democratic congressional candidates, who weren't exactly banging down her husband's door. "We all thought a woman who has loved Bill Clinton would dramatically influence the midterms," wrote John Cloud in *Time* magazine. "And we were right. It just wasn't Monica. Most people might have gone into therapy or hiding after what Hillary suffered this year. She tore up the campaign trail instead. The operative analogy best describing her ceased to be Tammy Wynette. It became Jackie Joyner Kersee."

She recorded one hundred telephone scripts and radio spots, hit twenty states, did fifty fund-raisers, spoke at thirty-four rallies. Well over half the candidates she stumped for won. There were, around America, 172 chapters of the Hillary Rodham Clinton Fan Club. Her approval ratings shot to 70 percent.

Two weeks after election day, the December *Vogue* hit the stands. Annie Leibovitz's *Vogue* cover shot, the first ever of a first lady, revealed a woman who had suddenly metamorphosed into someone far grander and more interesting than she'd ever been before. It wasn't merely that she looked elegant, and even, for the first time, a little sexy, posing demurely on a sofa in the White House Red Room, wearing a blood-red velvet Oscar de la Renta gown. It was the moment of ascendance the picture captured. "Hillary is no longer history's most humiliated wife, and has skillfully crafted a new image," reported the conservative *Daily Telegraph* of London, quoting *Vogue* editor Anna Wintour, who called her "an icon to American women." The accompanying story, by Ann Douglas, a New York author best known for a study of the Harlem Renaissance and its relationship to modernism, invoked no less than the philosopher William James in characterizing Hillary's "will to believe" and her "fresh contact with the ideals on which America was founded." She told Douglas that she kept a commonplace book, of the sort many educated nineteenth-century women carried, filled with quotations to help her "derive support from what somebody else has gone through and how they articulated it."

Hillary's butterfly emergence was happening at exactly the same time that New York Democrats were casting about for a Senate candidate. It was only the collision of these two fortuities that made her candidacy possible. If, say, Pat Moynihan had waited until the summer to announce he was leaving, it's hard to imagine that New York's Democrats would even have wanted Hillary Clinton. By the summer of 1999, as we'll explore in a future chapter, her great moment had already begun to curdle. Without the happy meeting on time's graph of Hillary's rebirth and New York Democrats' search for someone worthy of their own self-regard, her candidacy would never have come about.

From this starting point, events flowed with a momentum approaching inevitability. Most observers still considered her candidacy a long shot, but the press was egging her into the race ("Run, Hillary, run!" wrote Bob Herbert on November 12, 1998). After the new year turned, the *Meet the Press* segment set off a frenzy in the New York media. A poll showed her coming within five points of Mayor Giuliani. And Democrats bent over backwards not to discourage her. At one point, Judith Hope told the Associated Press's Marc Humbert, one of the state's most important political reporters, that she thought the chances of Mrs. Clinton running were remote; a few hours later, after she checked in with Sheldon Silver, the Democratic speaker of the State Assembly, she called Humbert back to paint a rosier picture. Silver had suggested that Hope respin. Charlie Rangel was everywhere, on New York 1 and in the papers, saying things like, "We can guarantee funds and no primary opponent. Ain't nobody going to run against the first lady." Since the reform movement, Democrats had prided themselves on open primaries; Rangel himself had been a direct beneficiary of that reform, because in the machine days he never could have gotten himself a spot on the ballot to take on and ultimately topple Adam Clayton Powell in 1968. But neither Rangel nor most other Democrats, in those besotted days of January 1999, stopped to consider whether sacrificing that principle to seduce their celebrity candidate was at all troubling.

The Force of Nature

On the Republican side, meanwhile, there was only one candidate. This Lazio, some congressman from Long Island, was making noises. But to those who were serious, the nomination was a foregone conclusion. On January 5, just two days after the *Meet the Press* segment, Rudy Giuliani announced that Bruce Teitelbaum, his chief of staff, would leave City Hall to become the director of Solutions America, a political-action committee Giuliani was setting up to raise money for a possible Senate run. The mayor played coy, seizing on the double entendre when asked by a reporter if he was "interested" in Hillary: "No way I'm going to answer that question. Not in this day and age. Oh boy!" Behind the playful badinage, though, he was very interested in her, at least as an opponent.

"He wasn't really very hot on running until the Hillary stuff started," a source close to the mayor says. "There was nothing in it for him to beat Carl McCall or Andrew Cuomo. So what? Nothing against them, but that's not a big deal. But beating Hillary Clinton . . . *that's* a big deal."

He was nearing the midway point in his second term, which would be his last, because voters had passed a term-limits referendum while he was in office. His mayoralty would end on New Year's Day 2002, which meant that, if he did seek a Senate seat and win in 2000, he would be AWOL for nearly half of his second term. But this didn't seem to matter all that much. By general agreement, he had accomplished, as mayor, what he was elected to accomplish—he cut crime. To the grateful 57 percent of the population that supported him, he had earned his pass. And as far as the other 43 percent were concerned, he couldn't leave town fast enough. There was also a hankering on the part of the political establishment to watch him try to move up, and undoubtedly an element of pride on his part: The only New York City mayor who had ever gone on to higher office was an obscure fellow in the mid-nineteenth century who became governor. New Yorkers knew that if anyone could break the mold, it would be Rudy. Among insiders, "What will he do next?" became a parlor game. There was talk of a cabinet position in a Republican presidential administration. One of his advisers, in late 1998, laid out to me his own plan for trying to nail down the vice presidency for Rudy in 2000. There was even talk, given his glowing national reputation, about the presidency, which he did little to discourage.

But Moynihan's retirement made the Senate the obvious choice. Some observers did raise caution flags. Insiders were quick to note that the iron fisted and autocratic Rudy was not exactly a perfect fit for the collegial Senate. Furthermore, there was the question of whether Governor George Pataki would try to block his candidacy. The tension between a New York State governor and a New York City mayor is built in, stemming mostly from the fact that the governor is the higher-ranking of the two, but the mayor, being in New York City, gets far more attention. But the tension between Pataki and Giuliani was off the charts; basically, they hated each other. In 1994, Rudy had crossed party lines to endorse Cuomo over Pataki, and he did it in his usual remorseless way, traveling the state and warning that a Pataki administration would be corrupt to its core. (Pataki was the hand-picked candidate of Al D'Amato, and Giuliani hated him, too.) Once Pataki took office, they made nice from time to time, but for the most part the tension only grew worse. Giuliani exploited the advantage of being in the state's media capital with casual perfection. In January 1997, for example, Pataki had scheduled his State of the State address—the governor's moment in the sun, the one speech he gives a year that is guaranteed to be carried live in the city. Giuliani, on the same day and with only a day's notice, decided to hold a press conference unveiling his plans for a new stadium for the Jets on Manhattan's West Side. You can guess which event drew more coverage. The two even reached the point, after Joe DiMaggio's death, of bickering over which highway in the city should be named in the great batsman's honor.

Even their chief aides hated each other. Pataki was more genial than Giuliani by nature, but, even if he wore a happy face in public, his communications director, Zenia Mucha, was delighted to serve as his private, snarling face. She detested Giuliani. She detested Cristyne Lategano, her counterpart on the mayor's staff. Lategano detested her. A story went around City Hall once that Giuliani staffers were celebrating Cristyne's birthday and, as she was handed the knife to cut the cake, someone yelled: "Pretend it's Zenia!"

If you didn't know better, you might assume that a Republican governor, whatever his personal feelings, would want a fellow Republican to win an open Senate seat. But if you did know better, you'd understand that for Pataki and Mucha, control of the party, and even the governor's future, was at stake. They—and D'Amato, who despite his loss to Schumer still held tremendous sway in state GOP politics—knew that if Giuliani got to the Senate, especially by defeating Hillary Clinton, he would become a virtual Republican godhead. This was certainly the thinking inside the Giuliani camp. "Play it out," one Giuliani partisan told me. "Say Gore beat Bush. And we beat Hillary. We defeated Hillary Clinton! In 2004, who would be talked up more as a Republican presidential candidate, Pataki or Giuliani? Not even close. We were thinking presidency. No question."

Pataki and his side understood all this too. Their greatest concern was not about the presidential sweepstakes but about power in New York. If Giuliani beat Hillary, he would surely try to leverage that power into a takeover of the state Republican Party by dumping Bill Powers, the state GOP chairman, who was an ally of the governor and D'Amato. Come 2002—the next gubernatorial election—Rudy could throw his support behind a different candidate, or maybe even run himself. Such was their enmity that they wanted Giuliani out of the way—yes, even if it meant that Hillary Clinton became Senator. One Pataki associate expressed their view to me at the time: "If you try to be friendly with this guy, the first chance he gets, he'll knife you in the back."

Of course, in politics, even the deepest resentments can be quickly released to the winds if expediency demands it. And sure enough, in the second week of January, Joseph Bruno, the Republican leader of the State Senate, announced that he would back a Giuliani candidacy. Back in 1994, when Giuliani endorsed Mario Cuomo for reelection as governor, it was Bruno who had dealt his fellow Republican the heaviest rhetorical blow of all—"Judas" Giuliani, he called his fellow Catholic. But now, the mayor's problem with the state GOP, Bruno told Albany reporters, "is history."

Obviously, this was not true. Bruno was perhaps positioning himself to play a role in a Giuliani campaign, or to play peacemaker between Pataki and Giuliani down the road. What was true was that even the governor was not big enough to stop Rudy. Bruno recognized this, and so did Bill Powers, the state Republican Party chairman, who was helpful to the Giuliani campaign from the start.

Giuliani was a force of nature. The only thing that could get in his way was a countervailing force. On February 4, one hit. Just after midnight, four white cops searching for a rapist in the South Bronx approached an unarmed black man as he stood in the vestibule of his apartment building. They ordered him to put his hands up, but Amadou Diallo—maybe because he didn't understand them, or maybe because he was reaching for his wallet to show them his ID—did not. They fired forty-one shots, hitting him nineteen times and killing him where he stood. The city exploded in anger.

The cops were members of the NYPD's Street Crimes Unit, which, newspapers revealed, had been badly trained and had thrown inexperienced cops together as partners without veteran leaders. It had, moreover, engaged in aggressive stop-and-frisk operations in poor neighborhoods that had resulted in a successful collar only once out of every sixteen stops—all in an effort, it seemed, to pad the arrest statistics. Even voters—the Giuliani Democrats—who had tried to turn a blind eye to the mayor's relationship with black and poor New York had to acknowledge that this was the dark side of the war on crime, and that the war needed some drastic rethinking.

The Diallo tragedy could not prevent Giuliani from becoming the Republican nominee for the Senate. One more dead black man, however blameless he may have been, has never been the kind of thing that would force the Republican Party to take moral stock of itself. But it could create more favorable political conditions for a potential Democratic candidate, one on whom all eyes, as winter eased, were still fixed.

"I'm Doing This"

The president's acquittal in the impeachment trial was delivered around noon on February 12. That same day, even before the vote was taken, Harold Ickes found himself back at the White House, at Hillary's invitation, talking about the Senate race. He recalls the scene as "surreal." "Here this woman had been through this hellish year," he recalls, "and the Senate was voting on whether to convict or not. It was a pretty mind-bending day, and it was the day we were talking about whether she was going to run in New York." Down Pennsylvania Avenue, Senate Republicans were humiliating Bill Clinton. And yet at one point Bill walked in, wearing sweat clothes—having just finished working out in the White House gym—greeted Ickes as an old friend, and joked around.

After the president left, Ickes and Hillary talked for about five hours. "Why in God's name would you want to do this?" he asked her. "Do you know what it's like being a U.S. Senator, the work that's involved, the just unglamorous and very hard work?" He told her in detail about the size of the state, its sheer complexity, the money the race would take, the various constituencies that had to be stroked. He said, "These are very thick, thorny, historically freighted issues." He also talked with her about the press, saying, "You've been very sheltered from the press, even though you think you haven't been. And you've got to be more open with them. You've got to think of them as people who have a job to do, working stiffs who have to file a story every day. And if they don't, they get laid off."

Hillary nodded. She asked questions and sought advice. But she never said much to indicate what her real thoughts and feelings were about running. Even so, it was clear to Ickes that even at this early point from the kinds of questions she was asking that "she was going to have to be talked out of it." The two best things she had going for her, he told her, were that it was a presidential election year, which tended to bring out Democrats in large numbers, and that New York had been her husband's best state after Arkansas. But Ickes let her know that it was going to be tough. "If losing is going to devastate you," he counseled her, "don't even think about running."

Ickes had no illusions; she could well lose, and he didn't want to see his old friend be embarrassed. He had his own reasons to be wary, too. He knew that a Hillary race would take a rather big chunk out of his life for the next two years, just at the time when he was trying to get his new lobbying business off the ground. But the bottom line was that if Hillary wanted this, he'd help her, so he spent the rest of February thinking about how this thing could work. He began calling around to his old New York contacts, and, as word of his efforts seeped out, doubters started to think again.

Ickes also made one important Washington pilgrimage. He and Mark Penn, the president's pollster, had never been on the best of terms. Penn had come into the White House through Dick Morris, Ickes's nemesis, and although Penn and Morris weren't particularly close either, the association meant that Ickes and Penn kept their distance from each other. But shortly after his February 12 sit-down with Hillary, Ickes—knowing that Hillary would want to rely on Penn's polling as the president had—went to Penn and said, "It looks like we'll be together on this one." Penn did a poll showing that, as he put it, "she could win—not would win—but could win by about five points." That was not as clear-cut as he, or Hillary, might have hoped, but nevertheless Penn says that "it was clear even from that point" that she was running.

Most of Ickes's conversations, though, were with New Yorkers. "What totally changed my mind about it," says one Democratic insider, "was these discussions that started to go on. Harold started having discussions with people you don't have discussions with unless you're serious about something: Bill Lynch, Ken Sunshine, Kevin McCabe. The uber-operatives. These are wired-in guys. You don't go to them with folly." Lynch had been a union organizer and David Dinkins's chief political operative. With three phone calls, Lynch could line up the unions and the black vote. Sunshine ran his own public-relations firm, representing Barbra Streisand and Leonardo DiCaprio among others. But his roots in New York politics went back more than thirty years, to the glory days of the reform movement. He could help arrange the support of a key labor leader like Dennis Rivera of the Hospital Workers' Union, or reach out to his many contacts in the press. McCabe had been the chief of staff for Peter Vallone, the speaker of the City Council, and had deep connections in Irish-American circles and in certain blue-collar unions. My source might have added a few other names to this list. George Arzt—in the 1970s, a *Post* City Hall reporter; in the 1980s, Ed Koch's press secretary; now the head of his own PR and consulting firm. George was the kind of guy who knew what political stories were running in the papers days before they appeared. Also, John LoCicero, Koch's chief political operative and a friend of Ickes's since the late 1960s.

Ickes wasn't the only one making calls. Hillary herself called or visited more than two hundred New York Democrats in the spring of 1999. There are no more than a dozen important Democrats in the entire state. If you get the people I've named above on board, and throw in Schumer, McCall, Sheldon Silver, Judith Hope, Bronx County Democratic leader Roberto Ramirez, and maybe one or two others, you've bagged the state. Still, Hillary called mayors of small towns and party chairmen of rural upstate counties that no Democrat had carried since Woodrow Wilson. Whatever else she brought to this task, she certainly carried along her over-achieving, good-Wellesley-girl earnestness. She asked, says one pol she consulted, "intelligent questions, lawyer-like questions." What were the issues upstate? What were the key counties? Where was the Democratic strength outside the city? What motivated suburban voters, swing voters? Who do I need to talk to in such-and-such a place? What's the history between this person and that person? This Democrat noted, though, that she kept her thoughts to herself.

She ladled out the kinds of perks that only someone who lives in the White House can. McCall and his wife, Joyce Brown, were White House guests, staying in the Lincoln Bedroom. Roberto Ramirez did the same. Sheldon Silver declined a White House invitation, but he met Mrs. Clinton in New York and stayed in touch throughout.

McCall and Brown were only two of several guests present at the White House on March 5 and 6, perhaps the most crucial days of Mrs. Clinton's decision-making process. Summoned to the White House that weekend was a handful of the state's top Democratic elected officials and operatives; a group that represented, as well as any other, the New York Democratic brain trust. Bill and Hillary sat down the night of March 5 with McCall and Brown; Victor and Sarah Kovner, long-time reform activists and close friends of Ickes's (several of the meeting's participants lived within blocks of one another on the Upper West Side); Harold and his wife, Laura Handman, one of the city's top libel lawyers; Bill Lynch; Dennis Rivera and his wife, Maria; and Randi Weingarten, the head of the city teachers' union.

It was the only high-level powwow between Hillary and leading New York Democrats that took place that spring. Over a dinner of poached fish in a private upstairs dining room, the group discussed what it would be like if Hillary got in the race. Again, Hillary asked many questions; and, again, she barely opened a window on her own thoughts, even to this group of intimates. Her reticence was interpreted in different ways. "People were not pleading with her to come," Victor Kovner says. "It was advice—what to expect. She was, I think, far from decided." Two other attendees came away with a different impression. The first: "It was basically a cheerleading . . . you know, 'You ought to run.' People put out the basic cautionary footnotes so they could be on record as having done so, but it was basically, 'You should do this.' " A second participant felt the scene was not exactly conducive to unvarnished assessments: "I felt it had no real focus. I guess that's the way those things go, though. Everybody's trying to make the most profound point. But I thought we were blowing smoke at her. Who wants to talk tough and talk reality in a setting like that? Eventually I turned to Harold and said, 'Thanks for getting me in here, but this is not me.' " This source remembers Rivera as the most outspoken and encouraging—which would jibe with Victor Kovner's memory that at one point while Rivera had the floor, the proto-candidate's husband tried to cut in, and Rivera told the president of the United States, "Wait, I'm not finished yet." After dinner they retreated to the screening room and watched *October Sky,* a movie about a young man who got out of the coal mines of southern West Virginia and became a NASA engineer. The sentimental but movingly developed theme, about the nobility of pursuing large dreams against long odds, was lost on no one.

It would be a while before it was clear that Hillary was running, but McCall left the White House persuaded that she'd made up her mind. So did Bill Lynch. Mark Green, who spoke with her on the phone around the same time, felt the same way. Hillary peppered Green with a series of questions about Giuliani. "I told my wife that I didn't think she was on the phone for fifty minutes to get a dinner invitation," he says.

The public posture of Judith Hope and the state Democrats at this point was to give her time. They feared that if she was forced to make a public decision too soon, her answer would be no, even though Hope knew the answer was already very close to yes. The public enthusiasm for Hillary was at its zenith then, and Giuliani, by contrast, was at his post-Diallo nadir. Polls matching Hillary against Rudy in February and March showed Hillary six to nine points ahead. She would never hold such a lead over Giuliani again.

Nita Lowey, meanwhile, was getting antsy. The Westchester congresswoman, who was incredibly popular among her constituents and came across as everyone's nice Jewish grandmother, was traveling around the state lining up support. She had always said that if Hillary wanted in, she would get out. But until that time, she had every intention of making the rounds and positioning herself as the candidate. Pressure was building on the Democrats to decide.

The Lowey situation came to a head in mid-April, when Democrats were having their annual Jefferson-Jackson Day dinner at the Manhattan Hyatt. Invitations had gone out featuring Lowey as the honored guest. Ickes told the AP's Marc Humbert that Hillary would not be attending. Humbert wrote that her refusal to attend probably meant she wasn't running after all, precipitating a heated argument among Democrats about whether Hillary would, or should, attend. Then, suddenly, word came from the White House that she'd be there. This caused the state party people no small amount of grief—they had to add security, they had to pay for her to come, and, as one party functionary put it, "we could have charged twice the price for a ticket if we'd known." To insiders, her attendance that night was "the clincher," as one told me, "especially since it was in response to Humbert and others writing that if she didn't come, she wasn't serious."

In May Judith Hope, her press aide, Matthew Hiltzik, and Mike Schell, a member of the state Democratic Executive Committee from upstate Watertown, took a drive through the Finger Lakes region and the state's southern tier, along the Pennsylvania border. Their ostensible purpose was to do some outreach to local Democrats. The hidden purpose was to scout out places for Hillary to swing through during the summer. The trip concluded at the Syracuse home of assemblyman Mike Bragman, with Hope, Hiltzik, and Bragman huddled over a map plotting three possible trips Hillary could take.

Finally, in late May, Harold Ickes's phone rang again. "I'm doing this," Hillary told him. "She well understood how short the half-life of a 'former' could be," Ickes says. "She didn't want to work for anyone. She wasn't interested in money. She didn't care for the lecture circuit. She had no passion for academe or foundations. She said to me that being one out of one hundred, she could have a tremendous impact on shaping policy. She spoke often of Ted Kennedy, as a sort of model of someone who had passed enormous amounts of legislation and had really had a major effect on the country." Ickes began looking for Manhattan office space and putting together an exploratory committee.

So it was happening. But it was almost as if it were happening in some parallel universe, or as if it were some fantasy campaign. Rotisserie-league politics. There was the candidate who told almost no one, with any deep emotional conviction, why she wanted this—the candidate who seemed, somehow, to think that if she just showed up, and she was nice, things would be all right. There was no clear line of action laid out for supporters to follow. There was too much consultation, too much advice, too many conversations, too much good news. There was too much discussion of issues, and far too little consideration of the fact that many New Yorkers—and not just right-wingers—would find the candidacy of this non–New Yorker preposterous. "We would talk about that," says one insider, "and we'd say, 'Well, she's right on the issues for New Yorkers.' We always thought, you know, who are the New Yorkers from New York? So many people are from somewhere else. Maybe upstate it's a little different, but in the city and the suburbs, I think we felt people wouldn't see it as a major issue." In the next six months, though, the carpetbagger problem, and others that no one could have envisioned, became pretty major after all.

CHAPTER 3

Mid-1999:
The First Steps

A Brand New Start of It

THE SCENE WAS a nearly perfect pastoral. A white wood-frame farm-house, with chimneys and rocking-chair porch, at the bottom of a shallow dell; behind it, a small shed; a few yards up the hill, a barn, classic deep red but needing a paint job; and, about a quarter-mile beyond that, up a narrow, unpaved road, a one-room schoolhouse dating to 1854 where Daniel Patrick Moynihan writes his books and thinks his thoughts. Glorious oaks and maples, spaced just so. A velvety curtain of mountains in all directions. The hay had been baled, and one could imagine, looking out over the neatly spaced bales on the far hillside, that in the right kind of sunset or dawn light the scene might resemble one of those famous Monets.

On the hillside where we were standing, however, the scene was one Monet would have had some trouble recognizing. There were more than two dozen satellite trucks, their dishes forming a jagged sky-line before the distant peaks. Another half-dozen or so buses, idling and belching out fumes. A complement of cars, all parked this way and that on the matted tall grass. And about 250 journalists. The soil of Antietam was consecrated by the blood of soldiers. On this loam, of Pindars Corners, New York, we and our exhaust fumes and television cables and mult-boxes and thoughtless footprints were leaving a rather less noble legacy.

Earlier in the week, word had come down from the exploratory committee's headquarters that hotel arrangements had been made for the press at a Marriott on the outskirts of Albany. The night before the event, we gathered there—the beat reporters from all over the state and from Washington, the leading columnists, a guy from *Editor & Publisher* who was covering us covering the event—and mingled in a mood of anticipation that recalled the first night of summer camp. (The ennui— we had no way of knowing yet just how long the next sixteen months would seem—settled in later.) About six of us sat in the hotel lobby, having drinks and predicting who would win and by how much. The waitress, fully untouched by Hillary mania, said Giuliani by ten. At eight o'clock the following morning, we boarded a bus to bring us here, near Oneonta in the west-central part of the state, about an eighty-mile trip. We touched down on the Moynihan property and immediately busied ourselves with that most common of campaign ac- tivities, charging off the bus and then standing around and waiting for something to happen.

The general understanding among political reporters is that you can usually count on Republicans to be on time and Democrats to be at least a half-hour late, each habit reflecting the neurosis of the party in question with respect to the idea of order. By this measure, no one would ever be able to accuse Hillary of being a Republican. Hillary had flown that morning from Washington to Binghamton aboard an Air Force jet, and her motorcade, as we settled in on the Moynihan hillside, was on its way from there. Hillary, they told us when we ar- rived, was about forty-five minutes away. Forty-five minutes came and went. Then it was twenty minutes. Twenty minutes came and went. Kids were selling lemonade near the barn. German TV was here, and Japanese TV, and who knows who else, and people were shouting into cell phones in various languages. Rory Kennedy, one of Bobby's daughters and an award-winning documentary filmmaker, was shoot- ing footage.

Finally, some activity. A bus pulled up. The pool reporters. The handful of people—usually from the big dailies, or the weekly news magazines, or the wire services—who follow the candidate around all day, gathering the quotes and anecdotes of the day's events to share with the rest of us. They ambled off: Adam Nagourney from the *Times*, Joel Siegel from the *Daily News*, Marc Humbert from the Associated Press Albany bureau, Eric Pooley from *Time*, and several others. Their presence meant the entourage had arrived, and the show should start soon. In the meantime, the rest of us gathered around them as they gave a rundown of everything that happened from the time the plane touched down until they arrived.

"She got off the plane. There were maybe twenty, twenty-five people there. Most supporters, but some protesters—"

"How many?"

"Don't know. Five or six. Six. 'Hillary, Go Home!' signs."

"With an exclamation point?"

"Uh, yeah. Exclamation point."

"Just one sign? How many, then? What else?"

"Anti-abortion activists. One of those dead-fetus signs."

"Okay. Anything else? What about her?"

"She shook a few hands."

"Did she say anything?"

"Yeah. To a little girl. Happy to be here."

"Is that 'happy to be here' or 'I'm happy to be here'?" A brief huddle ensues, and upon general assent, the "I'm" is inserted.

And so on. It's the most mundane stuff you could imagine, scribbled down with frantic intensity. Journalists often get the big things fabulously wrong, but at least we're scrupulous about getting the small things exactly right.

Meanwhile, Hillary and Moynihan were hiding away in the senator's little schoolhouse office. Finally, at eleven o'clock, they emerged. The microphones had been placed along a road about 200 feet down the hill from the schoolhouse. They were placed there more at the behest of the television crews than the campaign's. But their placement was the best thing that happened to the campaign that day, because it created, amid the din and clatter, a two-minute space of almost reverent silence as Moynihan and Hillary strolled toward the microphones. The reason for the leisurely pace was in fact prosaic— Moynihan was recovering from back surgery. But the effect was striking. Seen purely as image, the scene evoked the kind of social ceremony and ritual we are all taught to respect reflexively. In fact, the two of them reminded one of nothing so much as a father walking his daughter down the aisle. For a moment, the snickering stopped; all was silence, save the camera shutters, buzzing and whirring and clicking.

The driving emotion here, though, was something other than father-daughter tenderness. Moynihan was known to be less than thrilled by this potential candidacy, as he had never been an admirer of the Clintons, and had criticized Hillary over the threat her health-care proposal posed to funding for teaching hospitals, of which New York has many. He and Liz, his wife, had been persuaded to host this event by Mandy Grunwald, the Hillary advisor who had come from New York and worked on his past campaigns, because Hillary, with no old homestead or other traditional venue from which to begin her candidacy, needed a launching pad with at least a little potential to produce positive symbolism. Thus this stroll was at once a tender moment and a fraught one, and the time it took permitted us to ruminate on the arc traveled over the last thirty years not only by Moynihan but by the Democratic Party—how Clintonian New Democrat politics had reshaped the party and transformed Moynihan from scourge of the Left, which he had been ever since his controversial 1965 report on the "Negro family," into someone who was now more likely to be thought of, in the political atmosphere created by Hillary's husband, as one of Washington's leading defenders of the welfare state. This simple image of two people walking down a country lane turned out to be not simple at all. Journalists love to affect having seen it all. But no one could claim to have seen this.

Moynihan welcomed us, and spoke of the Plutarchs and Bunyans on his bookshelf, and the seventeen books he'd written wholly or partly in his little room, relying on its potbellied stove for heat. He was a gracious host, although one couldn't help but suspect that perhaps his reservations about all this did have something to do with the fact that he almost forgot, before he turned to introduce Mrs. Clinton, that, oh yes, he was there to endorse her candidacy.

Hillary approached the microphones and began to speak. She was obviously very nervous. It seemed odd that Hillary Clinton should have a case of nerves; it was only in retrospect, after we'd watched her make a series of amateur-night mistakes along the trail, that this would make sense. She began almost meekly. Since this was her Listening Tour, she said, she thought there was no better New Yorker to listen to first than "probably the wisest New Yorker we can know at this time."

She was "very humbled and more than a little surprised to be here." She guessed the questions that were on people's minds were, "Why the Senate, why New York, and why me?" She didn't answer them, but at least acknowledging them showed a self-awareness that it hadn't been clear she possessed. She took nine questions. One, about a controversy in Buffalo over the building of a new bridge to Canada, Moynihan judged too parochial and cut off. The only one she whiffed completely was a question from David Lewis of New York 1, about whether she saw herself as a victim of the Lewinsky scandal. Just hearing that name seemed to send her into some sort of paralytic trance, and she fell back on platitudes about being focused on the future and coming to New York to listen to voters' concerns. Moynihan had to help her out at one point by directing her attention to Gabe Pressman, the dean of New York's press corps, who by tradition gets the first question. Mrs. C. had shown her rookie colors by calling on the Washington-based NBC correspondent Andrea Mitchell first.

Pens were held at the ready in the event that she said anything objectionable or stupid—not knowing which county she was in, for example. This was a mistake Ed Koch had famously made when running for governor in 1982. Koch had finished a successful event in Cooperstown. He was getting in his car, recalls Marty McLaughlin, a New York PR man who was then his campaign press aide, when he spotted one last reporter and decided to go talk to him. "Mr. Mayor," the scribe asked, "what county are you in?" Koch stammered. He was stumped. "Thank you," the reporter said, and walked merrily away. "Do you think this will make news?" Koch asked McLaughlin. "How about the front page of every newspaper in the *goddamn STATE?!*" It did. Many of us on the Moynihan farm that day remembered that story. The senator surely did, too, and he put ice on the tension by noting, early on, that we were in Delaware County.

The day's sights were of a sort that Pindars Corners is unlikely to see again. But the most interesting thing about the day was something to be sensed, not seen: Hillary Clinton took that stroll to the microphones carrying astonishingly little baggage for someone with her history. The day after the Moynihan farm appearance, she had her first sit-down interview, in Cooperstown, with nine reporters from the state's major dailies and wire services. She took twenty-six questions. Exactly one was about the past, and it referred only vaguely to "everything that has been coming out in the last couple of years." She was asked, instead, about Mayor Giuliani; where she'd live; whether her husband would campaign with her; what tax increases she might support; jobs in central New York; why she was running; that sort of thing. She'd never shake the past off her shoes completely. But when she arrived at Pat Moynihan's farm that day, after having remade her public image—and having it remade for her—three or four or five times in the previous seven years, here she was with a chance, as the song says, to make a brand new start of it.

"The Smaller the Circus, the Better"

So began the Listening Tour. Consisting of about a half-dozen trips over the next four months, the tour was designed by Ickes, Penn, and Grunwald with state Democratic leaders to get her around the state and show her to New Yorkers—especially upstaters, who needed more wooing than downstaters—at her best advantage: earnestly talking policy with earnest citizens asking earnest questions. The off-the-record goal, as it was described to me at the time, was twofold: first, to show voters that she wasn't the scheming harridan of their imaginations; second, to bore the press into submission, thus beginning the process that *The New York Observer*'s Tish Durkin would later name the first lady's "controversectomy."

With respect to the stated goal, earnest policy talk was safely within her comfort zone. The events featured Hillary sharing the stage with her host—the president of the local college, or the manager or owner of a plant—and five or six local residents whose biographies intersected with the topic at hand. Most were arranged by local Democrats, working in tandem with Hillary's people, to find reasonably friendly venues. The audiences were handpicked by the local host committees, and, though they did include both Democrats and Republicans, invitees were instructed that questions off the topic would be unwelcome. Before each event, says one person who was along on many of the stops, Hillary was given a briefing book full of facts and figures about the venue and background information on any local issues that might come up. Not surprisingly, she quickly "knew the issues better than we did," this person says. Thus armed, Hillary would walk into the room, give the audience a little smile and a wave, and take her seat. She arrived at each venue with pen in hand and a notebook on her lap. Ever the responsible student, she constantly scribbled notes as people spoke. At a SUNY Oneonta forum on education, a woman asked a question about an advanced reading program. Hillary happened to know that the program had originated in New Zealand but, somewhere between there and America, had undergone several changes for the worse. At a senior center in Utica, I interviewed a woman named Ann Fusco, who had arrived "skeptical," but who, after the event ended, had a look of wonder on her face: "She was just so . . . smart and intelligent. My goodness!"

Hillary also used the events to inch her way out, very selectively and subtly, from under the weight of the White House. At a session on the economy in Rome, at a decaying air base that was a standard stop for politicians who wanted to sing the upstate economic blues, a man asked about the Northeast Dairy Compact. She said she would support New York's dairy farmers being permitted to join (and thus to get a stable, agreed-upon price), which wasn't the administration's position. Interestingly, she didn't bother to emphasize that her position represented a break with her husband on the question. Her handlers knew that reporters could check with their desks and learn that this was indeed a break with the administration. This trouble was saved by Michael Grunwald of *The Washington Post,* who actually knew what the administration's position was.

The Listening Tour was easy to make fun of, with a name like some cloying children's show on PBS. And the events were usually about as dramatic as quilting bees. The fact that she was visiting towns only to "listen" and "learn" insulated her from having to take many positions. She took few, and getting specific answers out of her or her aides about what she supported or opposed was hard work indeed. But the tour was a success in this respect: It revealed to voters a far less minatory figure than they had expected. There was about her not the slightest hint of threat or superiority. People had expected Hillary to instruct and talk, and, let's face it, to come across as pushy and judgmental. So when she paid genuine attention to the things people were saying, she really threw them. Ann Fusco of Utica talked about

Hillary's brains, but her enthusiasm, her eyes, made it clear that she just sort of *liked* Hillary, and was shocked because she hadn't expected to.

This was and would remain one of the most remarkable, and wholly unexpected, aspects of the campaign, something that people, if they hadn't seen it with their own eyes, could never be persuaded to believe. But it was true: With smallish groups of people, say 150 or fewer, she was personable, chatty, and reasonably straight-talking. She looked people in the eye, and she nodded as they talked, with a nod that was grandiose, like a stage actor's; whether she was taking people seriously or not, the nod sure made it *look* as if she was. This 150 figure, it turns out, has a basis in social science. Group dynamics, as Malcolm Gladwell explained in a *New Yorker* article some months later, change for the worse when an assemblage exceeds that magic number. And this fact of social science played out perfectly during the Listening Tour. With the press, Hillary was suspicious and uncomfortable. You could see it as she approached a circle of reporters: Her jaw would tighten, and her small hands would form into fists. Before very large crowds, she stuck passively to a script of banal clichés that could have been assembled by chimpanzees, and she had no instinct for how to carry a crowd with the cadences of her speech. But in more intimate and controlled settings, she found a way to connect to people, and they were almost always impressed. If only, I thought, she were running in Rhode Island, or on Guam, where she could meet every voter.

The newspaper accounts never quite managed to convey this. Newspapers don't reserve much space for describing that sort of texture. They want news. And the listening events were not news. In fact they were designed *not* to make news. From the campaign's perspective, one person traveling with her told me, "the smaller the circus, the better." So it was, I suppose, a moral victory for the campaign when, at the SUNY Oneonta forum, the listening session dragged on, even after most of the camera crews had packed up; it was an even bigger one three days later, in Syracuse, when the press throng had thinned from 250 to about 70.

And so while the second unspoken goal of the Listening Tour, to bore the press, was met, it was less blessing than curse. Most politicians understand that if they're being followed around by a column of reporters, they need to give them news, not out of duty, but self-interest:

If you don't give journalists a story to write, they'll go out and find one. Hillary, though, was basically inaccessible to reporters. She was granting no sit-down interviews. Her press availabilities were usually brief and bland. Occasionally, even a question from an audience member that she sensed might lead to an uncomfortable moment, or headline, was ignored. In Jamestown, at a furniture factory, a woman said with some scorn in her voice that her husband had lost his job because of NAFTA. Hillary thanked her for her comment and looked immediately away to the next questioner.

Hillary's knowledge of hospital-reimbursement formulas might have impressed doctors in Cooperstown (it's in Otsego County, by the way), but it was of little use to the newspapers. The New York press corps may have given Hillary Clinton the benefit of the doubt when she started out. But it wasn't in the beast's restless nature to stay polite for long.

What "the Vicious New York Press Corps" Really Means

When the Hillary-for-Senate story started in full force in January, and when the subject was knocked around on the op-ed pages and the cable shows, many people felt moved to say that the "vicious New York press corps" would eat her alive, or words to that effect. It's true that the New York media glare is awfully harsh, if only because of the intensity of the competition. Consider the menagerie in New York City alone: three newspapers, four if you count Long Island's *Newsday,* which circulates in and covers the city, five if you throw in *The Wall Street Journal;* nine local television news operations; two all-news radio stations and a handful of other news-talk stations, among them the conservative WABC, Rush Limbaugh's home base, and, for the liberals, WEVD (the call letters stand for Eugene Victor Debs); the Associated Press and Reuters; a complement of weeklies and magazines—*New York, The New Yorker, The New York Observer, The Village Voice.* The city is also the home base of *Time* and *Newsweek,* and of other national magazines that sometimes report or comment on New York politics: *The*

Nation, The National Review, Vanity Fair, Talk, even, sometimes, *The New York Review of Books.* There are countless ethnic newspapers, several of which can muscle their way into the front rank by dint of breaking the occasional story—*The Forward* and *The Jewish Week* chief among the Jewish papers, *The Amsterdam News* leading the black press, *El Diario* at the forefront of the Spanish-language press. Finally, there are dozens of community newspapers that employ the fresh-out-of-j-school go-get-ters who, if they show some spark, will soon enough work their way up the food chain to the bigger titles.

All that is just New York City. A few other major papers around the state—*The Buffalo News* (owned by Warren Buffett), *The Albany Times-Union,* the *Rochester Democrat and Chronicle,* two Syracuse news-papers, and the Gannett-owned newspapers of Westchester County—complete the roster.

A huge machine of many parts, this New York press corps. But two parts mattered more than the others.

The New York Times, obviously, is the state's most important news-paper. To paraphrase Chevy Chase, the *Times* is the *Times,* and you, whoever you are, are not. It's the *Times*'s attitude, and the attitude of many of its readers, that until it hits the *Times,* it isn't really news. The day after the *Meet the Press* show, for example, just about every news-paper in America ran a piece picking up Russert's mini-bombshell. Except one. The *Times* waited until that Friday to run its first Hillary-for-Senate piece—until, that is, Hillary had had four days to issue a blanket denial but had not done so—so as not to dignify what at that point could only have been regarded as gossip.

That story was by Adam Nagourney, the paper's chief correspon-dent on this race. He was, to Team Hillary, the most important reporter in the state; when Hillary started giving interviews in February 2000, Adam came first. The rest of us would sometimes chuckle, along the campaign trail, as Howard Wolfson would walk over to Nagourney, making sure Adam had all the information he might possibly need, sneaking a peek at his copy over his shoulder, trying to get a hint as to how the day's events might be relayed to the readers of the world's most important newspaper.

Nagourney was one of more than dozen journalists from print, television, and radio assigned to follow Hillary more or less perma-nently—a far cry, admittedly, from the 250 who showed up on Moynihan's farm, but two or three times the number normally given over to a Senate candidacy. And for a length of time that was totally without precedent. A Senate race in New York is usually covered intensively for seven or eight weeks—from Labor Day to election day. This race received that kind of coverage for sixteen months, from the Moynihan farm appearance onward. Never had a race been so picked over by so many for so long.

Naturally that much scrutiny would give the candidates less room than usual for error. A blunder by a candidate in the autumn of the year before the election would mean, in most cases, a one-day story on a back page. In this election, such blunders resulted in stories that ate up the front pages for days at a time. This was the case in all the papers, but especially so in one newspaper in particular; a newspaper that understood its mission and carried it out with glee; a newspaper that, as one person who used to work there once put it to me, "saw the world through the gunsights" and reported on it accordingly. The *Times* may be New York's most important newspaper, but this particular competitor is the loudest.

From the New Deal until 1976, the *New York Post* had been the city's leading liberal paper. Under the editorial direction of Dorothy Schiff, the *Post* championed the Roosevelts and harassed their foes. Later, the *Post* lampooned Joe McCarthy, and broke the story about the Nixon slush fund that led Nixon to deliver the Checkers speech. The *Post*'s columnists were some of America's leading liberal intellectuals— the unparalleled Murray Kempton and, back when they were still liberal, Max Lerner and James Wechsler. But by 1976, Mrs. Schiff was getting on and was ready to retire. Her decision to sell the paper was not a shock; the news about whom she was selling *to* certainly was. Her mind, though, was made up, and so, in the week between Christmas and New Year's of 1976, the paper's masthead, under "Publisher," was changed to read Rupert Murdoch.

Murdoch completely remade the paper in a matter of weeks. There was now a photo of a celebrity on the front page nearly every day, leaving Studio 54 or arriving at JFK in a disheveled state. He started up two new gossip columns; today the paper has four that run daily, and others that run once or twice a week. He introduced the kind of punning headlines and lead paragraphs that define tabloid journalism today (the famous HEADLESS BODY IN TOPLESS BAR, or, on the death of *National Enquirer* editor Generoso Pope, NATIONAL ENQUIRER OWNER GOES TO MEET WITH ELVIS). And most of all, he turned the *Post* fast, and hard, to starboard.

New York had had conservative newspapers, but never one quite like this. As a rule newspapers do not allow their editorial policy to bleed into their news pages. At the *Post,* though, the rule is the precise opposite. The editorial policy is everywhere. The various wars the paper wages on a daily basis—hero cops versus sissy civil libertarians; working stiffs versus busybody liberals; and most intensively, Greater Israel versus anyone who doesn't toe the complete Likud line—it fights with every tool at its disposal. So the paper's targets find themselves on the receiving end not only of harsh editorials, but of bombastic headlines, frantic columns, unfriendly news stories, unflattering photographs, snarky captions, gossip items about their messy divorce or latest nightclub debauchery, even the odd gratuitous whack in the sports pages or the arts section.

As for the paper's friends . . . Al D'Amato ran into an ethics problem or three while he was senator. The reportage of the allegations, thoroughgoing and salacious in the other papers, was, in the *Post,* scant. But when D'Amato's brother Armand was acquitted at trial, and when D'Amato himself was cleared of one matter by the Senate ethics panel, the exonerations were big news indeed. The most comic extreme came in 1992: The *Post,* as you might guess, had been, and is, no fan of Al Sharpton's. But suddenly, in the summer of that year, there appeared a handful of favorable stories about Sharpton. At the time, Sharpton was running for senator in the Democratic primary against Bob Abrams, considered tough competition for D'Amato (who eventually beat Abrams by one percentage point). Anything that was good for Sharpton was bad for Abrams and thus good for D'Amato. In the sense that the initiated reader can see who's in, out, up, or down based on how much and what sort of coverage they receive, the *Post* is akin to what *Pravda* must have been like.

Why do I dwell on the *Post* so? Because it's the only paper that announces its agenda with such clarity—the *Times* is liberal on its editorial page, but for the most part sober and evenhanded in its news pages. The *Daily News,* owned by Mortimer Zuckerman, is moderate editorially; it's a more serious paper than the *Post,* but one that possesses far less flash and attitude. All of which means that the *Post* does more than its competitors to drive the news coverage in New York. The *Times* influences the thinking of the ruling class—potential campaign donors, prime voters. The *Daily News* is the paper of the working class, with a circulation almost twice that of the *Post*. But it's the *Post* that knows how to turn a story into a STORY: keep it alive, make it Topic A, get it yakked about on MSNBC and Fox (which Murdoch, conveniently enough, also owns). The *Post* may refer on its wood— the cover headline, in tabloid-speak—to a "furor" over something; whether there has been such a furor, one tends to ensue, at least in its own pages.

And it all works because it's fun to read. Norman Mailer, speaking at one of the many "Save the *Post*" rallies organized in behalf of this constantly in-the-red operation, once said that he read the paper first every morning, before even the *Times,* because "it's alive; you can bite it." Even liberals who hate its politics acknowledge that you cannot resist its brazenness and cheek. A key ingredient of the paper's formula in recent years has been persuading more and more members of New York's elite—*Times* readers—to take the *Post* as their second paper. These readers are well aware of the *Post*'s agenda, and they might not believe everything, or most things, they read in the *Post*. But they remember them, and talk about them, and repeat the catchphrases that enter the local lexicon through that blocky, insistent typeface.

And so, when people talked about the vicious New York press corps eating her alive, what they really meant was: The *Post* will kill her. Which it immediately and joyfully set out to do.

The day after the Moynihan farm event, the *Post* had a total of eight pieces knocking her in one way or another. A "news analysis" by Deborah Orin argued that, since the latest polls showed George W. Bush ahead of Al Gore (sixteen months before the election!), New York, if it wanted to have any clout, would do poorly to elect a Democrat as its senator. An item in Page Six (the paper's influential gossip column) described how the residents of posh North Salem, New York wanted no part of the Clintons, who had looked at a house there. A column on Hillary's shortcomings as a female role model ran in the Living section. And so on. Shortly after the Listening Tour started, the paper asked its readers to name the most noble and most evil people of the century that was drawing to a close. On the Most-Evil list, Hillary came in seventh and Bill fourth, right behind Hitler, Stalin, and Saddam Hussein. They were write-in votes, but written in by readers who took their cues from the newspaper to which they mailed their ballots. Later in the campaign, after the *Post* had scored a few knockdowns against Mrs. Clinton, a Clinton campaign aide told me: "We have to take it into account with virtually every major decision we make: 'What can the *Post* do with this?' It's like having a second opponent."

The *Post* could drive coverage. But its ability to influence election results had waned in recent years. It was crucial to Ed Koch's election as mayor in 1977, when Koch faced a runoff against Mario Cuomo. Interestingly, Koch once told me, the *Post* helped him by devoting many favorable articles to him, not by lobbing daily grenades at Cuomo. But this positive reinforcement strategy would, by the time Hillary hit town, seem absurdly quaint. The paper helped save D'Amato's skin in 1992, and it was crucial to the victory of George Pataki in 1994. It could not, however, put D'Amato over the top against Schumer in 1998, notwithstanding the unprecedented appearance of four consecutive front-page editorials in that campaign's final week. And of course, it had not managed to hurt Bill Clinton, either at election time (he carried New York in 1992 and 1996) or during the Lewinsky scandal. Hillary's Senate race would be the paper's great proving ground. It was reasonable to expect, as Hillary started her campaigning, that at the *Post* no holds would be barred. One columnist—the occupant of a special place in the history of New York politics and the Clinton saga—was so vitriolic, and usually so wrong, that he bears special mention.

The Bad Seed Sprouts

In 1968, Harold Ickes was a co-chair of Eugene McCarthy's New York operation. Hubert Humphrey was anathema to the West Side reformers, because of the Vietnam war and his association with Lyndon Johnson. And so—this was before Bobby Kennedy got into the race—all the clubs and local activists wanted a piece of the McCarthy campaign.

By 1968, the first wave of reform-movement people had been around awhile. Offstage there were younger turks, anxious to give the oldsters the message that their time had passed. Chief among the turks were five or six young comers whose mark was indelible enough that they would quickly be dubbed "the West Side Kids." Simon Barsky is now the general counsel of the Motion Picture Association of America. Dick Dresner and Joseph Mercurio are political consultants. Dick Gottfried is a New York state assemblyman. Jerry Nadler is a Democratic member of Congress. And, finally, there was Dick Morris.

He grew up a true New York kid—in a Manhattan apartment at West End Avenue and 85th Street, the son of a real-estate lawyer and a magazine writer. When Dick Gottfried met him—they were both just 14, beginning their freshman year together at the prestigious Stuyvesant High School—he was already a total political junkie. "When we met, Dick basically organized us into a political unit, so we could control both the debating team and the student government," Gottfried recalls. Which they did, quickly.

In 1968, they were still in college. Some, like Gottfried, saw in Morris "a genius," a man totally obsessed by winning, mostly for the right reasons. "He was always scheming, always plotting, trying to do things," Mercurio says. "Always on top of the numbers. Who made how many phone calls? You woke up in the morning getting a call from him saying, 'Here are the things you can do to be a better politician, a better neighborhood person.' And you went to bed at night with him going over the list." Others saw a man with no scruples at all. "We saw Morris early on for what he was," says Victor Kovner. "Sarah [Kovner] called him The Bad Seed."

The Kids, led by Morris, were recruiting high-school and college students to go up to New Hampshire to work for McCarthy. Ickes, just a few years their senior himself but allied with the older generation of Reformers, didn't care much for this "McCarthy Army": He felt it might hurt that the kids weren't from New Hampshire, and that people's doorbells were being rung maybe just a bit too often. And, of course, he couldn't have appreciated the fact that shots were being called for the campaign by someone other than himself or co-chair Sarah Kovner.

Nadler remembers a meeting in New Hampshire in early 1968 in which they plotted strategy for the last weekend before the primary. Ickes was there, and Curtis Gans, who was in charge of the McCarthy New Hampshire effort; and Mark Alan Siegel, another of the Kids who later became a Manhattan assemblyman, and Nadler and Morris. Ickes,

Nadler recalls, had laid down the law about how many buses the Kids could charter to take pro-McCarthy college students to New Hampshire. They argued it back and forth, with Morris especially pressing the case for more. But Ickes and Gans, being in charge, won the argument. The number was about half what Nadler and Morris wanted. "Then," Nadler recounts, "Harold looks at us and says, 'I don't trust you. I'm gonna stand with you in Nashua Friday night and count the buses coming in with you.' And he did. What Harold probably doesn't know to this day is that we diverted the buses, and brought a lot of kids up in cars via other routes."

"There was an internal struggle in Gene's campaign," Gottfried says. "There was us, with the tons of kids. Them, fearing backlash. And Dick and Harold were the two key debaters in that fight. There was a lot of competition as to who was going to be seen as the bigger hero of the great struggle."

There followed less-great struggles—local races on the Upper West Side during the full flowering of the reform movement, when Ickes and Morris ran opposing slates of candidates. Still later, in 1974, they clashed during the Democratic gubernatorial primary between Hugh Carey and Howard Samuels. Ickes was with Carey, Morris with Samuels. Morris crafted some ads for Samuels attacking Carey's brother, Ed, who was in the oil business. Carey won, the primary and the general. The new governor, says Victor Kovner, "would spit at the mention of Morris's name."

Morris started a partnership with Dresner, which ended badly in 1982 the way most political consulting partnerships end, with a fight over money. He moved to Connecticut and hung out his shingle. Throughout the 1970s he had remained, at least outwardly, a liberal; he wrote a book in 1978, *Bum Rap on American Cities,* a straight-up liberal defense of urban America that argued that urban ills weren't the result of the profligate Great Society but of federal and state governments withdrawing money from the cities. But just a few years later, Morris started working with Republicans—Trent Lott, Jesse Helms—and, of course, with the young Democratic governor of Arkansas and his battle-ready wife.

The Clintons went on to dump Morris in the late 1980s, but they brought him back into the fold in 1994. The later Morris-Ickes feuds, the ones that took place in the White House over Morris's triangulation strategy, are by now well known. But their enmity had been set in stone years before, in New Hampshire and the political clubhouses of the Upper West Side. "After the '94 debacle," says one New York friend of Ickes's, referring to the GOP takeover of the House, "I called Harold and I said, 'Harold, what the fuck? Dick Morris?' Harold said, 'Well, they have a relationship. There's nothing I can do about it.' " There wasn't. It was mostly Hillary's decision to bring Morris back in 1994. Not a decision her New York admirers care to defend; not one that she herself, if she would ever speak honestly about such things, would probably care to defend; certainly not one she would relish having made, come 1999.

After his own sexual peccadillo was exposed in 1996 during the week of the Democratic convention in Chicago, and Clinton was forced to bounce him, Morris began a new life as a commentator and columnist. But for which side? He had few fans among liberals, who were familiar with his track record with Lott and Helms and who resented his influence over Clinton. He was not admired by conservatives, because he had worked for Bill Clinton and because, they now knew, he was evidently some kind of pervert. That story, incidentally, was broken in *The Star,* a supermarket tabloid owned by Murdoch, by a former *Post* reporter. This was where the Clinton henchman stood in Murdoch's orbit in 1996, and for a while thereafter. In November 1997, *New York Post* columnist Steve Dunleavy called him "the Rasputin Whore-Monger." In January 1998, the *Post* editorialized, in attacking Morris, that he "could write a book entitled 'The Man Who Loved Feet Too Much.' " If the *Post* was *Pravda,* say the late-1920s version, Morris was Trotsky.

Within a year, he would be one of the paper's chief columnists.

He was hired for one reason: To assassinate the Clintons. In 1997, in his memoir of his years with the Clintons, he had written that he would be forever grateful to Hillary. Not simply because she had brought him in from the cold, but for personal reasons. When his mother was dying, he wrote, Hillary "was a major support in my grief and I can never forget that." Somehow he managed to, and he accepted his *Post* assignment happily. February 9, 1999: Bill is going to fire Ken Starr. February 21, 1999: Hillary doesn't belong in New York. March 2, 1999: Hillary probably won't run (because of one poll, taken by

Murdoch's Fox News, which also paid Morris to be a pundit). May 4, 1999: Hillary has no chance, because look at all these accomplished women who've run in New York and lost. June 4, 1999: She'll take the money she's raised and go run in Illinois in 2004. June 15, 1999: The "chutzpah she shows in thinking she can pull one over on us shows why we must and will reject her." July 15, 1999: Her candidacy "died yesterday" with the release of another poll; she won't run. Et cetera. Relentlessly.

There were other columnists, at the *Post* and elsewhere, who had little use for Hillary—conservatives like John Podhoretz and Eric Fettmann at the *Post,* and William Safire at the *Times.* Still others made it clear that, while they didn't consider her Lady Macbeth, their enthusiasm for this project of hers was minimal. But only Dick Morris's columns read as though they were grounded not in ideology or belief—because after all, what did he believe?—but in a taste for revenge: against the First Couple, who had sacked him; against the liberal establishment of New York, which had cast him out those many years ago; against Harold Ickes, who had sparred with him three decades before over the number of college students who would travel to New Hampshire to prove themselves Clean for Gene. Morris would have nearly two years to settle those scores. He would make the most of the opportunity, letting readers in on conversations he and his clients the Clintons had had years before, putting the most anti-Clinton spin possible on each of the campaign's developments, and then going on the Fox News Channel to reinforce his message. On one occasion we'll get to in a future chapter, he made a preposterous but serious charge against Hillary's campaign for which he acknowledged he had no proof. The man who had hoisted his sail thirty years ago as a fire-breathing young liberal out to change the world had become Rupert's chief warmaker.

It was a milieu in which Hillary Clinton was a neophyte, this New York of 1999. But in another sense New York had already had a hand in shaping her destiny, and that of her husband. The Ickes-Morris feuds that played out in the Clinton White House had started here, a generation before. A prominent New Yorker, Pat Moynihan, had been one of her husband's leading Democratic critics, but he still had enough of an old, Tammany-style idea of party loyalty that he seemed prepared to put any animus aside and go to bat for her. Still another

New Yorker, Alfonse D'Amato, had run the Senate Whitewater hear-
ings that threatened to lead to her indictment, egged on by the *Post,*
pursuing a story that had originally been broken, during Bill Clinton's
first presidential run, by another New York paper, the *Times.* So she did
have connections to New York, albeit not the kind that politicians can
brag about. The next few months would be devoted to trying to establish those. She could hardly have done it more clumsily.

4

Late 1999: Reality

CHAPTER 4

A Rare Selfless Gesture

As HILLARY was wrapping up her first face-to-face with New York voters, the Republicans were facing a showdown of their own. On June 2, at one of those semi-nice, semi-cheesy suburban waterfront restaurants on Long Island, Republican Congressman Rick Lazio hosted a fund-raising luncheon with about four hundred supporters. He flew in Oklahoma Congressman J. C. Watts, the former Sooner quarterback, to be at his side. Watts, the only black elected official of any note the Republican Party could offer to the public, appeared at lots of these events around the country. Watts and Lazio were friends, but Watts, wary of stepping gracelessly into another state's internal politics, offered only measured encouragement. "I'm not here to say he should be the candidate," Watts said. "I am here to say he's a great congressman, a good friend, and would be a terrific candidate for the Senate if that's what he decides to do."

Not much was known about Lazio. I had met him a few years before, over lunch in Manhattan, my chief memory of which is that, the House just having passed a bill strictly limiting the size of gifts members of congress could receive, he inspected the check to make sure that his portion, with tip, did not exceed fifty dollars. He struck me much as he would later strike the rest of New York, and the country—smart enough, nice guy, pleasant company. After the June 2 luncheon he invited me downstairs for a private interview. He clearly believed he had the right kind of profile—Catholic, moderate, suburban—to make a statewide race. He also seemed to believe that, Giuliani or no, this was his time. And he seemed, that day, to have a handle on how to go about jumping in the ring with figures who, he surely understood, were larger than he was. "I had conversations with a couple of friends in the House who've run for the Senate unsuccessfully," he told me. "And they said the same thing: Be true to yourself. Let the chips fall where they may, based on who are you are and what you believe in."

Since winning his House seat in 1992 by upsetting a well-financed Democratic incumbent, Tom Downey, Lazio had hungered for a crack at the Senate. The specificity with which he had designed his course, and the care he took to cast a moderate vote here, a conservative one there, were not yet general knowledge. Except for Long Island's *Newsday,* the papers didn't tend to pay much attention to the activities of Long Island congressmen. It was clear, though, was that he was ready to jump into the race against Hillary if Giuliani decided not to run, or even to run against Giuliani in a primary. It was also clear that whatever maneuvering he was currently engaged in couldn't be happening without a tacit blessing from the governor.

And so, throughout July, with Giuliani making few visible moves toward actually running—he hadn't done much campaigning, and he would not call Mike Long, the head of the small but influential Conservative Party, to line up Long's backing—Lazio played the smaller dog nipping at the mayor's heels. On July 13, he announced that Trent Lott and Kentucky's Mitch McConnell, who headed the National Republican Senatorial Committee, would be hosting a $1,000-a-head fund-raiser for him. On July 19, two Giuliani supporters told the *Post*'s Fred Dicker, a columnist with better Republican sources than any other journalist in the state, that if Lazio ran Rudy would back out—a warning to the governor and to others in the party that they'd better commit to the mayor if they wanted to keep their party intact. The next day Joe Bruno, the state senator who had gone from "Judas Giuliani" to "that's history," put on the record what the two Giuliani supporters had said on background. "[Giuliani]'s not going to walk into a bloodletting that is going to damage him, damage the party, and damage the chances of a Republican beating Hillary Clinton," Bruno told Dicker.

The message was intended in part for Pataki, but especially for Zenia Mucha and Al D'Amato, the leading apostles of the anti-Rudy gospel who had the governor's ear. It was being delivered by Republicans who had the party's best interests in mind and who cringed at the thought of having to watch Hillary stroll into the Senate over the corpse of a divided GOP. And it was coming from Republicans close to George W. Bush, who feared that W.'s chances against Al Gore in New York would be killed by a bitter GOP senatorial primary (at the time, Bush was running even with Gore in New York).

The drama reached fever pitch by late July and early August, the phone lines of New York's insiders on fire with gossip and speculation. Lazio was saying publicly that he planned to announce his candidacy by mid-August, no matter what the mayor did or didn't do. Giuliani, more vaguely, was indicating he'd probably have some sort of announcement to make by September. His aides were saying privately at the time that, if Pataki wouldn't put his foot down and tell Lazio to cool it, the mayor just might say to hell with it and walk away from the race. With another politician, this talk would have been gibberish that no one took seriously, but with Rudy, it was anything but idle. Matters had reached enough of a head that McConnell went on *Meet the Press* to talk about the situation on August 1, saying that Pataki would be "the major player" in deciding which man the GOP would run and that he would surely do the right thing.

McConnell couldn't have known it when he was talking to Tim Russert, but something would happen that very afternoon to force Pataki's hand. It happened, as so many August political developments in New York seem to, in the Hamptons, at a birthday party for D'Amato at the Bridgehampton home of Charles Gargano, the Pataki appointee who headed the state economic development agency. Among the guests were D'Amato, Mucha, Pataki, gubernatorial aide Bradford Race, and Neal Travis, a *Post* gossip columnist. Travis went up to others, he recalls, started talking about the Senate race and Rudy, and "I said to them, 'Surely you want to run the candidate who can beat her.' But they just didn't give a shit." Pataki, Travis says, was lighthearted about the matter; D'Amato "kind of reasonable"; Race and especially Mucha intensely anti-Giuliani. On Tuesday, August 3, the lead item in

Travis's column described the party and quoted Pataki as saying, in response to the question Travis posed about backing the candidate with the better chance, "You mean Rick Lazio, of course."

When he read the item, says a source who works for Pataki, "the governor went batshit." The day after Travis's item ran, Pataki insisted publicly that it wasn't accurate, but to anyone who knew the players, it was obvious that truer words were never written.

The governor hunkered down—for a day. On Friday morning, a little after ten, Mike Long's phone rang. It was the governor, calling to tell him that he'd decided to endorse Giuliani and urge Lazio not to run. Long, whose relations with the mayor had always been icy and who had joined D'Amato and Mucha in encouraging Lazio to jump in, was "taken aback, definitely taken aback." Shortly before two that afternoon, with no advance warning, state capitol reporters in Albany were summoned to a press conference at which the governor made his announcement: "The party must unify behind one strong candidate," he said, "and I believe that Rudy Giuliani has earned the right to be that candidate. . . . I will support him and do everything I can to help him get elected. . . . I don't think a primary will be in the best interests of the Party."

Almost no one knew about this in advance. The governor didn't even call the mayor, sources say, until about an hour before his press conference. That afternoon I spoke to Teitelbaum, who was in Colorado lining up a fund-raiser for the mayor and had no idea about the announcement. "I'm totally shocked," he kept repeating. I talked to First Deputy Mayor Randy Levine, who was unprepared enough for the afternoon's developments that he was on a golf course in Dutchess County, about two hours north of New York City, where he and his wife had a country house. I talked to a gubernatorial aide who'd sauntered back to his office after a latish lunch and been hit with the news.

It turned out that for some weeks D'Amato had been navigating behind the scenes to try to bring the governor and the mayor to terms. D'Amato hated Giuliani as much as anyone, but he was the contact person in New York for national Republicans such as McConnell, who, their fund-raiser for Lazio notwithstanding, really wanted the mayor to be the candidate. It turned out that, on the very day Travis's item ran, D'Amato was sitting down with Giuliani in Gracie Mansion, the mayoral residence, to talk rapprochement. The talks were so secret that even Bill Powers and Joe Bruno didn't know about them until the day before Pataki's endorsement.

Lazio still made noises about declaring his candidacy on August 16, but after Pataki's announcement, no one gave them any credence. Giuliani, who thanked the governor for his backing, still spoke of the race in the subjunctive: "If" I run, "assuming" I'm the candidate. Given the mayor's equivocations, Pataki had traveled as far out on a limb for Giuliani as he possibly could. True, he was getting heavy pressure from the national GOP. But given the two men's history, Pataki could fully have justified not backing Giuliani and making him endure a primary. It was a rare selfless gesture by Pataki, who followed his genial nature and put the past behind him. Nothing could justify Giuliani's walking away now.

Four-Part Disharmony

Hillary's concerns at the time were well outside the traditional realm of politics. She had no need to bother herself with anything so quotidian as lining up endorsements and getting the Democratic Party behind her. Such was her celebrity and position that all that took care of itself; all she had to do was show up. What Hillary needed, instead, was first, a smooth transition from first lady to candidate that would develop the sympathetic story line of early 1999, that of the strong (and wronged) woman converting her national humiliation into hard-won power; second, a moderately plausible conversion from Illinoisan/Arkansan/ Washingtonian to New Yorker.

She chose odd methods.

On the first point, the issue, in a phrase, was The Marriage. It wasn't long after the impeachment dust settled that the public's conception of the marriage, and her role in it, began to shift ever so subtly. It could be seen in the polls, which over the course of the spring and summer of 1999 began to show the president's, and Hillary's, public approval ratings dropping off, because they were no longer threatened with being booted out of the White House. It could be heard in the way liberals who had risen to the Clintons' defense during the scandal began to talk about them: We went to the mat for you. We disagree with you, on the death penalty and free trade and lots of other things, but we saw your attackers as dangerous, and we stood with you. But you've drained the life out of us, and now we're tired of it. Spent. We held up our end of the bargain over these last months. Now, you hold up yours. Give us a little peace.

This attitude was only subtext in the spring of 1999; the *uber*-text, especially in official Democratic circles, was unalloyed enthusiasm. But all the same the subtext was real, and Hillary and Ickes and everyone else around her knew it. They knew that, if she did this thing, she would have to show she was aware of these tremors of discomfort and even resentment and respond to them lest they become an earthquake. She would have to come clean about her marriage, explain her attraction to Bill—which, fairly or not, was news—and, in crude campaign terms, take the issue off the table. What could be a better venue than *Talk* magazine? It was launching that summer to a huge buzz. And Hillary could have asked for no friendlier editor in America than Tina Brown. Brown had made her admiration of the Clintons clear in the pages of *The New Yorker*, which she ran before she left to start *Talk*. Tina and Hillary were pop-cultural soul mates, each charging into male-dominated arenas and asserting, with good results and bad, her will. With their similar ages and hairstyles, they even sort of *looked* alike. So, over the course of the first half of 1999, Hillary sat for a series of interviews with *Talk* contributor Lucinda Franks, whom she had previously met socially on Martha's Vineyard and who was the wife of Democrat Robert Morgenthau, the venerated Democratic district attorney for Manhattan.

The Franks piece hit, as fate would have it, the day after Al D'Amato's birthday party, and while most New York political reporters were spending their time chatting up GOP sources, their stories were buried under this avalanche. The *Post* started it off—the paper actually got a leaked copy of the interview, a day before anyone else—with a story headlined HILLARY: BILL CAN'T HELP CHEATING; EXPLAINS HIS FLINGS AS A "DYSFUNCTION." The next day, the paper's Deborah Orin reliably weighed in with another "analysis," arguing that Hillary was "trying to paint herself as the victim of a cheating husband" because it had helped her in the polls before and she was now "sliding." The paper also found shrinks who thought Hillary was offering a "sham excuse" for Bill's behavior. (Hauling out shrinks and quoting them in sidebar stories to justify a paper's position on the topic at hand is an old tabloid warhorse; the *Daily News*'s shrinks, not surprisingly, were altogether more sympathetic to Mrs. Clinton.) In *The Washington Post,* Howard Kurtz noted that "she never blames him for the affair or for deceiving her and the country." All over America, opinion was virtually unanimous. "Tacky," said *The San Diego Union-Tribune.* "Psychobabble," snorted *The Plain Dealer* of Cleveland. "Another dollop of Clinton-speak," sighed *The Arizona Republic.* Gene Weingarten, in *The Washington Post,* and Clarence Page, in his syndicated column, both wrote pieces to the effect that they were going to go home and tell their wives they'd been damaged as children and were therefore going out that night to find some nookie. There were only two defenses, by Robert Scheer in the *Los Angeles Times,* and by Sally Kalson in the *Pittsburgh Post-Gazette,* who gave lots of space to a Baltimore clinical psychologist who tried to analyze Hillary's remarks without judging them.

What Hillary actually said, in a very flattering and sympathetic article, was that she saw a psychological and emotional link between the circumstances of her husband's childhood and his present behavior. That traumatic past events have power in all our lives is obviously true. But politics and journalism have never found in Freud a very graceful partner, as Tom Eagleton learned, and so it was a short and easily managed march from Hillary saying there was a link to claims that Hillary had said Bill's childhood trauma "caused" his tomcatting, which Maureen Dowd wrote in the *Times,* or that Bill's mother and grandmother were "responsible" for his behavior, as Steve and Cokie Roberts rendered it in their syndicated column.

Still, Howard Kurtz had a point. What Hillary *didn't* say was revealing. She expressed no anger at Bill, either on her own behalf or the country's. And she said nothing of her role, during the Lewinsky matter and over the years, in controlling the political damage his affairs caused or threatened to cause. Before Ken Starr's office found the blue dress, it was all the work of the famous "vast right-wing conspiracy"; after, it was explained away in the dispassionate and impersonal language of psychology. She dealt with the issue by really only half dealing with it. Those of us who covered her for the next year became wearily familiar with the style, whether the topic was her health-care initiative or her position on the death penalty. Most savvy politicians know how to answer questions in a way that puts them to rest. With Hillary, there was something about the way she answered questions that only raised other questions.

It was a shock to the pundits, but, in the wake of the *Talk* interview, her poll numbers *did* shoot up. Two weeks before the interview came out, Giuliani was ahead of her by 10 points in a John Zogby poll for the *Post*. After the interview, they were at 44 points apiece. (Zogby, whose star had risen when he called the Clinton-Dole race on the nose but who in 1998 had published "tracking polls" in the *Post* showing D'Amato overtaking Schumer as election day approached, pronounced himself "mystified and confounded . . . the only revolt seems to be amongst the public against the pundits.") But the poll numbers weren't the important thing. The barrage of headlines about the interview was. And her attempt at damage control, at a press conference in Jamestown, was tight and unrevealing: "I'm a very strong proponent and believer in personal responsibility. That's what I hope people will take away from it." Hillary was beginning to look something other than sympathetic.

If her effort to keep her favorable public image on course was wanting, her attempts to convert herself into a New Yorker could be embarrassing. Hillary was in Utica, on the first leg of the Listening Tour, when *The Forward* broke the story that, in response to a questionnaire from a New York Jewish group called the Orthodox Union, she had said she would support the principle that Jerusalem should be the "eternal and indivisible" capital of Israel. It was leaked to the paper not from the Hillary camp but from somewhere inside the Orthodox Union. The Jerusalem question is always an issue in New York campaigns, and anyone running for dogcatcher in New York signs on to the position Hillary took. So her people were happy to have it out there. But coming from a candidate who had little track record on Israel's security aside from her remarks in support of Palestinian statehood in 1998, it bore the ring of a pander. The next month, *The Forward* broke the story that, lo and behold, Hillary's maternal stepgrandfather was Jewish! The conservative editorial directorship of the paper at the time was not inclined to lend Hillary Clinton any form of succor, and the paper got the story on its own. Yet not everyone believed that. Even when she *wasn't* pandering, it looked like she was.

Those were awkward moments, but they were one- or two-day

stories. Other matters, though, lingered far longer than that. One was the question of the Yankees. Probably no episode better expressed the hysteria of this phase of the campaign than the question of whether Hillary was a Yankees fan. At a labor luncheon at Manhattan's Tavern-on-the-Green in May, Randi Weingarten, the teachers' union president, gave Hillary a Yankees cap. She put it on. Photos were taken. The next month, at a White House ceremony honoring the World Series champs, she donned another one, this time given her by manager Joe Torre. Photos were taken again.

Those pictures were a visual stake in her heart. Think back to Rudy Giuliani, wearing his little Yankees outfit on the streets of Brooklyn. Consider the experience of a friend of mine, who back in the 1950s used to do door-to-door canvassing in Manhattan for Democrats and who made absolutely certain that he remembered, from election to election, who was a Yankees fan or a Giants fan or a Dodgers fan, because to invoke the wrong team was to risk a vote for the GOP. Consider that the old line in Brooklyn was that the three greatest villains of the century were Hitler, Stalin, and Walter O'Malley, who moved the Dodgers (originally the Trolley Dodgers, after the early-century youngsters who used to make a game of dashing in front of streetcars just before they passed) to Los Angeles. To New Yorkers, intensely parochial about their state, their city, their borough, and even their neighborhood, things didn't get much more serious than which baseball team you rooted for.

Hillary tried to say she'd actually grown up a Yankees fan. Her first love was the Chicago Cubs, of course, but she "needed an American League team to root for," she said, and she chose the Yanks. The number of people who bought this was roughly zero. It was the perfect emblem of her fraudulence and gall to her detractors, embarrassing even to her admirers. "I've been to Yankee Stadium a thousand times in my life," said the mayor, who had done everything in his power to identify himself with the team's success short of throwing a few innings of relief, "and I've yet to see Hillary Clinton there."

But here's the thing: It was, apparently, true. There was a *Washington Post* story from 1994—three or four years before her running for office in New York was even a remote fantasy—noting that she had grown up a "big-time" (her phrase) fan of the Chicago Cubs and the New York Yankees, idolizing Ernie Banks and Mickey Mantle. If you think about it, it does follow a certain logic: A person who is a Cubs fan presumably hates the White Sox; a person who hates the White Sox would tend to pick the American League team that is the most likely guarantor of their continued mediocrity; hence, the Yankees. (Besides that, a Cubs fan needs to cheer for a team that wins.) At any rate, this little nugget from 1994 wouldn't be unearthed until the next July, when the *Post* ran a brief item mentioning it, and by which time few New Yorkers would notice it and fewer still believe it.

And here's the stranger thing: Hillary's people had this clip the whole time, but never put it out. Joel Siegel of the *Daily News* told me later that he had it, too; when he had his first interview with Hillary and asked her about it, she tried to state her case, and then said she had "just given up" trying to persuade New Yorkers that it was true. Maybe so. All the same, it's the first time I've ever come across a candidate being murdered over something, having documentary proof that truth was on her side, and not offering it up.

And so it went. After baseball, the next New York lesson would take place on the jagged terrain of the city's ethnic politics. In mid-August, eight days after Pataki's endorsement of Giuliani, Bill Clinton announced a plan to grant clemency to sixteen imprisoned Puerto Rican nationalists, members of the Fuerzas Armadas de Liberación Nacional (FALN). At first it wasn't much of a story. Giuliani called on Clinton to release the pardon report from the Justice Department, which would have shed light on the grounds on which the president had made his decision. But the mayor took no position on whether the president was doing the right thing, beyond adding that similar consideration should be given to Jonathan Pollard, who'd been convicted of spying for Israel. Wolfson said Hillary would be "supportive, provided that the terms of the parole are strictly adhered to."

Nine days later, though, New York City Police Commissioner Howard Safir, intensely loyal to Giuliani, stood at One Police Plaza with a former NYPD detective who'd been blinded by an FALN bomb in the mid-1970s, and accused the president of doing this to help Hillary. "This is really, truly pandering to the Hispanic community," said the detective, Frank Pastorella. The same day Giuliani, at a fundraiser in Rochester, came out harshly against the deal. The spin cycle was restarting.

The *Talk* story dominated the papers for about a week. This one

went on for two. As the prisoners stalled on the renunciation of violence that was a condition of their release, Giuliani kept on the issue
full-bore, mentioning it at every press conference and appearance, and
on his radio program, and pressing for the pardon report. Safir joined
in. The *Post* played the story huge day after day. Cardinal John O'Connor jumped in, criticizing Clinton and backing off his earlier pleas for
consideration of clemency (he had written a letter to Janet Reno in
March 1996; he selectively reused portions of this letter for his column
in *Catholic New York,* leaving out the part where he'd asked Reno to
consider pardon or clemency). Hillary's campaign had no idea how to
move against this onslaught. Mark Penn, the campaign's pollster, was on
his honeymoon at the time. Ickes was trying to pay at least some attention to his new lobbying business. Hillary, as was now her custom, said
nothing.

The assumption that Bill must have done this for Hillary is debatable at best. The clemency process had begun years before and had
been a project of White House counsel Charles Ruff, who was quit-
ting his job and who was anxious to have the deal struck before he left.
"This caught us completely off guard," a source close to Hillary insists.
"Team Hillary did not know this until a phone call came that the
White House was going to offer clemency to these prisoners. Now,
nobody believes that. 'Oh, she's the president's wife, how could she not
know, he's doing it to help her.' Well, it sure didn't help her." She did
not need help with a constituency among which she was polling at 75
percent or higher. And presumably, Bill Clinton has not survived as
deftly as he has in politics by doing things like handing his opponents a
blind police officer for their future campaign commercials. But few believed the Clintons' arguments.

By Labor Day, the pressure was monstrous, and Hillary came out
against Bill's offer. But she did it without warning any Latino elected
officials, who were flabbergasted. Fernando Ferrer, the borough president of the Bronx and New York City's highest-ranking Puerto Rican
official, recalls being at home with his wife the night after Hillary
changed positions, when she called him to say she was sorry she hadn't
called beforehand. "I am, too," he told her. "You could have saved us all
a lot of grief." A few days later, Hillary met with Ferrer, Congresswoman Nydia Velazquez, Bronx Democratic leader Roberto Ramirez, and about a dozen other Puerto Rican officials at a private location

in Greenwich Village to patch things up. With an exception or two, they tried to put a nice face on things, chalking it up to her inexperience. She was lucky, too, at times like this, that she was running against Giuliani. Hillary would have to do far worse to make most Latinos drop their support of her against him.

The next mistake was the most devastating yet. Some months before, Hillary had promised Leah Rabin, the widow of assassinated Israeli premier Yitzhak Rabin, that she would visit Israel. The nascent campaign got in the way, but now she was prepared to honor her commitment. The trip would include a stop in Jordan to call on the new king and queen (King Hussein had recently died), and, for diplomacy's sake, in Ramallah, in the occupied territories.

New Yorkers, long accustomed to seeing prospective candidates coincidentally "vacationing" in Israel, Italy, or Ireland, assumed at first that this was a nakedly political trip. In fact it was a first-lady trip, not a candidate trip. There was tension throughout 1999 between Hillary's White House staff and her campaign staff over her time and schedule. Usually, the campaign staff won. But not this time. Consequently, she left for Israel with several members of her White House staff and no members of her campaign staff. "Israel," a campaign aide told me shortly after she returned, "was the last place we wanted her to go."

With good reason. On Thursday, November 11, she appeared at a day-care center in Ramallah with Suha Arafat, Yasir Arafat's wife. As Hillary sat, and as an interpreter translated Mrs. Arafat's words into English, Suha made mention of the "daily and intensive use of poison gas" by the Israeli army against Palestinians and of Israel's poisoning the Palestinian water supply. When Mrs. Arafat finished, Hillary greeted her and kissed her on both cheeks.

Mrs. Clinton would try to say later that the translation wasn't clear. To the reporters, though, it was clear enough; they heard what Mrs. Arafat said. They knew that Mrs. Arafat had used Hillary's appearance to grab headlines with her inflammatory words, and they expected that Mrs. Clinton would issue a statement denouncing those charges and reiterating her support of the peace process.

It took almost a full day for the denunciation to come, finally issued to reporters in Amman. It took about five seconds for The Kiss to make the cover of that Friday's *Post*. The picture was all that was needed. SHAME ON HILLARY ran the headline. A sub-headline mentioned "blood libel." A kiss, an act with such profound Biblical (albeit New Testament) significance. As New York political symbolism, it recalled Jesse Jackson's bear hug of Yasir Arafat, an act that caused him considerable grief in the 1988 New York presidential primary.

Congressmen Jerry Nadler and Anthony Weiner called around to reporters to make sure that their stories would include supportive quotes from officials with Jewish surnames. Ed Koch said "she handled herself correctly" given that she was there in a diplomatic role as the president's wife. Their view was a minority one. Giuliani—who, during the week of celebrations marking the United Nations' 50th anniversary, had had Yasir Arafat tossed out of a Lincoln Center concert hall during a performance, just in case any of those Giuliani Democrats were confused as to where he stood on the Middle East—said he would have denounced Suha immediately and forcefully on the spot, sensitive peace-process negotiations or not. Hillary's own response, like her defense of the *Talk* interview, was half a response: She, as the president's wife, didn't want to create an international incident, which was a credible argument. But she couldn't bring herself to admit that maybe she'd made a mistake, by not denouncing Mrs. Arafat more quickly or by going to Ramallah in the first place.

In a state where a Democrat who wants to win needs two-thirds of the Jewish vote to do so, the photograph was a catastrophe. The anger could be gauged that Friday morning on Bill Mazer's radio show on WEVD. Mazer's was the only program in the city whose (heavily Jewish) audience was almost uniformly liberal and pro-Clinton. But that Friday, both the host and his callers expressed dismay and disgust. "The damage it did on the West Side, among people who are Democrats, people who should have been Hillary supporters, was immense," Nadler told me later. "I'd talk to my constituents. They'd say, 'She's anti-Israel.' 'Why? Based on what?' 'Well, she kissed Suha Arafat.' And that was it. You just couldn't argue with it."

These four dramatic missteps—the *Talk* interview, the Yankees problem, the FALN, and Suha—were the markers that defined Hillary Clinton that fall. She certainly didn't manage to do much to define herself. Even when Giuliani handed her a chance to do it, she passed. On September 22, the mayor, in response to a question that his press office had urged a reporter to ask, launched into a tirade against the Brooklyn Museum of Art, whose new exhibit, "Sensation," featured a painting in which the Virgin Mary, her breasts formed of dried elephant dung, was surrounded by cutouts from pornographic magazines. Paroxysms burst out of the mayor for two weeks about what "sick" stuff it was; about how if he could do it, it wasn't art; about how he was going to cut off the museum's funding, even though doing so would obviously flout court precedent, as he must surely have known (a court eventually ruled against him, as the courts generally did on First Amendment matters). Public opinion, and editorial opinion everywhere but in the *Post,* was against the mayor. It was a nice chance for Hillary to put Giuliani on the defensive. A strong statement of some sort would have helped her with the liberals and Jews who were cool to her. Instead, four days into the controversy, she said she found the show "deeply offensive" but believed Giuliani's threat to shut down the museum was "a very wrong response." Trying to please everyone, she naturally pleased no one.

The Legend Implodes

This was the left-wing warrior of repute? She came to New York, by reputation, as a woman who saw the world in stark good-and-evil terms. As she saw it, there were those who wanted to make the world a better place for children and women and the human spirit, and those who got in the way. But the Hillary New York was seeing was anything but a courageous woman taking stands. Preternatural caution, rather than conviction, was her governor. And there was also, it was becoming clear, a breathtaking naiveté in her view of what a campaign was. She honestly believed that campaigns were pure environments for ideas, and that the superior ideas would out. And so when she did seek to "define" herself, it was entirely on matters of policy. She attacked Giuliani on the minimum wage, forcing him to flip-flop on his position. She hit him on the Nuclear Test-Ban Treaty, which the Republican Senate had just voted down, and had him on the defensive. She knocked him on the congressional Republicans' huge tax cut, which he had come out in support of and which wasn't popular in New York. She rebuked him for his policy on the homeless. These substantive arguments, she won.

But these victories were two-day stories, three-day at best, and, generally speaking, were covered in detail only in the *Times*. Meanwhile, the controversies—traveling the well-worn route from the *Post* to the *Daily News* to the chat shows, nearly all of which were hostile to her—stayed alive for a week, ten days, more. She had no intuitive knowledge of how to run a campaign's obstacle course, or how to counter bad publicity. Her campaign was something of a shambles at this point. It was being managed out of Washington, by Penn and Grunwald and Ickes. She had a bare-bones staff, some of whom she barely knew. Wolfson and Karen Dunn, in the press office, had only recently signed on and gotten to know her. Karen Finney, another press aide, had worked in the first lady's office and knew her, and Neera Tanden, who ran issues research and shared speechwriting duties with Wolfson, had also worked in the White House. But as a team they were just getting used to one another, to their candidate, and to the snake pit in which they found themselves. The exception was Wolfson, who had earned his New York campaign stripes in Schumer's race, but even he hadn't really been through the wars. Any number of old-pro New Yorkers, the kind of people who had years' worth of relationships with reporters and pols, could have applied a tourniquet to the campaign's bleeding. George Arzt, for example, an old *Post* reporter who still had lots of friends at the paper, could probably have planted at least a few favorable stories there, or seen to it that the tone of some stories was more balanced. Team Hillary worked without that sort of benefit.

Things reached such a pass, after the Suha debacle, that even some of her backers started openly asking the political version of the old Casey Stengel question, "Can't anybody here play this game?" Charlie Rangel, who had done as much to egg her into the race as anyone, said publicly that she'd better "announce and get a professional campaign team. I don't work with exploratory committees." To quiet such talk, Hillary did hire a campaign manager. Bill DeBlasio, the New York regional director of Andrew Cuomo's HUD and an experienced hand in local politics, was someone Rangel and other Democrats knew and trusted. His hiring put an end to Democrats' complaints of amateurism, but such carping had already reopened for Hillary's opponents the line of attack that she wasn't going to run. Dick Morris, who'd been writing this since early summer, hammered the point in a couple of more columns. I spoke on a panel with Dick that October at Columbia University. Afterwards, we rode the subway together down the West Side. C'mon, I said to him; bet me $10 that she won't run. He wouldn't take my bet, but he would continue to write it (October 26, 1999: "My bet is that she will take the money—and not run."), and the argument developed a nice head of steam. The story line on the race that went out across the country was, Is she really running? Just before Thanksgiving, Mrs. Clinton was forced to react.

At a November 23 press conference at the Park Avenue head-quarters of the United Federation of Teachers, Randi Weingarten, in what was obviously a staged moment, asked her: "So . . . Mrs. Clinton . . . what will it be? Is it yes, or is it no?" "The answer is yes, I intend to run," Hillary replied, as thirty or so staffers, hauled into the dreary meeting room to give the occasion a little oomph for the cameras, cheered. Even that, though, Hillary got wrong; "I in*tend* to run," she said, with an inflection that seemed to leave open the possibility of a last-minute reversal.

There was a month to go before the year ended, and so, of course, time for one more gaffe. At an Irish breakfast, where Irish pols and labor leaders applauded her work in the Northern Ireland peace nego-tiations, a reporter asked her if she planned to march in the St. Patrick's Day Parade. Her eyes popped to innocent life, and she smiled: "I sure hope to!" Everyone realized, as soon as the words came out of her mouth, that Hillary had stepped in it again. As a rule, most Democrats did not march in the parade. Marching in that particular parade had been an act of controversy throughout the 1990s, ever since the Irish Lesbian and Gay Organization petitioned the holders of the parade permit, the Ancient Order of Hibernians, for the right to march under their banner and were refused. Every St. Patrick's Day of the decade was rife with invective, ill-will, and multiple arrests of gay activists and their supporters who protested the event. After the breakfast ended, Wolfson, aware of what his candidate had done, tried to spin it that it was Hillary's hope to march—if things between the Order and ILGO could be worked out. But it was obvious from the way Hillary an-swered the question that she had no idea, and that her staff hadn't prepped her.

She'd had about as bad a six months as a candidate can have. Her attempt to refashion herself from distant first lady into flesh-and-blood pol was by turns earnest, amateurish, sad, disastrous. The Hillary Clinton of the 70 percent approval ratings and the 172 active fan clubs and the praise-winning 1998 barnstorming and the historic *Vogue* cover—the Hillary Clinton whom New York Democrats had begged to enter this race—was scarcely even a memory now. I don't often find myself nodding in agreement as I read the *National Review,* but I had to admit that there was something to Noemie Emery's observation that "that odd sound you hear is a legend imploding; the short, saintly stardom of Hillary Clinton, as it sputters to a halt." Even in *The Nation,* the more sympathetic Andrea Bernstein had to concede that "the school of smaller steps"—Hillary's chosen locution for her aggressively modest, post-health-care-fiasco view of political possibility—was "only slightly inspiring."

And yet: There she was, at year's end, still just a few points behind Giuliani in the polls! If there were ardent Clinton haters, there were evidently ardent Clinton admirers as well. But even this question—of who admired her, and who did not—would yield some very surprising answers.

CHAPTER 5

January 2000:
Struggling

The Woman Problem

AT THAT IRISH BREAKFAST, I was chatting with James Traub of *The New York Times Magazine* about the race. We got around to the subject of Hillary and women. After the dust of Hillary's fall disasters began to settle, we'd both been noticing that a lot of women were reacting to her candidacy with visceral hatred and contempt. The reaction was perhaps most intense among Democratic white professional women—that is, women like Hillary. Traub, in our conversation, remarked that he had a friend who was a therapist on the Upper East Side, and that many of his friend's female patients would plop themselves down on his couch and use the time not to explore the mysteries of their relationships with their mothers and husbands but to vent about Hillary. "Can you imagine?" Traub said. "These women spending $165 an hour to talk about *Hillary?*"

Eva Moskowitz, the city councilwoman who represents the Upper East Side, says she began noticing the phenomenon in the fall of 1999, when she was running for the council. She was shaking hands with voters, she recalls, at a supermarket on First Avenue when she got into a conversation with a woman who praised Moskowitz's work on education and other Hillary-ish issues. "We had this very nice conversation," Moskowitz says. "Then she said, 'By the way, you don't support Hillary Clinton, do you?' 'Well, yes, I do.' And she launched into this incredible tirade, and I thought, 'Oh, my God, this is going to be hard.' And this was a woman who cared about education and uninsured children and all these issues on which Hillary has been a leader."

Such tirades were a common occurrence around Manhattan at the time. What Moskowitz learned along the campaign trail the previous October, the press finally discovered in early January. Hillary had a problem with women. She still led Giuliani among women in polls, because black women, like black voters generally, backed her ten or twelve to one. But among white women, she trailed Giuliani, according to one January survey, by seventeen percentage points.

The "woman problem" was actually several different problems. Republican women hated Hillary, as you'd expect. Older women, the campaign's private polls showed, were especially skeptical of her; she represented an idea of womanhood well outside their frame of reference. Suburban women tended to find her cold and unfeminine. But by far the most striking defectors were white, professional Baby Boomer women. These women were her most logical base constituency, the natural and reliable launching pad for any woman seeking statewide office. And they wanted no part of her, and to ask one why was to risk spending the next twenty minutes on the receiving end of a Gatling-gun stream of consciousness.

But *what* didn't they like about her? "They just didn't like her, and they never articulated it, really," says City Councilwoman Ronnie Eldridge, who represents the Upper West Side. Across Central Park from Moskowitz's district, Eldridge's was a very liberal district that should have been the most fertile Hillary territory in the state. Eldridge herself had taken a verbal shot at Hillary's candidacy already when, during Hillary's autumn of discontent, she said Hillary should not run. Eldridge, who had been one of New York's most prominent Democratic women since 1964, when she was one of Bobby Kennedy's most enthusiastic supporters (and who was now married to the columnist Jimmy Breslin), was more concerned that her party was running an inept candidate than she was about anything else. But she heard quite a lot of Hillary animus from her female constituents in late 1999 and early 2000 on other grounds. "I felt, from what these women did say, that there was just this sense of entitlement that they wanted to reject," she says. "It was like, 'Enough of this already.' "

Enough of what, exactly, was hard to say. There was Eldridge's Entitlement Theory: the suspicion that Hillary expected professional, white women to support her in whatever she did and not ask questions. Harold Ickes was partial to the Enabler Theory, according to which these women were furious at Hillary because she had abetted Bill's philandering and had thus participated in a marriage that didn't advance feminist ideals. Others in the campaign believed that elite women were jealous of Hillary's exalted place in the world and felt, as they watched her deal clumsily with her marriage and the various allegations that arose against her, that they could have occupied that place with more aplomb. "There's this thing," one Clinton aide says, "whereby no person from Harvard ever says any other person from Harvard is excellent. It doesn't happen."

Ellen Chesler leaned toward the theory that professional women believed that all of Hillary's power derived from her marriage. Based in New York, Chesler is a woman with unique experience in the field of women and power, having both written on the topic and lived it. She is the author of *Woman of Valor,* an acclaimed biography of pioneering birth-control advocate Margaret Sanger. She has a long background in New York politics, as chief of staff in the late 1970s to Democrat Carol Bellamy, the first woman elected to citywide office in New York City. Chesler also knew Bill and Hillary quite well—she had worked for Hillary during the 1992 presidential campaign, and she once traveled to Haiti with Hillary and George Soros. Chesler believes that elite women "had only seen the derivative aspects of her power" and felt that Hillary hadn't earned anything on her own. "Many women who hadn't had it both ways," Chesler says, "who gave up either career or family, were confused or resentful of the fact that Hillary did have it both ways. I think as first lady maybe she didn't fully understand that."

All these notions represent aspects of an attitude toward the Clintons that is peculiar to liberal Baby Boomers and that produced, by the time of Hillary's candidacy, an animosity toward her that was in some ways even more passionate than the hatred of her by people on the Right. It's an attitude that stems from the fact that Hillary was the first professional woman, the first woman like these elite women who were now so hostile to her candidacy, to become first lady. These women never cared very much about what Nancy Reagan or Barbara Bush did; they were as remote from the experience of these New York City women as Anita Bryant. But Hillary was supposed to be *theirs*.

So they paid more attention to Hillary, and they expected far more of her. She was supposed to represent their generation—their mores, which were not their mothers', and the morality of the 1960s. That phrase, the morality of the 1960s, will sound jarring to those who reflexively equate the decade with a ribald and decadent amorality, and with the sort of social decline with which the Right has always associated the Clintons. But the young liberal elite students of that decade did have their own morality: the morality of authenticity. Be yourself, not who society demands that you be. The morality of authenticity was evident in the women's movement, which thrived on the conviction that "politics" was not about deal making and compromise, but about life choices—leaving the kitchen, breaking down the walls of the best professional schools, securing the right of abortion. ("Choices," not coincidentally, was a word Hillary invoked every time she spoke to women's groups.) It was evident in the gay rights movement, the moral foundation of which was the demand by gay men and lesbians to be able to be who they were and live accordingly, without fear. It was evident in any number of tracts and speeches from the era—among them, the famous Wellesley commencement speech by one Hillary Diane Rodham: "We're not interested in social reconstruction," she said. "It's human reconstruction."

Human reconstruction somehow never came to pass. And by the time of Bill Clinton's election in 1992—by the time the young activists of America's elite campuses bore children, took on mortgages, and slowly came to admit that their parents might have been right about a thing or two after all the Boomers' truce with bourgeois convention had taken firm hold. Yet they still wanted to believe that their mode of living would be better than their parents', and that the world they would make once they held power's reins would be better as well.

By 1993, it fell to Bill and Hillary Clinton to fulfill these expectations. This was, in political terms, an unusual, not to say oppressive, demand. To the rest of America, which either did not share or utterly rejected the ethos of the 1960s liberal elites—that is to say, to the vast majority of the country—the Clintons were expected, once in the White House, to uphold traditional values and respect traditional boundaries. But to liberal Baby Boomers, they were supposed to transform those values and boundaries in accordance with the Boomers' very different priorities. Who could possibly do both those things at once? Over time, Bill Clinton turned out to be just another politician (albeit a very talented one), willing to cut deals and corners, then trying to make up for his shortcomings with his charm (that most inauthentic of qualities!). Then, when it emerged that his character was not what it might have been (the generational transfer of power would have gone down far more smoothly if the first Boomer president had been a man of almost puritanical rectitude), the liberal Boomer journalists who had supported him so fulsomely in 1992 began to turn, and Clinton's moral collapse became a metaphor for the collapse of the hopes of the generation of Baby Boomer liberals. It was no accident that nostalgia for Tom Brokaw's "greatest generation" arrived when it did, after Clinton and his generation had been given almost six years to prove the superiority they had arrogated to themselves in their youth and had failed to do so.

And Hillary? One can say that it was the cattle futures, or Whitewater, or health care, or the marriage that repelled so many New York women. But the reaction elite New York women were having to her, beginning in that fall of 1999, suggests something more. They saw her as complicit in her husband's personal failings; complicit, therefore, in tarring the good name of the whole generation. Insofar as their reaction to Hillary revolved around how she represented them, it was a very narcissistic assessment. And it produced a striking irony. Hillary had once been an exemplar of that liberal-elite narcissism, poking fun at Tammy Wynette and cookie-baking. Now she was emerging as its victim. She had made mistakes and compromises these women considered unacceptable.

One suspects more Baby Boomer women than wanted to admit it had made similar mistakes and compromises. It may be that many of these women, as the novelist Mary Gordon told me in January, saw in Hillary someone who "forces us to understand the contradictions of our own generation" and to see "the reality of ourselves rather than the fantasy of ourselves." That was the view of a Boomer and avid Hillary supporter. Less generous interpretations would emphasize, as one feminist did to me, that Hillary "never said, 'I can't condone what my husband has done.' " These interpretations were vastly different, but both were about Hillary's relationship to the cohort that fate had designated her, of all women, to lead. (It was interesting that younger women, free of Baby Boomer women's expectations, supported her much more strongly in the campaign's polls. This prompted her pollster, Mark Penn, to adopt the quip: "If women don't know why to vote for Hillary Clinton, they should ask their daughters.")

These women represented a small fraction of the vote, but a potential disaster to the campaign. If her most logical constituency hated her, how could she possibly persuade other voting blocs? "It was a pretty hard wall of resistance," says one adviser. "This whole thing was like a transplant—you didn't know what kind of rejection you were going to face. And it was distressing to her. Having fought so long to dissociate her private life from her public life, and to establish a public track record on issues of importance to women, she was kind of hurt by it."

As to what to do about it, Hillary's campaign was frozen. Since it wasn't a strictly political problem, it didn't lend itself to the usual kinds of solutions. She was hesitant to try to impress these disillusioned women by being too much the ardent feminist, lest that repel other voters. And she was too guarded to confess her true emotions about her marriage, or pretty much anything else for that matter.

So she set about seeking to address the problem in early 2000 through a dogged iteration of the issues and sketchy references to her resumé. The issues were abortion, child care, education, health care, gun control, and other matters that pollsters tell us "cut favorably" with women. Unfortunately, on abortion, she had no leg up on the mayor— if anything, he was to her left on the question, because he opposed parental notification in the case of abortions for minors, and she backed it. She had nothing on him with respect to gun control, either. Health care was, for obvious reasons, a dodgy thing for her to bring up. This left her with kids. Concern for the welfare of children had been a constant in her career, going back to her Yale Law School days. So the phrase, "For more than thirty years, I've been an advocate in behalf of children and families" began popping up in every speech. When it came to the part of the speech, though, where she was supposed to fill in the details, she would again retreat into generalities, selling herself, I felt, rather short: She *had* been one of a handful of liberal legal scholars in the early 1970s who pretty much invented a new area of law, children's rights, arguing that the law in some instances should give weight to the views of minors. Garry Wills had reviewed her writings on the subject in a famous 1992 article for *The New York Review of Books* and had virtually canonized her. One might have expected her campaign people to bring this article back into circulation, highlighting the salient bits for the benefit of reporters who tend not to linger over six-thousand-word treatments in the *New York Review,* but they must have kept it in the same filing cabinet as those old Yankees clips.

With regard to her resumé, whatever concrete experience she had tended to get lost in the vagueness of her rhetoric. She would say to people, "I find as I talk to women that I'm a very unknown well-known person." It wasn't a bad opener, but it was never compellingly fleshed out. She had been named one of the top one hundred lawyers in the country in the 1980s, which might impress somebody some-where, but which to New York ears sounded like some sort of scam, since awards, as blasé New Yorkers know, so often are. She had headed the Legal Services Corporation, which provides legal defense to the in-digent. It was an appointment requiring that she be "confirmed by the United States Senate," a factoid she liked to drop in. That had a little potential as a selling point. It sounded like a real job, being in charge of a budget, operating with congressional accountability. But what did she *do* as head of the Legal Services Corporation? She didn't really say. And the two best-known items on her resumé, her partnership in Arkansas's leading law firm and her attempt to reform health care, were not the kinds of accomplishments around which winning campaigns are built. Many people had been elected to the Senate having done less, but it was getting hard to avoid the conclusion that maybe she didn't have that much of a record after all.

She made these points in her speeches, and in interviews, when she started doing them in February. And most crucially, she said them to groups of women at private conclaves arranged by her campaign staff and supporters. Ann Lewis, the longtime White House aide and sister of Massachusetts congressman Barney Frank, helped put these events together. Working from Washington, Lewis had helped Hillary embark on the Listening Tour. By early spring, she had moved to New York to work on the campaign full time, helping to coordinate these meetings with women. Ellen Chesler was also active in this effort, as was Libby Moroff, a longtime liberal activist in Manhattan who had worked for Ruth Messinger for many years. One such meeting, between Hillary and a select group of women at the offices of the power-ful Manhattan law firm of Skadden, Arps, Slate, Meagher & Flom, took place on March 13. The venue was chosen by Ellen Chesler, whose husband is a partner at the firm. The meeting brought together around a hundred women, most of them professionals, to meet with Hillary. Cheryl Mills, who won fame as a shrewd defense attorney for Bill Clinton during the Senate impeachment trial and who moved to New York after she left the administration, was there. She introduced Hillary to the group, and Hillary gave her spiel.

Eva Moskowitz, the city councilwoman, was there. She remem-bers that Hillary called on her afterward for the first question. Mos-kowitz made a basically sympathetic comment about how the women in this room needed to find ways to go out and pass this message along to their doubting sisters. "That was the only positive comment," Moskowitz says. "And this was a meeting of the so-called converted. But even at this meeting, one woman asked her how she could stay with him."

Chesler's recollection of the event is more upbeat. "The reception became very positive," she says. "She converted people. Women began to understand that, for starters, she was invited to run here, which no-body remembered. And it was an important meeting because many of these women, wherever they came from, represented women's groups. Even as large as New York is, word of mouth is important." There were other meetings, too, hosted by Hillary backers but without Hillary, at which women who were supportive of Hillary tried to persuade an in-vited group of skeptics. These meetings, usually of twenty or twenty-five women, were held throughout the spring and met with varying degrees of success. The Woman Problem would persist far beyond the spring, though. And when it finally began to fade, it did so less because of anything Hillary did than because of two things that were done to her, one by Rick Lazio and the other by Tim Russert. But that was months away.

Even if these women had adored Hillary, she faced a formidable challenge in another respect, one that not just Hillary but every woman who ran in New York had to confront. No woman had ever been elected to statewide office in New York in fifty years, not since two women served brief terms as members of Congress elected at large. In more recent times, one could look at each election in which a woman had come close and cite specific and pragmatic reasons why it hadn't happened. In the 1976 Democratic primary, in which Pat Moynihan narrowly defeated Bella Abzug, one could argue that Moynihan squeaked by because the left-leaning primary vote split between Abzug and Ramsey Clark. In the 1980 general election, conventional wisdom held that Elizabeth Holtzman, then a Brooklyn congresswoman admired for her work during the Nixon impeachment, would have beaten Al D'Amato if Jacob Javits hadn't stayed in the race, running on a third-party line after he lost the GOP primary to D'Amato, taking from Holtzman just enough of the moderate-liberal vote.

So there were always plausible explanations for why women failed. But the real reason is that, despite its enlightened and trail-blazing image, New York's political culture is uniquely hostile to women. Think of the adjectives one reflexively associates with New York: fast-paced, aggressive, hard-edged, rude, loud, a little obnoxious. New Yorkers revel in these qualities. And, in the very male tabloid culture that sets the tone in New York, they're not necessarily considered bad qualities for men who aspire to lead. But a woman who's aggressive and hard-edged and rude? That doesn't play, not even in New York. In other words, we might say that the political culture of New York values exactly the qualities that can make women seem, in the euphemisms most regularly employed, "pushy" and "shrill." Women could win congressional seats and other legislative seats, because those races never got much coverage. But expose a woman to a few months of intense press scrutiny, and it was almost inevitable that she would either end up being characterized by the press as too weak (if she couldn't adapt to the political culture's rules) or too tough (if she could).

Hillary's problem, then, was twofold. It was tough for women in New York in the first place. And tougher still for a woman whom so many women seemed to hate.

Into the Drowning Pool

Hillary paid two homages in mid-January. The first was show business with a dash of politics. The second, politics with a show-biz fillip. So it said something about the state of her candidacy at the time, and the way in which she was still feeling her way across New York's political landscape, that she managed the former with aplomb, while the latter proved rather more complicated.

Since December, David Letterman had been hectoring Hillary on air for not appearing on his show. Rudy Giuliani had done the Letterman show more than a dozen times over the years, sometimes hopping onstage just to read the Top 10 List. His cooperation helped turn the show into a rite of passage for politicians both local and national. Al Gore, in his "reinventing government" phase, broke a glass ashtray with a hammer and nail on Letterman to see whether it would shatter into more than thirty-five pieces, in which case said ashtray would be judged unfit for government use. Just after Christmas, Letterman had engaged in a humorous exchange with Howard Wolfson, on air, over the phone. Wolfson got off some decent lines ("Does the Carnegie Deli deliver to the green room?") that Letterman didn't expect from a political flack. ("I do the jokes here!" he said.) From that moment, "When is she doing Letterman?" became one of those questions that can distract a campaign for several days until it comes up with an answer.

In this case, the facetious question pointed to a more serious problem the campaign was facing. The press had grown increasingly impatient with Hillary's closed posture. She hadn't granted a sit-down interview since that first one in Cooperstown six months before. On January 3, the *Daily News* editorialized that she'd been behaving "more like a celebrity than an office-seeker" and complained that "her campaign has declined repeated invitations for months to visit the *Daily News.*" The editorial struck a nerve. The *News* wasn't hostile to her in the way the *Post* was, so insiders were watching the *News* closely to see which way it would lean in this race. It was a given that the *Post* would endorse Giuliani, and it was generally assumed that the *Times,* though anything but a great defender of Bill Clinton during the Lewinsky scandal, would in the end back Hillary. The *News* was the open question; its publisher, Mort Zuckerman, was probably a Democrat, but of a very centrist stripe: strongly pro-Israel, contemptuous of the Left or anything smacking remotely of it, suspicious of the teachers' and public employees' unions. He was a supporter of Bill Clinton's, which argued for a Hillary nod, especially if Bill really put the squeeze on him in October. On the other hand, Zuckerman had twice endorsed Giuliani, and in 1998, he had waited until three days before the Senate election—laughably late for an endorsement—to back D'Amato over Schumer. Insiders amused themselves by trying to guess which wind would fill Zuckerman's sails when the moment of decision came.

She did the show on January 12. Walter Cronkite came out during Dave's monologue and told him to try "not to be a jackass." Letterman was deferential. She got off one reasonably funny line. When Letterman noted that, since she'd just moved into the new house in Chappaqua, "every idiot in the area is going to drive by honking," she pointed at him and said, "Was that you?" It wasn't much, but one unscripted laugh was really all she needed to deliver, and so the appearance was judged a success, notwithstanding a mini-controversy the cable shows tried to stir up around the fact that the Letterman staff had warned her in advance that she'd be getting an on-air quiz about things like the state bird and tree (bluebird and sugar maple). She'd memorized the answers months before anyway, expecting that some reporter would try to trip her up on them. Letterman got his highest ratings in years.

The Letterman appearance was one piece of good news—her poll numbers shot up—in what was otherwise a vexing month for the Clinton camp. First there was the woman problem. Then there was the housing problem. She moved into the house in Chappaqua in January, and while establishing residency was inarguably a good thing, the house had been a running issue throughout the fall and winter, because the Clintons had asked Democratic fund-raiser Terry McAuliffe to provide collateral for their loan. On this matter, as on many others over the years, the Clintons made an unnecessary mess of things, choosing the complicated and malodorous alternative (involving a party moneybags) over the simple one (getting a mortgage). The move also gave the yakfests another chance to speculate on the marriage and ask whether Bill would move there when his term ended. (He had decided, at the last minute, to accompany her on move-in day, so that the cameras would convey not a lonely spouse striking out on her own but a happy couple embarking on a new adventure.) And finally, the day before Hillary's Letterman appearance, a new poll showed Giuliani ahead of her 49 to 40; also, it showed her favorable rating dropping below 50 percent for the first time. The errors of the previous months had taken their toll.

Her line of attack against Giuliani at the time was to argue that he lacked the temperament to be a good senator. If you have a disagreement with your fellow senators, she would say, "you can't sue them or fire them." Her polling had shown, and simple common sense suggested, that this could be a successful line of attack against the blustery chief executive. It might have been more successful coming from anyone other than the most controversial woman in the United States. After all, voters could reasonably wonder whether she herself could achieve comity with the likes of Trent Lott and Jesse Helms and the fifty or so other men who'd voted to throw her husband, and her, out of the White House.

The avenues of attack on Giuliani were narrowing. She couldn't paint him as a Gingrichite, as he wasn't. She couldn't get very far, either, with the sanctity of *Roe v. Wade,* because Giuliani was pro-choice and because, as regarded future Supreme Court nominees, everyone who watched the man operate knew that when the time came to vote on nominees, Giuliani would follow his own compass rather than the party line. Now that the previous January's luster had worn off this candidacy, and her campaign was engaged in the hard work of cobbling together a coalition that might get her to 51 percent, there were few strategies that seemed winning, and few voting blocs on which she could completely rely.

In fact there was exactly one: African-American voters were backing her by overwhelming margins. Black New Yorkers detested Giuliani, and though it might not be fair to say he detested them back, he made no efforts at all to seem the least bit friendly to them. In a city where nearly 30 percent of the population is African-American, he had no high-ranking black deputies. The prominent black elected officials in the state—Charlie Rangel, Carl McCall, Manhattan borough president Virginia Fields—he not only refused to meet with but regularly belittled. And black voters loved the Clintons. The African-American vote in New York was the difference at this stage between the race being a blowout for Giuliani and Hillary staying within striking distance.

The one day of the year on which even Giuliani paid obeisance to black New York was Martin Luther King Day. Usually, he attended the largest King Day celebration, at the Brooklyn Academy of Music, and even though he was always greeted with a smattering of boos, he managed most years to drag himself there and say, as Republicans are wont to do on King Day, that King's "real message" had to do with color blindness and individual responsibility. This January, though, the mayor did not attend; the organizers—chiefly, the office of Brooklyn's Democratic borough president, Howard Golden—had invited Hillary, so the mayor announced a scheduling conflict. Hillary went to BAM, gave a fine speech, and then to a church on Convent Avenue in Harlem, as a few of us in the press followed along in a van. Her third and final stop was at the upper Madison Avenue headquarters of the National Action Network's House of Justice—the home office of the Reverend Alfred Sharpton.

Only New York City could have created Al Sharpton. And the New York white establishment needs him as the Pentagon needed the Kremlin during the Cold War. He has done some monstrous things. There are certain episodes in his past that he'll never live down, or acknowledge. I have little doubt that he knows, and likely knew at the time, that Tawana Brawley was not telling the truth about having been raped by six white men. But he has never admitted it, and probably never will, because to admit he knew the truth would expose him to more legal damage from those he impugned, and because his base constituency would read such a confession as a sellout. That constituency, by the way, is comparatively small, even among black New Yorkers. In a city with around 1.5 million black voters, Sharpton, in his two major runs for office, never drew more than 130,000 votes. But Giuliani's recalcitrance on race matters—his reflexive defense of the police in every cop shooting, for example—and the newspapers' irresponsible tendency to cast racial tensions in the sharpest terms possible have made Sharpton's influence greater than the size of his constituency.

And yet, Sharpton fills a vacuum in a way that no other political leader seems willing to do. In New York City, when a young black man is shot by a cop, or killed by whites, he's the only really prominent black politician who's there every time. Over the years, he has become, though some will never acknowledge it, a legitimate political player. He ran a respectable Senate race in 1992, when he proved himself conversant on a range of issues far broader than those he normally talked about, and a mayoral race in 1997, when, in a low-turnout Democratic primary that was held shortly after white police officers in Brooklyn sexually assaulted Abner Louima, he nearly forced Ruth Messinger into a runoff. He had a base that did, or was perceived to do, his bidding en masse. So, after that Senate race, the National Action Network became a whistle-stop on the trail of most any Democrat seeking votes, and Sharpton became—like the Hasidic rebbes in Brooklyn—a person to whom establishment pols paid heed. I remember being in his car with him once, in the early 1990s, when Governor Cuomo called. I had the sense, given Al's unimpressed demeanor, that this wasn't such a special occurrence. Besides all this, he was funny and sharp, and he understood the game with the kind of instinct that you can't teach. In the late 1980s, he had permitted the unfriendly *Post* to photograph him under the dryer at his hair salon, getting his process; he even obliged the paper by picking up a copy of the *Post* to appear as though he was reading it while getting his hair done, which naturally ensured that the picture made the wood. Three years later, when he announced his Senate candidacy, he did so by saying, "I'm officially throwing my hair into the ring."

The obligatory call on Sharpton could still be controversial; the *Post* could be relied upon to let its conservative Jewish readers know that Democratic pols were sharing the stage with a man who had shared other stages with Louis Farrakhan and Khalid Muhammad. But it was more controversial for some than for others. Chuck Schumer and Eliot Spitzer, who were Jewish and whose position on Israel could not be questioned, could get away with it. Hillary was another matter.

For months the *Post,* and once in a while the *News* and the *Times,* had reminded readers that the day would inevitably come when Hillary would break bread with Al. Like the Letterman question, "When will she meet with Sharpton?" became a standard inquiry she faced on the stump. The Rev had been known to use the leverage he gained through such anticipation to make white politicians squirm a little, issuing a demand or two that might cause them grief with moderate white voters.

But Sharpton's hatred of Giuliani was such that he was in no mood to make mischief for Hillary. Sharpton had met with Harold Ickes and Bill Lynch on November 2, Lynch says, and had negotiated the Hillary meeting in what Lynch calls a "very friendly and very accommodating" way. "It was Sharpton who suggested she do it on King Day," Lynch says. "He said he wanted to be helpful and his main agenda was to defeat Rudy Giuliani." Sharpton's version of the meeting has just a little more edge. Ickes, Sharpton recalls, asserted that Hillary could win the black vote without Al Sharpton. "I said, 'Fine,' " he says.

" 'If you think she can do it with the team that couldn't reelect David Dinkins, the first black mayor of New York City, who was the only black mayor in America who once he got elected couldn't get re-elected, but couldn't do it with him and according to you could do it with a white lady from Arkansas, be my guest.' I don't think he expected to hear that."

Having flexed that muscle, Sharpton turned out to be a pussycat. He'd even given some thought to how to spin her appearance sympathetically if big trouble arose. The week before the event, he told me that "if Rudy and the Republicans want to say she's in Al Sharpton's pocket, I'll pull out the clips—and I have them—of me meeting with George Pataki and of [state GOP chair] Bill Powers calling me a responsible leader. That should quiet that down."

It was in the teens that day, officially, but with the ferocious wind it felt much colder. New York City has about eight or nine days like that every winter—the kind of cold that gives you a headache. But up the creaky and sagging stairs of the National Action Network headquarters, and inside the packed room—three hundred people in a space designed for half that—suddenly it was 100 degrees. No air. Radiators clanging. Cheap particle-board paneling, the kind that buckled when you leaned against it.

It was an audience quite unlike any other Hillary Clinton had faced. She could generally count on black audiences to look on her rapturously, with a defensive, she's-our-girl, when-you-pick-on-her-you-pick-on-us kind of adoration, as they had at BAM and the Convent Avenue church. The NAN partisans were a different crowd. To this audience, Hillary Clinton was just another pro-workfare, pro-death penalty, play-to-the-white-soccer-moms centrist Democrat. And it was a smart audience—serious NAN people would tend to know things like the history of the Garveyites in Harlem and own heavily thumbed copies of C.L.R. James's *The Black Jacobins*. They would turn out for Dr. King's day, especially with a celebrity coming to call, but they would much prefer Malcolm X.

As I listened to the warm-up speeches, knowing that Hillary would deliver the same sort of anodyne tribute to Dr. King she had given twice that day already, a tribute that would have played as well with upstate Rotarians as it did at BAM, I actually felt a little sorry for her. This audience would not adore her. It would tolerate her. And there was always the chance that *something would happen.*

When her car pulled up, Sharpton went out to greet her. At the time, Reverend Charles Norris of Queens was at the microphone. His talk, about his youth and his path to the ministry, started out unremarkably enough. Then suddenly he caromed into an anecdote about having worked at a clothing firm owned by a man named Miller, "a Jew." A few in the audience muttered responses like, "We knew that." Then Miller sold it, to "another Jew." Reporters hadn't been paying much attention to Norris at first. We were now. He paused, and finally said, "I was then employed by another Jew, by the name of Jesus." Applause.

On the blacks-and-Jews shock meter this was only about a six out of ten. You couldn't really call it anti-Semitic venom; it seemed more like a bewildering and tasteless attempt at a joke. But it created A Situation: once again, Hillary had waded into the drowning pool of New York ethnic and racial politics, where substance counts for little and symbolism and response mean everything. Congressman Eliot Engel of the Bronx was in the room when Norris made the remarks and immediately went down to where Sharpton was greeting Mrs. Clinton, who had arrived with Ed Koch. He reported that, while they were downstairs, "Norris made some terrible statements," Koch recalls. After a brief damage-control session, a sentence denouncing anti-Semitism was inserted into the First Lady's speech, and though it wasn't exactly a major applause line, it went down well enough.

After the speech, in a back room, there was a longer damage-control meeting that included Hillary, Koch, Lynch, Engel, David Dinkins, Charlie Rangel, Bill DeBlasio, and Patrick Gaspard, who worked at Local 1199, the hospital workers' union. Koch recalls Dinkins arguing that there was no need for Hillary to comment on Norris's remarks directly, and "I said, 'Oh no, this guy's got to be answered,'" Koch says. "And she said that, too. She was very forthright." Lynch's memory is that "she was just kind of listening. I'm assuming this was a new dynamic for her." Sharpton says that Hillary "said she was going to denounce any statements of insensitivity, and I said I would too, if I found it insensitive, which I did. I think that surprised her a little."

When Hillary came down to the sidewalk where reporters had

been waiting, she denounced Norris's statement without being asked. The next day's papers, even the *Post,* made little of the remark. Sharpton denounced Norris the following day himself, which killed the story completely after just two days. Maybe, finally, she was starting to figure this town out.

One other comment from that day would linger more than Norris's remarks. The parents of Amadou Diallo, whom Sharpton had been squiring around town ever since their son was shot, were in the audience. Toward the beginning of her remarks, Hillary expressed her sympathy to them for the "murder" of their son. Although "murder" may not have been the wrong word morally with respect to forty-one shots fired from six feet at an unarmed man, "murder" was very much the wrong word legally, since the trial of the officers was not yet underway. She said it so quickly, and so obviously without thinking, that hardly anyone noticed; among reporters, only Nagourney caught it and mentioned it toward the end of his article the next day. Sharpton, Koch, and Lynch all say none of them noticed it, and it was not even discussed at the meeting where they talked about the Norris matter. But the following week, *Daily News* columnist Jim Dwyer, normally a pretty liberal (and definitely anti-Rudy) voice, wrote a scathing attack on Hillary over it, and the next month, long after Norris was a distant memory, a police fraternal organization took out a full-page ad in the *Post* reminding readers that Mrs. Clinton had convicted the cops before trial. Callers to radio shows, in whose minds Hillary was no doubt screaming the charge at the top of her lungs to incite the Sharptonites, would mention the remark for months.

Giuliani had a rather strange King Day himself. As was his custom, he attended the dinner of the Congress of Racial Equality. CORE, once a mighty warrior of the civil rights movement, operated now under the sponsorship of Roy Innis, an erstwhile black nationalist who'd tacked sharply to the right over the years and was generally regarded as a pretty bizarre fellow. He had a habit of inviting to his King Day dinner a series of guests whom Dr. King in his lifetime would no doubt have found appalling and then facing down the inevitable questions from the media by invoking the spirit of Christianity and forgiveness and brotherly love. This year, he had invited Atlanta Braves pitcher John Rocker, who couldn't make it, and Austrian rightist Jörg Haider, who could. Haider had once praised Hitler's economic policies and the "brave men" of the SS, and was at that moment poised to join the governing coalition of Austria. Mayor Giuliani worked the dais and shook every hand, Haider's among them.

It took a few days for word of the handshake to leak out, at which point the mayor said he hadn't known who Haider was. This was ridiculous, since Haider had been the subject of a lot of media coverage, and since he had planned the previous fall to run in the New York City Marathon. Even though he'd pulled out at the last minute, the NYPD had held meetings to discuss the security and logistics of a Haider run, and it's virtually impossible to imagine that Giuliani hadn't been privy to those concerns. But Rudy spent two weeks saying he didn't know.

The coverage of the Sharpton and Haider incidents made an interesting contrast. If Hillary had shaken Jörg Haider's hand and pretended for two weeks she didn't know who he was, you can be sure it would have been front-page news in the *Post* and the lead topic on every talk show in America for days. But with Rudy, the *Post* didn't dare whip it into a controversy. One of the most hilarious *Post* moments of the entire campaign came on February 4, the day Haider's Freedom Party was sworn in as part of the new government. Under normal circumstances, the specter of Haider sharing power in Austria would have made for at least a two-page spread in the *Post*. It was the lead story in *The Times* that day. But under these circumstances, with Hillary trying to rally New Yorkers to denounce Giuliani for appearing with Haider, the *Post* buried the story on page 24, under the headline AUSTRIA OK'S REPENTANT HAIDER.

New York is an ethnic place, but, as Hillary was learning, some ethnic squabbles are more important than others.

The Hillary-Haters Pitch In

At month's end, both campaigns were to release their first financial reports. The common view had long been that Hillary would be taking in checks faster than her people could open them and would probably end up raising about $25 million. Giuliani, it was presumed, would do well, what with all the Hillary-haters around America, but not that well—maybe $20 million. It was all going to add up to the most expensive Senate race ever, eclipsing the 1994 California Senate race, in which Dianne Feinstein and Michael Huffington spent $44.4 million. But Hillary was supposed to have the edge.

So when Bruce Teitelbaum called a press conference for January 19, a full twelve days before the papers were due to be filed, most of us suspected he had something surprising to say. And he did. In a mere six months, Giuliani had raised $8.9 million. Adding that to the $12 million he had raked in the previous year, and factoring in a probable late infusion as the race heated up in the fall, it was clear that Giuliani could easily raise $25 million, maybe $30 million. Teitelbaum's announcement forced the hand of the Clinton campaign, which quickly had to disclose its number—just $8 million. Raised over a period of about nine months, this amount put her on track for a total of less than $20 million. Giuliani, in other words, could come out by November with an advantage of $10 million or so.

No matter how Team Hillary tried to spin this, it was a disaster. The various advantages with which she had started the race—a lead in the early polls, the admiration of people in general and women in particular—had vaporized. The lone remaining advantage she had was money, and now even that was a mirage. As Teitelbaum stood before us that day, pointing proudly at his charts and his plastic mail bins crammed full of envelopes, one could begin to imagine Rudy Giuliani taking his place on the floor of the Senate.

Teitelbaum was coy on the subject of how much money had come from out of state, and from people whose interest in the race had rather less to do with their enthusiasm for his candidate than their loathing for the opposition. And he didn't acknowledge the man who had helped mastermind this coup. The day after the press conference, Greg Sargent and Josh Benson broke the story in *The New York Observer*'s online edition: Rudy's direct-mail guru was none other than Richard Viguerie, the Virginia-based arch-conservative. Viguerie had been enlisted by the Giuliani camp to rent various right-wing mailing lists, including, among others, the 37,000 Americans who had purchased neckties, coffee mugs, and mink gloves from Rush Limbaugh's "No Boundaries" collection.

Viguerie's name called forth memories of Oliver North, Barry Goldwater, Jesse Helms, George Wallace, and Pat Buchanan, the high-profile clients he had worked for in the past. The name Giuliani seemed an unlikely addition to this list—a pro-choice, pro–gay rights mayor of a city that was anything but a Republican citadel. Giuliani, as the mayor of a five-to-one Democratic city, had toiled in the early 1990s to forge for himself an acceptably centrist image. Now he was running against the city he governed.

In strategic terms, it made sense for Giuliani to do this—a Republican's votes in a statewide election won't come from the city, so he had to make a new and more conservative image for himself to satisfy suburbanites and upstaters. And, since there were obviously piles of money to be made from Clinton-haters across America, why not go and get it? If he had to run to the right, so be it. He had run to the left when doing that was expedient; he knew how to execute such maneuvers without being too obvious about it.

Still, one last bridge needed crossing for Rudy's conservative conversion to be complete. That bridge led to a liquor store in the Bay Ridge section of Brooklyn, presided over by a fellow named Mike Long.

CHAPTER **6**

February 2000:
The Launch

He Wrestled Mario Cuomo Over Philosophy

ONE FREEZING COLD NIGHT in February 1972, Mike Long and a friend went to an Irish dinner-dance at a Catholic church in East New York, Brooklyn. Mike lived in East New York and, with his brother Tom, ran an ice-cream parlor he had bought when he returned in 1961 from a hitch in the Marines. The neighborhood's most famous son may be Danny Kaye, but don't be fooled by that; East New York was and is one of the city's toughest sections. Historically Jewish, it was one of the last neighborhoods in the city to experience white flight—I have an old campaign poster for Norman Mailer's mayoral candidacy in 1969 that celebrates the city's quilt of neighborhoods, and even then, the designers of this poster thought it appropriate to render the words "East New York" in a faux-Yiddish typeface.

By the 1970s, when the neighborhood's racial makeup had changed, its 75th precinct suffered from some of the city's highest rates of homicides and thefts and other somber indicia. And the neighborhood was home to crime of the organized as well as the street variety: the bar where Henry Hill was drawn into mob life in *Goodfellas* was in East New York.

That February night, Tom Long was locking up the shop and noticed that Mike's friend's car, which he'd parked out front before the two hopped into Mike's car to go to the dinner-dance, was smashed in and mangled. Someone had sideswiped it hard, driving down the street too fast and probably too drunk. Mike and the friend returned, and they all got in Mike's car to prowl the neighborhood streets and see if they could find their perp. Right around the corner from the ice-cream parlor was a place called the Crystal Room. "It was a known place," Long recalls. "Clearly a mob joint." And, parked right across from the Crystal Room, they saw a car with parts of the friend's vehicle in the back seat.

The Long brothers and their friend called the cops and stood outside waiting for them to arrive. While they were waiting, the door of the bar opened up, and out came around twenty people. One thing led to another. A man punched Long. Soon the whole gang was on top of him. He somehow managed to break away, but then suddenly someone drew a gun and, at point-blank range, shot Long in the side of his abdomen. The bullet narrowly missed his vital organs and spine.

The police never did collar the shooter, but, two weeks later, Long went back to the Crystal Room with several plainclothes cops and identified the man who'd punched him. He was a hood named Richard Gomes, who was connected to the Vario crime family (immortalized in *Goodfellas*) and who at one point was the driver for none other than John Gotti. Years later a Manhattan lawyer named Ed Hayes was talking with Long and told him, "Mike, I'm gonna track that bastard down." Hayes called a corrections official in Rhode Island, and was told that Gomes had been convicted of two stabbings and was in a penitentiary. "Why do you want to know about this guy?" the official asked. "Because," Hayes said, "a friend of mine had some trouble with him years ago." The corrections officer paused. "I'll tell you something," he said. "If your friend had trouble with this motherfucker and lived, I guarantee you he's the only one." And that is Mike Long.

He is not one to run from a fight. He got into a famous one in 1977, during a forum of mayoral candidates held at Fort Hamilton High School, in the Bay Ridge neighborhood to which Long moved in the early 1980s. Mario Cuomo was one of the candidates; he was running as a Democrat, but also on an obscure minor-party line that Cuomo boasted was the "only party in the state with a platform." Long, by then a rising operative in the state Conservative Party, didn't like hearing this, because, as he put it to me in an interview, "*We* had a platform." The event ended and Long, as he tells the story, confronted the future governor thus: " 'Mario. The Conservative Party doesn't have a platform?' And he was kinda, really, somewhat angry. And he says, 'That's what I said, you don't have a platform.' And I says, 'You're wrong.' And he says, 'You don't have a platform.' I say, 'You're a liar.' That's probably inappropriate for me to say that, you know? But as I say it, we're eyeball to eyeball, and he just took me with both hands and pounced on me, and I went through these two doors, but before I went—and he's a pretty big guy—I was able to grab onto his sleeves, so I dragged him through the doors with me." They tussled and shouted insults at each other; the cops broke it up. Cuomo—Long pronounces it "Como"—-and his entourage drove away, but, in a few minutes, his car circled back. Mr. Como had returned to apologize to the man who was likely the only person in New York State willing to use his fists to defend the honor of his party's platform.

Long lived, by then, in Brooklyn's Bay Ridge section, an altogether more placid neighborhood in the shadow of the Verrazano-Narrows Bridge, where he owned a liquor store. He became the head of the State Conservative Party in 1988. The respect for him, as nearly universal as respect for a political person in New York can be, derives from the fact that his party has principles, and would sooner endorse a loser than compromise them. His importance derives from the fact that New York is one of the few states in which minor parties can actually play important roles in elections. The state's election law defines a "political party" as any group that can nominate a person for governor and get that person 50,000 votes on its ballot line. That accomplished, the group attains official party status for the next four years, until the next gubernatorial election, when it has to do it all over again. And so New York's parties include not just Democrats and Republicans, whose candidates get 50,000 votes many times over, but the Liberal Party, born of the anti-communist labor movement in 1944, the Conservative Party, the Right-to-Life Party, the Green Party, the Independence Party, and the newest one, the Working Families Party, a liberal-left coalition started mostly by union and housing activists that won its status in 1998. Generally, these parties reach the 50,000 threshold by cross-endorsing the major-party candidates: The Conservatives endorse the Republican nominee and instruct their members to vote for that nominee on the Conservative rather than the Republican line, the Liberals back the Democrat, and so on. The minor-party ballot line can have appeal beyond the party's enrolled members; there are a certain number of people who, just to be different, or because they're ideologues, or to register distaste for the two major parties, cast a minor-party vote; people for whom it is somehow psychologically more comforting to vote, say, for Ronald Reagan on the Conservative line instead of the Republican. And even the parties that run quixotic candidates can corral 50,000 votes, in a state where gubernatorial elections usually draw five or six million voters, by showing some modicum of organizing ability.

The Conservative Party of New York was born in 1962, both as counterweight to the Liberal Party and as bulwark against Rockefeller Republicanism. It truly came into its own at the time of the 1965 mayoral candidacy of William F. Buckley, Jr. (Mailer and Buckley, only in New York: it's great both ran, and, as I'd bet they would agree, it's great both lost). In the years since, the party has been vital to the statewide chances of any Republican candidate. George Pataki beat Mario Cuomo in 1994 by about 290,000 votes. He won 329,000 votes on the Conservative line. The Conservatives, in other words, provided his margin of victory. The last Republican to win a statewide election without the cross-endorsement of the Conservative Party was Jacob Javits, in 1974, who ran as a Republican and a Liberal. Normally, a Republican candidate would pick up about 300,000 votes on the Conservative line, a number that would come in awfully handy in a close race.

Rudy Giuliani had always been at odds with the Conservatives. In 1989, when he first ran for mayor, the Conservatives had endorsed Ron Lauder, a former diplomat and a son of cosmetics magnate Estée Lauder. Best remembered now, if at all, for not knowing that the mayor did not control the Board of Education. Lauder was put in the race by D'Amato, to whom Long was close, just to attack Giuliani from the right and make him drain his treasury. In 1993, the Conservatives had run George Marlin, a far more articulate and interesting man, but one who also had no chance of winning. In 1997, Long was invited to Gracie Mansion to discuss a possible endorsement with the mayor. They left it that Giuliani would get back in touch with Long if he wanted to pursue an endorsement, but, Long says, "he never got back to me." When it was clear Giuliani would be reelected, and the Conservatives couldn't find anyone to take their line, they actually left it blank rather than back the socially liberal, Cuomo-endorsing mayor. Long says he thinks the mayor's done a good job, but in three elections, he's "never voted for the man."

By 1999, though, the game had changed. Giuliani and Teitelbaum understood that having the party in the mayor's corner would be more important in a statewide race than it had been in Giuliani's previous, citywide campaigns. The mayor wanted the Conservative endorsement, but he wanted it on his terms, and he didn't want to do much work to get it. Long thought it odd when, one night in April, he and his executive vice-chairman, Jim Molinaro, were invited out to dinner at an East Side Italian restaurant with Rudy, Randy Levine, and Cristyne Lategano, the mayor's communications director (and widely presumed paramour), and sat there for more than an hour discussing everything under the sun except politics. Finally, Long decided to start the conversation:

" 'Mr. Mayor, I assume I'm having dinner with you because you are considering running for United States Senate.' And he says to me, 'I haven't made up my mind yet.' That was the end of the statement. I said to myself, 'I'm not gonna let this go now.' And his people started moving around a little bit, like I wasn't supposed to speak like this. So I say, 'Then I assume I'm here in case you do run for United States Senate, and you'd like to know what we're gonna be doing.' 'Yeah, I'd be interested in that.' 'Well, let me just tell you that if our convention were tomorrow, Rick Lazio would have our support. But the other side of the coin is our convention isn't tomorrow. It's a year from this coming month.' 'Oh, that's good to know.' " And so on.

Long was confounded, and put off, by the mayor's diffidence. But he told Giuliani that night that there were only two endorsement deal-breakers: First, the Conservatives would never back a candidate who also had the support of the Liberal Party, which mayoral candidate Rudy had had each time he ran. Second, he would have to join them in opposing partial-birth abortion. Long understood that he had to bend on certain issues, but there was no way he was going to back Rudy without the mayor pledging a thing or two to him in return. " 'You give me those two,' " Long told Giuliani, " 'and if you desire, I'll move forward and help you get the endorsement.' 'OK, very good.' "

They went down the street to a cigar bar owned by the mayor's friend Elliot Cuker, had a smoke and a cognac, and said goodnight.

Lazio, though pushed to the sidelines the previous August by Pataki's endorsement of Giuliani, was still sniffing around for opportunities to jump in. He had Long's tentative backing because he had done things the Long way. The previous December, Suffolk County Conservative leader Pasquale Curcio brought Lazio to Bay Ridge, where the three men lunched for two or three hours with Long at a place called Skinflints, down the block from Long's liquor store. In February 1999, Lazio attended the Conservative Party's annual winter conference, made nice with the leaders, sponsored a coffee hour. Such gestures were important to Long: Someone who wanted the Conservative Party endorsement had to work for it.

Giuliani had no intention of working for it. Long could see that the mayor expected the Conservatives to back him simply because of the importance of beating Hillary. A Giuliani source essentially confirms this, saying that the mayor's people were working with other upstate Conservative Party leaders, such as Tom Cook of Rochester, to bring intra-party pressure to bear on Long and force him to come around to Giuliani—without the mayor having to meet Long's conditions. "We wanted the Conservative line, but we didn't want to lose the Liberal line," this source says. "We were thinking at the time that if everything went our way, we'd have the Republican, Conservative, Liberal, and Independence Party lines. Could you imagine that? So when a person walked into the voting booth, they'd see Rudy's name four times, boom boom boom boom, and Hillary's once, or maybe twice."

Long *was* under intense pressure to "do Giuliani" and keep the Republican-Conservative alliance intact. "My own wife said, 'You're not gonna get away with this,' " he says about his reluctance to endorse Giuliani. "I said, 'I'm not gonna flinch.' " Long also knew that state GOP leaders were leaning hard on upstate Conservative Party leaders to come out for Rudy in defiance of Long. They even tried, Long told me, to organize a charter plane flight of Conservatives down to the city to visit the mayor at Gracie Mansion. "One of my leaders tipped me off," he says. "And I had some people in my ranks saying, 'Look, we're gonna get killed if we don't go with Rudy.' And I said, 'If you come to the convention and outvote me, fine. Then you're going to have to find another chairman.' " The man who had walked into the Crystal Room to stare down John Gotti's driver did not play games.

Long had been less than thrilled in August 1999 when Pataki gave up his neutral stance and endorsed Giuliani. Long saw the governor the week before the endorsement, and he says he'd "gotten vibes" that Pataki would be backing the mayor. He persuaded the governor to hold off for a week, he says; then, the *Post* item about the D'Amato birthday party hit, and the rumors about D'Amato's role. Pataki called Long the Friday morning of his announcement—incidentally, before he reached out to Giuliani, whose call from the governor came in the afternoon. "I urged him not to do it," Long says of Pataki's endorsement. "He said, 'Look, I appreciate our conversation, but I'm going to move forward.' " Long, though, stood pat. He wasn't going to think about endorsing the mayor until Rudy met his terms, and until he asked.

Giuliani never did ask. He sent Long signals by moving rightward on certain issues—he came out for school vouchers, for example, and expressed support for George W. Bush's proposed $1.4 trillion tax cut. The fuss Giuliani made over the Brooklyn Museum's "Sensation" exhibit, especially, was seen by many as an act the mayor performed for an audience of one, Long. While Giuliani surely wanted Catholics around the state to take note of his line in the high-culture sand—Catholics represent nearly half of the statewide vote—he must have been gratified when Long was quoted in the papers as approving his actions.

But no sooner had the mayor made that overture than, on the first Saturday in October, just as the "Sensation" flap was ebbing, he went on CNN and said he would never change his position in favor of partial-birth abortion. Long had made it clear, in interviews with me and other reporters, and to the mayor himself at that April dinner, that even though he'd be willing to grant Giuliani more ideological leeway than usual in the interest of stopping Hillary, partial-birth abortion would remain a litmus test. And here was Giuliani telling Long to stuff it. Long would have to learn, as everyone who'd butted heads with the mayor had, that you played by Rudy's rules, or you didn't play.

As the year closed, Giuliani still hadn't called Long, but Lazio, itching to be the candidate, was calling Long once a week. It seemed that perhaps Giuliani didn't even want the Conservative Party endorsement; that his historical affiliation was with the Liberal Party, and that, as one operative put it to me, "he goes with the people he trusts." If you knew Giuliani, you recognized this as one of the central defining traits of his personality—it could manifest itself admirably as loyalty, less admirably as suspicion or just plain paranoia. It seemed clear that, if he was forced to choose between the two minor parties, Giuliani would run as a Republican-Liberal—that is, as a moderate—and try to push Mrs. Clinton, who had the Democratic and Working Families lines, to the left.

Such was the atmosphere on February 7, when the Conservative Party met in Albany for its annual conference. The mayor did not attend. Lazio did. And Long that day told reporters about Giuliani, "I think I would rather that he didn't run"—a dramatic change from his previous public comments, which had more or less suggested that he was sitting by the phone waiting for Giuliani to call. Giuliani shot back from City Hall that "generally, what I am interested in is not what a political party thinks, it is what the people in the state think." He added, in his casual, what-me-worry way, that if people "think I'll be a better senator, they should support me. If they don't think I'll be a better senator, they should support somebody else." From a strategic point of view, the mayor's stance made sense: If he didn't end up having the Conservative line, it would be awfully hard for Mrs. Clinton to paint him as a right-winger. At the same time it was a huge gamble; the Conservatives could choose another candidate, a move that could hurt Giuliani to the tune of 300,000 votes. George Pataki was too amiable to fight Giuliani, and Al D'Amato was too keen on always playing both sides to force a showdown. No one doubted, though, that Mike Long would force one, if it came to that.

The Blank Canvas

After weeks of planning—hunting down a venue in her adopted Westchester County both large enough and close enough to Westchester County Airport, where Air Force One would be landing—the

Hillary for Senate campaign had settled on the gymnasium at the State University of New York's Purchase campus for her formal announcement. This was an announcement unlike any the New York Democratic Party had held. Candidates' announcements usually take place in hotel ballrooms with about one hundred people. For this one, though, ten thousand filled the home gym of the Panthers—every major and minor Democratic politician in the state, a couple of thousand students, a few thousand union members and other party loyalists bussed in from around the state. It took more than an hour just to get everyone into the hall; enduring the lines at the metal detectors was one of the prices Democratic loyalists paid at large gatherings to get a look at their famous candidate and her husband.

The event was a magnet, too, for some notable faces not normally seen along the Hillary trail. White House aide Sidney Blumenthal was on hand, looking on with pride at this turnout for the woman to whom he was such a close confidant. And up in the bleachers behind the press, there were two for whom the event had the appeal a car wreck has for passersby: *Post* columnist John Podhoretz and his special guest, Linda Tripp confidante and Clinton nemesis, Lucianne Goldberg.

The speech was carried live on CNN, New York 1, and other cable channels. The President, Chelsea Clinton, and Hillary's mother, Dorothy Rodham, were all there on the stage. Hillary was using every piece of ammunition she had, and it was her best opportunity yet to make a clear and forceful case about why she was running and why New Yorkers should open their arms to her candidacy. Some opening speakers would hint at this: "When you need the best person for the job," Charlie Rangel bellowed, "you don't ask, 'Where are you from?' You ask, 'Can you serve?' " In a scripted but appealing moment that was designed to remind people that the first lady who made some people's blood boil inspired the opposite effect in others, Amity Weiss, a fifteen-year-old sophomore from Ithaca High School, recalled setting eyes on Hillary for the first time: "It never occurred to me that that impact could be felt from one person." Nita Lowey spoke, as did Chuck Schumer. The introductions built up to Pat Moynihan. Still assumed to be less than enamored of this candidacy, Moynihan nevertheless obligingly reminisced about visiting Eleanor Roosevelt at Val Kill, her Hyde Park home, and concluded by saying, "Hillary, Eleanor Roosevelt would love you." Party officials really smiled at that one, perhaps less out of enthusiasm than relief.

Hillary approached the podium. The crowd applauded her fiercely, and protectively; you could see in people's hopeful eyes that they wanted this to go so well for her. This assemblage, after all, was the hard-core Hillary defense team—her Maginot Line against a world that thought her opportunistic or corrupt, or both. You could sense, also, that they feared she would not quite rise to the moment—like the parents of a Little Leaguer at bat for the first time, praying for anything better than a strikeout. She managed to start out with a rare joke at her own expense ("I'm a little older now, a little blonder"). She ran through her standard issues catalog, a collection of initiatives and buzzwords that polled well for Democrats—gun control, family and medical leave, hate-crimes legislation, a comprehensive test-ban treaty—punctuating each, as closely as she could come to Jesse Jackson style, with a promise that "I'll be on your side."

In more intimate settings, she would enumerate the items on her resumé in an attempt to make the case for herself as a professional with accomplishments in her own right. In this speech, before a more general audience, she told would-be folksy anecdotes to reassure her listeners that she was not the distant first lady of their more skeptical imaginings, but a public servant attuned to the needs of regular people. She had, she wanted her audience to know, eaten lunch with teachers at a school in Queens. She'd visited businesses "from Jamestown to Great Neck." She'd spoken with breast-cancer survivors at Adelphi University. She had "sat on porches and backyards from Elmira to New Rochelle."

But the one thing she couldn't talk about was herself. Nothing about a brush with tragedy, nothing about a personal experience with hardship or discrimination, nothing to open herself up to her listeners and show them that she had an understanding of the human condition that went deeper than the relationship between citizen and state. It was weird. It was, for starters, utterly out of step with the dominant strain of contemporary American political rhetoric. That rhetoric in recent years has tended to emphasize the personal narrative—the act of turning the crucial events of one's life into an appealing, if often quite mawkish, personal story. To find the technique's master we need look no further than Hillary's husband—the Man from Hope, talking as he did in 1992 about his bounce-around childhood and having to punch his drunk stepdaddy and feeling people's pain. Hillary just didn't have it in her to do this. In this respect she was suited to an earlier age, a time when politicians talked more about the social order and less about themselves. Her rhetoric, when it rose above the bland recitation of specific issues, tended toward notions about civic ideals and the larger world that were profoundly rooted in her view of society. Discussing her ideals, she was comfortable. Discussing herself, she was anything but comfortable.

In never describing her real feelings, Hillary came before people as a blank canvas, on which they could paint anything they wished. Take, for example, her motive in running for the Senate, a topic of intense debate right up through election day. It probably was more honorable than not—she had surveyed her post–White House options and felt she could have her greatest impact on the issues she cared about in the Senate. But she never explained this in a way that sounded as if she actually meant it. In her announcement speech, her justification for why she was running took up all of one sentence: "I may be new to the neighborhood, but I'm not new to your concerns." People applauded this line because they knew they were supposed to (it was also the most often quoted sound bite from the speech). But you could tell by the speed with which the applause died that the audience found it a clever line, not an answer. Similarly, in other venues, she could not respond with any conviction to the simple question, "Why New York?" "Well, Bill and I always wanted to move to New York," she would say, scooting quickly along to her assertion that what you believe is more important than where you're from. Even if it *was* true, it didn't *sound* true—she wouldn't say why, or talk about their conversations on the subject, or add anecdotal evidence to give ballast to the statement.

We could call this tendency of hers admirable, if it were based on a genuine resistance to making appeals to voters based on bathos. And to some extent that was the case. She believed, earnestly, in ideas, and in a rationally ordered world in which those ideas, not smiles and personal narratives, should matter to voters. But as strong as that belief was in her, stronger still was her resistance to sharing, with the press or the public, any details of her personal life. According to the biographies, she had always been this way; seven years in the White House, years during which even her inoffensive utterances were sometimes twisted, once they reached talk radio and the cable shows, into declarations of war against traditional values, surely persuaded her to build the wall even higher. Her attitude, as people around her would sometimes describe it, was that wherever she went, she was there for The Event or The Theme. Breast cancer. The candidate she was stumping for. The children. She'd go, and she'd make her speech, staying relentlessly on message, and that was it. She feared that if she gave an interview, the story would be about her instead of about breast cancer or the candidate or the children.

It was hard to figure. People in politics understand that you have to show the press your good side as a defensive maneuver if nothing else. But Hillary wouldn't play this game. She operated inside a fortress of privacy from which little information emerged—not even the benign sort that could have rendered her more human and sympathetic. At one point along the campaign trail, with reporters pleading for some small morsel of harmless personal information, aides revealed that she liked spicy foods and hot sauce, and was even known to carry around a little bottle of Tabasco sauce on her person. From the Hillary camp, this was about all you got.

Kathy Kiely of *USA Today* told the story of how, on Hillary's Save America's Treasures tour, the reporters in tow had patiently waited days for an interview. Finally, at a dinner, they were told Hillary would join them at their table. She did, but when Kiely pulled out a tape recorder, Hillary "shot up as if she'd been stung by a bee" and announced that there was an old friend across the room to whom she had to say hello. Later, one of Hillary's press aides came over to apologize and told the reporters that Hillary would see them after all. The reporters were herded over to see her—not to ask questions, but to have souvenir pictures taken.

There's another story, famous among New York journalists, of one of the times she came to the city to campaign for Chuck Schumer. As she finished her speech, a reporter for New York 1 caught up with her, a feat in itself in those days. The reporter started asking a simple question about why she was appearing for Schumer, the kind television people ask in order to get their "sound," as they call it, so they can pack up the cameras and report back to headquarters that they got a quote. Most pols understand this, and oblige. All Hillary had to say was what a great candidate Chuck Schumer was and how important this election was for the future of America and New York. It would have taken her ten seconds. She brushed right past the reporter without a word.

A person with habits like that was not suddenly going to become Ms. Congeniality. And so the efforts she did make to open herself up were limp, half-hearted, and, because they were delivered in a spirit of mistrust, phony. At her announcement speech they showed a video, produced by Linda Bloodworth-Thomason, that was obviously intended to proffer Hillary at her best. Parts of it were stunningly effective. There was a retired colonel named Herbert J. Smith, who talked of her commitment to breaking through Pentagon bureaucracy and getting to the bottom of the causes of Gulf War Syndrome. He began by noting that his political views were of a very different order than hers, but he enthused about the work she did on the issue and the attention she lavished on veterans. Smith made it clear that she truly followed through on her promises in a way politicians are thought never to do, and he concluded: "She's a beautiful lady." A beautiful lady! From a military man! It was typical of the campaign's many missed opportunities that Col. Herbert J. Smith (Ret.) never reappeared throughout the entire race. But that day, at least, it was a remarkable testimonial.

The only scenes from the video that made the papers and chat shows were its clumsy attempts at humanizing Hillary. She made a "mean tossed salad" and a "great omelet" and couldn't carry a tune. It was a little unfair. But it was the story line the press decided on: the New York media, while not very interested in the billing records and Travelgate, were intensely interested in trying to solve the vexing riddle of who she was, and, until she offered some assistance in that pursuit, she wasn't going to get much of a break. Getting at the politician as personality was the New York way. And in a city of Italians and Irish and Puerto Ricans and Jews and blacks, midwestern Protestant reserve didn't go down so well. New York's most popular politicians had monstrously huge egos. Koch, Giuliani, Cuomo, D'Amato, Bella Abzug, even Moynihan in his more elegant way—all of them flaunted their personalities, styles, and tastes. Their favored turns of phrase or foods were touchstones of a shared world view or experience for New York voters. The New York press was used to politicians behaving this way, celebrating themselves and their city and their state with no apologies.

Obviously, this wasn't something Hillary could do. Advertisements for her salad-making abilities weren't a filling substitute.

It also didn't help that day when people noticed that the huge banner behind her said "Hillary." Not "Hillary Clinton," just "Hillary." She had left the "Clinton" off, pundits scoffed, the better to distance herself from her husband. "That 'Hillary' was really not deeply considered," an aide told me later, "though people thought otherwise. To the extent that it was, it was not to distance her from her husband, but to make her seem more . . . everyday-ish. Somebody you could call by her first name. If you're dealing with the issue of running as royalty, you want to try to make a person more approachable." The "Hillary" decision turned out to be all right. New Yorkers adjusted. But the brouhaha was a good example of the way in which every move she made, at this point, was regarded by the press as cynical and calculated. The press had decided that her leaving "Clinton" off the banner meant she feared being hobbled by Clinton fatigue. Of course, if the banner had said "Hillary Clinton," she'd have been accused of piggybacking on her husband's name—a far more likely strategy, given her husband's popularity in New York. So there was no good option.

The question of whether Bill should speak was a lose-lose proposition as well. He sat on the stage, alongside Chelsea and Dorothy Rodham and Moynihan and others, and smiled and applauded and looked proud, just like a candidate's wife. He did not speak, which this aide described to me as a decision based on the fact that "we knew we were only going to get so much air time on the news shows, and if he spoke, they'd take his sound bite, leaving less time for hers. I don't know if he was pissed, but he was a good sport about it." Again, the fact that he didn't speak was interpreted on the talk shows as a sign of her lust for independence and control. If he had spoken, the story would surely have been that Hillary was leaning on Bill to do her campaigning for her.

She was relieved and pleased to have made it through, aides said, but the day had not been what she'd hoped. For a few days afterward, in fact, the story that kept bouncing through the tabloids was about the background music for the event, which had included Billy Joel's "Captain Jack," about a college dropout who sits around getting high a lot of the time. Giuliani, knowing a wedge issue when he saw one, said the song's message was "let's say yes to drugs." The song actually depicts the emptiness of the stoner's life. But Giuliani had a keen sense of how to play the press. He knew how to utter one sentence—"let's say yes to drugs"—that would take up more headline space than Hillary's twenty minutes' worth of sentences. He elbowed his way into what was supposed to have been her story.

A Clean Shot Missed

The outlook did improve for Hillary the next day, when she began an upstate swing to lay out specific proposals. They didn't seem terribly significant at the time, but it was these speeches that laid the groundwork for Hillary's eventual success upstate, and for her endorsements from the upstate newspapers. In Buffalo, she talked of the upstate economy and offered a fairly detailed and sensible plan to improve Internet access and attract high-tech jobs. At a Rochester hospital, the message was prescription drug prices. Mentioning the far lower prices for many drugs in Canada, and arguing for their importation, went down well in a city so near the Canadian border; I noticed at least a half-dozen people who had not even applauded when she was introduced joining the standing ovation when she finished. In Syracuse, she laid out some education proposals that, incredibly for a Democrat, deviated from the teachers' union line on teacher testing and certification.

In each city, the coverage could hardly have been more favorable, which points up an amusing difference between the newspapers in the city and those upstate. When Hillary hit an upstate city, not only was her mere presence news, but the papers would actually lead with what she said in her speech. In the city, giving a straight account of what she said was considered earnest and provincial. The city papers—the tabs especially, but to some extent even *The Times*—tried to avoid leading with the speech at all costs. If she did a short press availability after the speech and took a question on a pressing topic of the day, *that* was the lead. The speech was the bottom three paragraphs.

In Rochester, something happened that was unarguably more important than the speech. It was a Wednesday morning, and in that week's *Village Voice,* Wayne Barrett reported that Giuliani had sent out a fund-raising letter accusing Hillary of "hostility toward America's religious traditions." Barrett's father, a rock-ribbed Lynchburg, Virginia, conservative, had received the letter, and Wayne read it while visiting him. The letter went on for eight pages, with a virulence unusual even by New York standards. It invoked a "relentless thirty-year war the left-wing elite has waged against America's religious heritage" and scorned "liberal judges" who had banned posting the Ten Commandments in the schools. The irony here was almost comic. Conventional wisdom always favors Republicans on matters of religion. But in this case it was Hillary who was the devout churchgoing Methodist. The notionally Catholic Giuliani almost never troubled himself with going to Mass, although the papers had generally been too polite to note it over the years. And, of course, he'd had six years to call for New York City's public schools to post the Ten Commandments and had somehow forgotten to do so. But Giuliani, relying on the conventional wisdom, and because he was fishing in the waters of right-wing evangelism to raise his money, was able to argue that Hillary was a godless leftist and he a God-fearing real American.

The day Barrett's story broke, both Hillary and the press were staying at a Crowne Plaza in downtown Rochester. The press van call was for 8:15 A.M. But aide Karen Finney came down to the lobby to tell us the candidate was doing a press conference in a corridor on the hotel's mezzanine. An impromptu availability from Hillary was rare indeed. She had heard about the letter the night before and read it that morning, and she wanted to react immediately. When she emerged through a set of double doors, her face was pale, her jaw locked, her brow tight, her eyes, so often expressionless, luminous. She was quaking with rage. I focused for a moment on her hands; they were shaking. Yet when she began to speak, the emotional intensity went out of her like air out of a balloon. She was "outraged that he would inject religion into this campaign in any form whatsoever," and he had to "take responsibility" for the letter. But the language she used was all measured politician's language—"inject religion," in particular, is press-release speak. She said nothing to indicate what her religious beliefs *were;* nothing about how she'd been going to church regularly since she was a little girl, even during her college days; nothing that carried any personal passion. Her campaign quickly handed out copies of a speech on her religious faith she'd delivered in 1996, but that packed none of the punch that her telling us directly would have.

Giuliani had had several clean shots at her over the months. This was Hillary's first clean shot at him. She could have strafed him and put him on the defensive for three or four days. Instead, she just rapped his knuckles. The story floated away, to be replaced by a story that restored things to their normal, Hillary-is-a-monster state. At a diner in the small upstate town of Albion, Hillary was treated to a meal on the house and forgot to tip the waitress. *The Washington Times* broke it on February 11, but the next day, the *Post* went bonkers with it, running not only a news story about it on page three, but a sidebar quoting etiquette experts to the effect that people who can afford to leave tips but don't are "spoiled" and "can't relate to everyday life." The story ran the usual and by now boring circuit from the *Post* to Fox to the other cable shows.

The tip story and her exasperating tightness notwithstanding, her first week as an official candidate had gone fairly well. Her rhetoric had changed. It was now more direct and specific, and she was talking more like a real candidate. The change was noted by Mort Zuckerman's editorial page, which opined that "at least she's putting her ideas out there," while the mayor "confined himself mostly to sniping from the sidelines." *News* columnist Michael Kramer declared her "the winner of week one."

A Problem of Authority

It had been a year since Amadou Diallo was shot by four police officers. On February 2, 2000, the trial finally began, and on February 25 a verdict was at last handed down: all four officers were acquitted on all charges. The acquittal hardly came as a surprise—the defense had won a change of venue from the Bronx to Albany, and legal experts had long predicted that the murder charge that the Bronx District Attorney brought against the cops would be tough to prove. Still, anger over the acquittal, among blacks in particular, was passionate.

Here again was a New York campaign moment that would tell us something about the candidates in this race. The fury the shooting had generated is hard to overstate. For a year, the consensus among political insiders had been that an acquittal would hurt Giuliani badly. Hillary supporters, while perhaps not outright hoping for an acquittal for political purposes, at least hoped that such a verdict would bring with it the silver lining of headaches for Rudy. If the justice system held no one accountable for what happened to Diallo, maybe the voters would hold the mayor accountable. When the verdict was delivered, observers wondered whether the mayor would be crass enough to gloat about it, defend the cops, and use the acquittal to taunt his and the police department's critics. But nothing of the sort transpired. Giuliani did just what a mayor is supposed to do. He expressed "very, very deep, heartfelt sympathy" to the Diallo family, and he called for calm.

Hillary Clinton was in Chicago for a fund-raiser when the verdict was announced. Nearly four hours passed between news of the verdict and a statement from the Clinton campaign. When it finally came, it was another example of the on-the-one-hand, on-the-other-hand style the campaign seemed perversely intent on perfecting: police should be more sensitive to the community, the community should understand how difficult police work was, and "we must all work together" toward some magical day when there would no longer be any problems in the world. Having already accused the cops of "murder" at Al Sharpton's headquarters, Hillary was left with straitened options. And she didn't really possess the vocabulary to talk about matters like cop shootings. Education or health care, fine; but this was a topic on which New Yorkers, whatever their point of view, shared an emotionally intense history with one another, a history to which she was not party.

This was a specific and tangible manifestation of what "the carpetbagger problem" really meant. A New Yorker—Nita Lowey or Robert Kennedy, Jr., or any of the other bypassed candidates—could have injected him or herself into a matter like a police shooting a little more aggressively, with a surer innate feel about what would and would not be appropriate to say. But Hillary could not. Other manifestations of carpetbaggerism she could address. She could learn the issues and travel the state and meet Democrats and voters. But there were certain things about New York life that could not be so quickly learned, not even by the eager Wellesley perfectionist. The continuing cops-and-minorities melodrama was one of them. It was an issue on which an outsider couldn't speak with authority.

This being New York, where one learns to expect the unexpected, the next month found her doing exactly that.

CHAPTER 7

March 2000:
The Argument

A Campaign Divided

HILLARY'S MONTH STARTED with another difficult swim through New York's ethnic and racial soup. In the aftermath of the Diallo verdict, she delivered what aides advertised as a major policy address on Sunday, March 5, at Riverside Church. The church, once presided over by the activist minister William Sloane Coffin, is one of the great historical centers of liberal ecumenicism in New York—the site, over the years, of many a rally or service devoted to racial tolerance, the nuclear-freeze movement, or the Left's proper role in the national debate. It was a place where the liberal conscience and the religious soul linked arms—in other words, a comfortable place for Hillary Clinton, one where she might have been expected to speak a little more freely than usual. But even here, before this racially mixed and extremely sympathetic audience, she delivered a speech that refrained from pressing any one point too hard—a speech intended not for the Riverside parishioners but for the larger audience of voters. She ended up saying in banal language that yes, we *can* have lower crime rates *and* better police-community relations. The audience received her words warmly, but without much enthusiasm.

The next Saturday night brought the arrival of a moment that politicos had been drooling over for months—for the first time, Hillary and Rudy met face to face. The occasion was the annual Inner Circle dinner, the New York journalists' roast of local politicians. The evening began with a long cocktail hour. Then, once the two thousand or so guests had taken their seats in the massive ballroom in the midtown Hilton, reporters took the stage, producing skits and parody songs—with widely varying degrees of skill—that poked fun at the pols. This was followed by an intermission, during which dinner was served and people mingled. Finally, after an intermission, the mayor fired back with his own parody, which was guaranteed to be (a) the last word, and (b) better, since the mayor had hired professional writers and was performing his skit with the help of the cast of an actual Broadway show. The mayor had wanted the *Chicago* cast to back him up. But that cast included Bebe Neuwirth, a committed liberal (and George Stephanopoulos's girlfriend at the time), and Neuwirth refused to share a stage with Giuliani, so the mayor settled for the *Saturday Night Fever* crew. The event was best known for lasting about two hours longer than anyone wanted it to.

To this mix was added the unprecedented presence of a sitting first lady, who would not be treated with reverence but lampooned as just another local pol—a symbolic transformational moment. The expectation was that Hillary was going to come in for a beating in the reporters' skits, and that expectation was met resoundingly. One skit, which made sport of Giuliani's penchant for arresting first and asking questions later, culminated in Hillary landing in jail with Jennifer Lopez, with Bill Clinton arriving with enough bail money for only one or the other and choosing Lopez. It was funny, but slightly sadistic. No other pol took shots nearly as harsh as she did that night. Giuliani—because reporters feared his wrath, or because they needed to preserve their access—was intentionally spared similar sallies. As Lars-Erik Nelson reported in the *Daily News,* when one skit had a reporter saying that Chappaqua, where Mrs. Clinton had moved, was Indian for "land of separate bedrooms," a rejoinder from another reporter that that "sounds like Gracie Mansion" was edited out at the last minute. (The mayor's marital problems, while not, like Hillary's, a matter of forensic science, were nevertheless well known.) And there Hillary was, sitting at a front table (a guest, people were intrigued to note, of Mort Zuckerman), having to smile through it.

The understanding, in the days preceding the dinner, was that Hillary, as novitiate to these rites, would be in no position to complain about her portrayals. The thinking was, "She thinks she's had it tough? Let's see if she can handle *this.*" And she did. Of course she had no option other than to sit there and smile, but you did have to say this in her behalf: She may not have been a good candidate yet, but she was tough. She could take just about anything, and she never lost her poise. George Arzt, the well-connected public relations man, met Hillary in the lobby when she arrived and escorted her backstage to say her hellos. He says that when he took Mrs. Clinton backstage to meet with journalists, they ran into Giuliani unexpectedly, and Hillary surprised Arzt by extending her hand first. "She was not taken aback at all," Arzt says. "He seemed to be. It was really something." And, though Giuliani was the star of the show onstage, one had only to scan the ballroom and catch sight of the circle of boom mikes and television cameras, bobbing over the crowd like buoys on the ocean surface, to know where the evening's real star was, in her full-length black satin gown.

The next week, Hillary marched in the St. Patrick's Day Parade. (She had finessed this appearance with the parade's gay and lesbian protesters by marching, the week before, in a parade in Queens that did allow gays to march.) The St. Pat's audience was not her crowd; the ringers her campaign managed to persuade to stand along the route and wave their "Hillary!" signs so things wouldn't look so bad were little match for the "Go home!" and "Where's Monica?" serenade through which she once again waved and smiled.

The truly interesting developments in the Clinton campaign were taking place out of view. Hillary's campaign to this point had spent around $7 million. It had nothing to show for it. Eight months had passed since the Moynihan farm event, and she had gained no ground on Giuliani in the polls, while her unfavorable ratings had moved in the wrong direction. Of course her difficulties were a function of the mistakes of the fall, and the relentlessly negative press, which scrutinized everything she did in a way it had for no other candidate in memory. But there's a reason campaigns call the press "free media": They have "paid media"—television and radio commercials created by their team of consultants—to try to counteract negative press.

Hillary's paid media was nonexistent.

Team Hillary, as her consultants fashioned themselves, was assembled in February. Mandy Grunwald was in charge of the commercials. Grunwald had lived in Washington for more than a decade, but she had grown up in Manhattan, a daughter of *Time* magazine journalist Henry Grunwald. Before establishing her own business, she had worked for the Sawyer-Miller Group, a New York–based Democratic firm, and had served as a media consultant for Pat Moynihan, which made her the key player in putting together Hillary's event at the senator's farm. Grunwald had won fame for her work on the 1992 Clinton-Gore campaign. But after Bill was elected, her relationship with the White House began to sour; the president had relieved her of her duties as a media adviser to him in 1994, after that year's wipe-out election. Hillary, though, had remained loyal to her. Grunwald was one of the small number of friends and advisers whose counsel Hillary had sought as she began to explore the possibility of running in New York. In some fundamental ways, Grunwald was very much like Hillary. She was tough, and she had a reputation for circumspection toward, not to say outright suspicion of, outsiders and journalists. New York newspaper reporters developed the habit, as the campaign progressed, of congratulating those few who managed to get through to Grunwald and have a substantive conversation with her. Or, depending on how the conversation went, of sympathizing with them.

Another such close confidant was Mark Penn, the president's pollster. Penn, another ex–New Yorker, had cut his teeth at the firm of David Garth, the legendary dean of New York consultants. Bill Clinton may have fallen out with Grunwald, but Penn, to the White House, was untouchable. It was Penn's polling method, in which he sought to sound out distinct clusters of voters on issues that affected their daily lives, that drove the strategy of the 1996 campaign. Penn's were the so-called "small-bore" proposals that made a case for a government that still did things, as long as they weren't big, expensive things. Penn, who worked out of an office on Pennsylvania Avenue just a block from the White House, spoke to reporters more easily and was less circumspect than Grunwald. But as a general rule he left the press relations to others, preferring to crunch his numbers.

Such was Hillary's, and the president's, trust in him that he was also in charge of Hillary's message, which was a highly unusual set-up. Typically, campaigns, especially at this level, would put one person in charge of the polling, asking potential voters not only their opinions of the candidates but also their attitudes on various issues. A second person would take those poll numbers and convert them into winning themes and messages. Traditionally, the two jobs have been regarded as separate. But such was Penn's status at the White House that, for this campaign, his dual role wasn't questioned.

Grunwald and Penn were assisted by a New York–based ad agency, DeVito-Verdi. To insiders it was a strange choice, since the firm had no experience in political campaigns. Yet it was also a refreshingly unorthodox choice, one that was out of character for this ever-cautious candidate. DeVito-Verdi had a reputation for nimble creativity. Hillary had been impressed by a series of award-winning ads the firm had made for a pro-choice education project. The firm also had a recent track record of making at least two provocative ads. It had had done a print ad for the American Civil Liberties Union after the Diallo shooting depicting forty-one black spots that were clearly supposed to be bullet holes. The police union was quick to denounce it. DeVito-Verdi had also produced a series of bus posters for *New York* magazine, one of which touted the mag as "possibly the only good thing in New York Rudy hasn't taken credit for." The mayor, predictably, sued over the use of his image, and lost. The agency—specifically, Ellis Verdi, who coordinated the firm's work for Hillary—was hired to bring an "edgy" (this from the campaign press statement announcing the agency's hiring) New York quality to Team Hillary's creative output. And, sources said, to apply a little competitive pressure to Grunwald, about whom the first lady was feeling skittish.

Still, it could hardly be ignored that Team Hillary included no New York heavyweights. There were three top-flight Democratic media consultants based in New York: the aforementioned David Garth, who had helped elect Ed Koch mayor in the 1970s; Hank Sheinkopf, who worked on Democratic campaigns all over America, including Bill Clinton's in 1996; and Hank Morris, who was Chuck Schumer's consultant. Of the three, Garth had the grandest reputation, but he was out of the question—he had also worked for Republicans, including Giuliani, in 1993. He'd had a falling out with the mayor over a variety of issues that boiled down to the fact that no single room in New York City was big enough to house both men's egos. But Bruce Teitelbaum was trying to persuade Garth to rejoin Giuliani for this election, so if Garth was going anywhere in this race, it was there.

Sheinkopf was a sometime partner of Dick Morris; he did meet with Penn and Hillary in an apartment in Trump Tower in November 1999, but the conversation didn't lead anywhere. Hank Morris was summoned to the White House in the summer of 1999, cashiering his standard ratty sweater for an actual suit. But, according to sources, Hank Morris and Hillary didn't see eye-to-eye on what the campaign should do; Morris, like most media consultants, wanted to be the chef, not one of several cooks. David Doak, a major Washington-based Democratic consultant, also had talks with Hillary, but did not sign on, for much the same reason as Hank Morris.

"Too many cooks" was, to be sure, a problem. Grunwald, Penn, and Ickes were all experienced, strong-willed, and accustomed to running things. The campaign manager, Bill DeBlasio, had extensive experience in New York campaigns, having worked for David Dinkins and Mario Cuomo, and for Bill Clinton's New York operations. He was also a protégé of Ickes. But Ickes's influence with Hillary did not result in much authority for DeBlasio, who despite his title was not a manager of this campaign in the sense that he could make broad strategic decisions and see them carried out. DeBlasio's contributions, especially as time wore on, focused more on dealing with the things he knew best—how to stroke the unions, which local pol to deal with in this or that city or neighborhood. Penn and Grunwald were really running things, but from their vantage point in Washington, they could scarcely gauge the rhythms and sounds and smells of the campaign. The campaign suffered from that, at times terribly; it would be months before the Clinton operation developed anything like a New York feel about it, months during which there would be little sense of energy or momentum around her campaign.

But the fundamental question facing the campaign was not the geographical placement of her counselors. It was how best to develop a message that made a persuasive case for Hillary. As of March, Hillary was trotting out her resumé to groups of women; before more general audiences, she went over her list of issues. But there was no sharp message that articulated her rationale and told people in a concise and plausible way why they should put her in the Senate.

This campaign needed a clear message far more than most, because distrust of their candidate, and suspicion of her motives, was so widespread. So any message Hillary's team developed had to acknowledge, at least implicitly, the many unique problems this race presented: The fact that Hillary was, no matter how one tried to sugarcoat it, a carpetbagger; the widespread misperception that she had steamrolled her way into New York, elbowing Nita Lowey *et alii* out of the way (despite the fact that New York Democrats had begged her to run); the fact that about 40 percent of the electorate, including large segments of women, said they hated Hillary; the challenge of giving this guarded candidate qualities like personality and humor and humility; the perception among far too many voters that she was, to be blunt, a bitch.

No sooner was Team Hillary assembled than the campaign was split over the basic question of how to confront people's reactions to Hillary. Everyone agreed that the campaign's chief argument to voters had to revolve around Hillary's positions on the issues. But, on the question of how, or indeed whether, to deal with Hillary's negatives, the team quickly fell into two camps. Ellis Verdi wanted to meet Hillary's negatives head-on. His experience was in advertising, not politics, and in advertising, it's common practice to acknowledge negative perceptions of a product, refute them, and dispense with them, often in a jokey way. "The most effective advertising deals with the truth and doesn't disregard it," Verdi says. "You can take negative perceptions and either disprove them or reinterpret them as strengths." Ickes agreed with Verdi.

Grunwald and Penn, though, did not want to confront Hillary's negatives at all. Grunwald believed, given the strength of people's emotional reactions to Hillary—actually, to both Clintons—that trying to address the negatives would accomplish little more than keeping them in play. "Throughout this campaign," Grunwald says, "there were people who said, 'You have to deal directly with the carpetbagger thing,' or 'You have to deal with your marriage.' But as much as people talk about all those things, it was our belief that if she would go out there and say, 'I know you're curious about why I stayed with my husband, and let me tell you all about that,' it would just be the last thing people would want."

Penn agreed. "You don't deal with negatives on trust by saying trust me," Penn says. "You deal with negatives on trust by doing." To Penn that meant staying strictly on the issues, and Penn's polling affirmed that a clear majority of New Yorkers agreed with Hillary on the issues. On education, the use of the budget surplus, the environment, and health care, New York voters were much closer to Hillary's positions than to Giuliani's and, later, Lazio's. When Penn asked voters which candidate would do a better job on these issues, Hillary came out ahead almost every time. Even on health care, it appeared that New York voters were less mindful of Hillary's disastrous 1994 health-care plan and more mindful of their agreement with her broad goals of universal coverage for children and a generous prescription-drug benefit for senior citizens. So Penn was right. If the race were an issues debate, she would win.

But would this race really be a pure environment for issues? From the moment Hillary set foot in the state, the race was about *her.* Everyone, inside and outside the campaign, knew this. But not everyone wanted to admit it. And so one could sense, from Penn and Grunwald and from Hillary, as she presented herself to New York voters in the campaign's early months, that the decision to try to work around Hillary's negatives was not merely strategic. There was an emotional resistance to dealing with voters' dislike of her. Certainly it was not Hillary's way—talking frankly with people about her shortcomings and accepting their criticisms was not exactly one of her strong suits. And the president, who was offering his wife regular advice, was hardly the person to suggest ways for her to justify her marriage to voters. With both the candidate and the president reluctant to dip into those waters, her key advisers did not want to be the ones to have to drag Hillary there. "The people who could make her feel comfortable about dealing with that were exactly the people who were not going to go there," a campaign source says. "Mark Penn is not going to go in there and say, 'Well, we should deal with the Woman Issue.' That's an emotional thing. He can't give her a number on that."

By March, Hillary had raised about $15 million, and had spent almost half of it. Much of it had gone to direct mail, which raises lots of money but is so expensive to produce that it eats up much of what it brings in. But wherever her money had gone, it had not gone on the air. Rudy Giuliani was already up with two different commercials in March, but such was the confusion and infighting within Team Hillary that her first ad didn't air until May. And May, for a race that had begun in earnest the previous summer, was seeming late.

A Secret Overture

Watching from the sidelines, Susan Thomases was deeply concerned about the campaign's lack of a message. Thomases was probably Hillary's closest friend; they'd known each other since the early 1970s. She was also, back then, Harold Ickes's girlfriend. Thomases had been a central figure in Bill Clinton's New York operations in his presidential campaigns, using her New York experience to advise Bill on which events he should do and what parts of the state he should hit. Thomases had not been closely involved in Hillary's decision to run and had not been enthusiastic about the idea. But once her friend decided to jump, Thomases, out of loyalty, jumped too—not as an official adviser, but as a sounding board. She wanted her old friend's campaign to succeed, of course, and to do that, she felt it needed a more coherent message than the one it was offering. Thus began an internal drama that would occupy the campaign for the next four months.

Dwight Jewson was the man who would occupy center stage in that drama. Jewson is the head of a consulting firm called Strategic Frameworking, based outside Seattle. Strategic Frameworking's clients were, by 2000, mostly corporate—the firm helped the Frito-Lay Corporation figure out how to sell Doritos, developed and introduced Red Wolf Beer, and marketed the Taco Bell Value Menu. But Jewson had a political pedigree. He, like Penn, had once worked in New York for David Garth—in fact, he and Penn had worked on campaigns together. One of his areas of concentration over the years had been the emotional and psychological terrain of politics. He had led a study in 1996 about voters' emotional attachments to the parties that examined how the Republicans had won voters over on an emotional level in 1994, and how Clinton had won them back in 1996. His expertise, in other words, was exactly what Hillary's campaign needed.

So, in March, Thomases, who had known Jewson since the 1970s, made a secret overture to him on behalf of the Clinton campaign. Thomases wanted Jewson to do two things: to conduct focus groups to determine Hillary's greatest weaknesses, and her strengths; and, based on those results, to develop a clear and credible message for the campaign. "I thought Dwight would give us a clear language to articulate why people should vote for her, and why she should be their senator,"

Thomases says. "Hillary was not running for president. She was running for legislative office, and we needed to figure out a language that dealt specifically with that." Thomases felt that Hillary's rhetoric, to that point, centered too much on her resumé and not enough on what specific things she would try to do for New York in the Senate. She enlisted Jewson to try to change that. So Jewson sent the Clinton campaign a letter describing what he would do, where, and when; and offering to do it for $87,000: $10,500 for videotaping, $6,500 for travel, $62,500 for research, and $7,500 for document preparation. The objectives of the focus groups were to include (all verbatim from the letter):

- Creation of a single consistent message for the campaign
- Development of a slogan and tag line
- Development of the framework of a stump speech for the candidate, and talking points for surrogate supporters
- Recommendations for defining the most important difference(s) between Mrs. Clinton and her opponents
- Recommendations for responding to charges made against Mrs. Clinton by her opponents
- Evaluation and review of existing and proposed commercials
- Suggestions for additional commercials for television, radio, and print

I would imagine those last two points in particular did little to convert Penn and Grunwald into Jewsonites.

Focus groups are one of those staples of the modern political campaign about which commentators love to complain—part of the overpackaging and overmanaging of candidates. But every major campaign uses them, because they're the most efficient way to get insights into people's feelings about the candidate. Polls give campaigns percentages of people who choose one of three or four available answers to a series of questions. In focus groups, people get to run off at the mouth. A campaign can hear in people's voices how they really feel about a candidate, and this campaign especially needed to hear that. Jewson had used focus groups before to help lift troubled campaigns. On at least two of these occasions, Jewson had worked with Penn. In 1978, Governor Hugh Carey, seeking reelection, was suffering in the

polls. Most observers, and even Carey's staff, assumed that it was because voters viewed him as running too much with the jet set (Jimmy
Breslin dubbed him "Society" Carey). The public did, in fact, view
Carey this way, but Jewson's focus groups found that, in addition, people had trouble associating Carey with specific accomplishments.
Based on Jewson's findings the Carey campaign developed a tag line:
"The more you know the facts, the more you know Carey's right." It
became one of the more memorable lines in New York election lore,
and Carey won in a landslide.

Jewson and Penn had also worked together for Jay Rockefeller in
West Virginia. In 1976, Rockefeller won the governorship against a
corrupt Republican incumbent. But in 1980, with inflation roaring
and the state's economy in the soup, he was facing a tough reelection
fight. Jewson's focus groups found that West Virginians continued to
view Rockefeller first and foremost as a Rockefeller, and a New
Yorker, even though he'd come to the state in the early 1960s as a
VISTA volunteer and stayed. From Jewson's focus groups, the Rockefeller team crafted an ad campaign that turned this liability into an
asset, arguing that the Rockefeller name and connections would benefit the state. Rockefeller romped. Hillary could surely make a similar
argument to upstate New Yorkers. Making people who live in forgotten and economically depressed rural areas feel that a candidate's fame
will bring them some clout is not the world's worst idea.

Hillary was less than eager to hear the ugly particulars about why
women and other voters didn't like her. But she was also frustrated
with the way her campaign was going, and intrigued enough by
Jewson's pedigree that she was on the verge of approving a check to
him in late March. But at the last minute she pulled back. In a memo to
one of my sources, Jewson fretted about getting a firm yes or no from
the campaign because he'd already booked space in a hall in Westchester County for the purpose of conducting his initial focus groups and
paid the deposit for its use. The same thing happened in April. Finally,
in May, Jewson was given the go-ahead. By then, the rancor inside
Team Hillary had become, as one insider put it to me, "cancerous." But
we're getting ahead of ourselves.

Ray in a Pickle

Harold Ickes had, over the winter and into the spring, been in regular contact with Raymond B. Harding, the head of the state's Liberal Party. Ickes wanted to see whether the remotest possibility existed that the Libs might endorse Hillary. He understood that Harding had endorsed Giuliani for mayor three times, and knew very well that Harding was in Giuliani's innermost circle of advisers. But Ickes thought that in a Senate race, the dynamic might be different. In municipal elections, the Liberal endorsement was a kind of power play—a bet on the winning horse, which, if correct, would give a few party regulars nice positions in the new administration (both of Harding's sons got jobs in the Giuliani administration). But on the federal level, the party usually operated according to a more ideological calculus. Throughout its fifty-six-year history, the party had always endorsed the Democratic presidential candidate, which meant it had backed Bill Clinton twice. And, with the exception of liberal Republican Jacob Javits, the party had always cross-endorsed Democrats in New York's senatorial and congressional races.

Ickes and Harding had often worked on the same side in the old days—both supported Hugh Carey for governor in the 1970s, and Harding went on to serve as a special assistant to Carey for five years. But all that changed in 1989. Ickes was a key adviser to David Dinkins that year, and Harding emerged as one of the Giuliani campaign's top lieutenants. Harding spent a lot of time in 1989 disseminating to reporters a charge that back in 1986, Dinkins had illegally transferred some stock to his son. For a few days, the scandal threatened to finish Dinkins off as a candidate. He was forced to endure a tense, sweaty press conference, with his accountant at his side; finally, his campaign produced a letter (some people still believe it was backdated, which the Dinkins camp always denied) indicating that the stock transfer was kosher and that Dinkins had not tried to hide it. Handling the damage control for Dinkins, just as he would for another more famous chief executive a few years later, was Harold Ickes.

The Ickes-Harding relationship actually went back further than most people understood. Ray Harding was born Branko Hochwald to Jewish parents in Herzegovina in 1935. This was not, of course, the most convenient time to be born to Jewish parents in Herzegovina; the elder Hochwald smelled the odor of Nazism then making its way to the Balkans, and in 1941 he took his family and escaped to Italy. But Italy, too, proved increasingly inhospitable to Jews as the war progressed, and in 1944, nine-year-old Branko and his parents ended up in a detainee camp. There seemed little hope for them until suddenly, in June of that year, President Roosevelt announced that one thousand refugees from Italy were to be given safe haven in the United States until the war ended. An intervention of this magnitude was utterly at odds with American immigration policy and with the prevailing U.S. policy on war refugees, neither of which was overly generous. As it turned out, the impulse for the move was not entirely humanitarian: Refugees were streaming into Italy at a rate of about 1,800 a day at the time. The chaos was putting increased pressure on the Allied forces just then marching past Anzio and up through the southern part of the boot.

Little Branko Hochwald was one of the one thousand lucky refugees who survived a harrowing boat ride across the Atlantic and attacks from Nazi U-boats and were ultimately delivered to a relocation camp near Oswego, New York. The story of their passage is told by Ruth Gruber, the Roosevelt administration official who traveled with the refugees, in her 1983 book, *Haven*. And the FDR cabinet official to whom Gruber reported, the man whom Roosevelt directed to oversee this project and who fought congressional opposition to the rescue, was Secretary of the Interior Harold L. Ickes, Sr. Once the war ended, the refugees were supposed to be returned to Europe. But Ickes again intervened, leading the fight to keep them here. He, Gruber, and others arranged a congressional hearing at a school in Syracuse, where the refugees testified as to their love for America and the tender hours of study they had put in learning the Bill of Rights. When the camp's Boy Scouts marched into the hearing room in their crisply pressed uniforms, carrying flags and reciting the Boy Scout oath in English ("I will do my best to do my duty to God and my country"), Branko Hochwald was among them. The hearing helped win over the skeptics, and the refugees stayed. Harold Ickes, Sr., had helped save the child who, forty-odd years later, in that 1989 mayoral race, would lock horns with Harold, Jr.

Branko Hochwald changed his name while still a teenager. His parents hated the Germanic last name, he told Gruber, and "there was a radio serial that I listened to with rapture, called *David Harding, Counterspy.* I suggested the name Harding and took the name Ray from a favorite cousin." Today, Ray Harding is one of the great character actors of New York politics, and probably of politics anywhere in America, leading a party that was founded by a group of anti-Communist union leaders the very year young Branko came to America.

Huge. Obese. Thick eyelids. Jowls. Unfiltered Camels. Zippo lighter. That's who Harding is, and that's how Harding talks: "Present tense, few pronouns. He speaks headlines," wrote Joe Klein in *New York* in 1989. Eccentricity and color are crucial to New York's idea of its political culture, and Harding has mountains of both. He also has humanity. His mere size, along with his curt manner of speech, can make him seem baleful and intimidating, and he enjoys coming across that way, when it suits his purposes. But it's his act, and he is endearing precisely because of it. "Throwback" is a word tossed around a lot in talk about Ray, who has run the party (with one brief interruption) since 1976. But it's accurate: He not only looks like an old-time political boss, he actually is one. In Mike Long's Conservative Party, endorsements are made by a process vaguely resembling consensus. By contrast there is nothing vague about the selection process of Ray Harding's Liberal Party. Ray decides.

Ray obviously wanted to choose Rudy—he was ferociously loyal to the mayor, and, like anyone else, he had to factor in Giuliani's considerable wrath and taste for revenge against those who crossed him. Usually, what Ray wanted, Ray got. But this time around, a significant chunk of the small party's executive committee wanted to endorse Hillary. Harding could not, in this case, ignore dissenting views. There's a long-standing joke that "the Liberal Party is neither," but during this election, there were Liberals for whom Rudy, a centrist as mayor, had moved too far to the right. If Rudy lost, and if there was enough resentment within the party about the endorsement, it was conceivable Ray could be ousted. This had happened before, in 1983, when Ray was banished to the wilderness in a party coup inspired by the newly elected governor, Mario Cuomo. It had taken him two years to regain control.

Furthermore, there was a view among Democrats, long advocated by David Dinkins, that Democratic candidates should refuse the Liberal endorsement in future races if Harding went with Rudy in this race, and that view was gathering some momentum. If the Democratic nominee refused Harding's cross-endorsement in the next gubernatorial election, the Liberal Party might expire. It was strange, perhaps, that the litmus test on which Democrats would judge Harding should be an out-of-stater to whom no one owed any particular loyalty, but that's what being first lady will do for you.

Ray was in a pickle. Never reticent about talking to reporters, he lay strangely low throughout the winter and spring. "Not . . . discussing . . . Senate," he would say, no matter how many different ways you tried to ask the question. But he was going to have to talk soon. March meant it was getting to be decision time. Whichever way he went, somebody would be furious at him; somebody was likely to try to end the career that never could have begun without the intercession of the father of the man who was now burning up his phone line.

The Nation Sees Local Rudy

In New York, and I think in the country, there had not been a recent politician who spoke with such unvarnished frankness as Rudy Giuliani. His was not a histrionic frankness—he was not driven by an inordinate need to draw attention to himself, as, say, Newt Gingrich sometimes was. Rudy, in contrast, just said what he thought. Maybe, before the media age, there were politicians who said whatever came into their heads. But television has largely vanquished that kind of spontaneity. People who are in front of cameras all the time naturally watch what they say and how they say it. Except for Rudy.

It wasn't that he didn't care about his image. Like all politicians, he cared about it profoundly, and he massaged it more than people think, especially when he found himself on a national stage. There were, indeed, two Rudys, Local Rudy and National Rudy. When he traveled out of New York, or did national television shows, he could be amazing—full of facts, as he always was, but also courteous, reasonable, the very face of congeniality. I remember seeing him on *Charlie Rose* once, talking about welfare reform and crime reduction. National Rudy smiled and cajoled and calmly explained the history of welfare policy since the 1960s, totally in command. A moderately informed (and politically moderate) viewer in Richmond or St. Paul or Tempe could not possibly see the National Rudy without wondering what all those crybaby New York liberals were carping about. The mayor behaved similarly dozens of times on other national shows—*Today, Larry King, Crossfire,* others.

Then, back on New York 1—at moments, that is, that he knew were for municipal consumption only—Local Rudy would return, telling people how silly they were, what jerks they were being, how they were embarrassing themselves, how he actually felt kind of sorry for them, they were so stuck in some pathetic, Marxist past. Both modes of performance were very image-conscious—the former to broaden his appeal to middle America by sanding down the hard New York edges, and the latter to appeal to New York by sharpening them.

So he was as concerned with his image as anyone. But his manner was different from any other politician I've seen or covered. He was not capable of speaking in cliché, or resorting to the kind of euphemism and implied meaning that politicians generally use (tropes through which Hillary spoke almost exclusively). If he meant to say something, he said it, flat out. It was in his nature. He was not averse to making trouble, preferably by getting under the skin of the liberal elites; he knew he couldn't lose that argument, since the conventional wisdom had it that the liberal elites had sent the city to ruin and he had saved it. So he constantly got after them, over welfare, or crime, or, especially, the cops, whom he always, always defended.

The early morning hours of Thursday, March 16, would bring the mayor one more opportunity to confound liberal piety. Police working the Midtown South precinct were doing "buy-and-bust" operations—buying small amounts of pot from street dealers and then arresting them. Undercover officers Anthony Vasquez and Anderson Moran were almost done for the night when they decided to go for one more arrest. Outside the Wakamba Cocktail Lounge on Eighth Avenue, not far from Madison Square Garden, Officer Moran approached Patrick Dorismond, a 26-year-old black man, and asked him if he had any pot. Dorismond, a big man, said no, got angry, and brushed the undercover cop away. A struggle began, and Dorismond ended up dead, shot by Vasquez.

It happened late enough that it barely made Thursday's papers,

but by Friday, it was the lead in every paper, with pages of stories devoted to it. The news accounts, in addition to detailing the circumstances of the shooting, included reports of Dorismond's past
arrests—robbery, attempted robbery, assault, criminal possession of a
weapon. Dorismond, in other words, was not a Boy Scout, one of the
two common metaphors invoked at such moments, the other being
"altar boy" (it turned out that he *was,* in fact, an altar boy, or had been
when he was teenager). In each case the charge had either been dis-
missed or he had pleaded guilty to a violation such as disorderly conduct, violation being a lower category of offense than misdemeanor.

There's a way politicians are supposed to react to police shootings: express sorrow, remind the public that fingers should not be
pointed until the facts are in (don't "rush to judgment" is the cliché),
and call for calm. Publicly, that's what they do. At the same time, it is
standard police procedure to release a victim's prior arrests, so that
newspaper readers across the city can get the pro-cop spin; the New
York Police Department had done it in almost every major shooting of
a black man who had a record, and not only while Giuliani was mayor.
Sometimes it was perfectly legal to do so, as when the shooting victim
had a felony conviction as an adult. But in Dorismond's case it was his
juvenile records that were released, and "juvie" records, in the parlance,
are the province of Family Court, and Family Court records are under
seal. Court precedent was clear: They could be released only at the
family's behest or by a judge's order. The Giuliani administration had
never been big on court precedent, and so the city's chief lawyer,
Michael Hess, was hauled out to explain that the courts were wrong on
this, and that the release was appropriate because the information was
relevant and because Dorismond's right to privacy "expired with him."
Even Giuliani's defenders cringed a little at that coolly clinical "expired," about a man whose only crime was to say no to drugs and lose
his temper.

Almost no one was buying this legalistic pirouette. But Giuliani
managed, for a time, to keep himself out of the debate. Friday brought
the St. Patrick's Day Parade, which always produced pro-Rudy headlines, and on Saturday, he left for a five-city, two-day upstate campaign
swing. The campaign trip might have been big news in itself, as it was
the most extensive jaunt this reticent candidate had taken to that point.
But Giuliani chose to make news in another way. That Sunday, from

Elmira, he did a live interview with *Fox News Sunday*'s Brit Hume. Hume asked Giuliani if he wasn't demonizing the victim. And the mayor cut loose.

Dorismond's "pattern of behavior" contributed to his death; the public had a "right to know" about his background; Dorismond had a long record of "arrests and convictions," the mayor said. But aren't we talking, Hume asked, about a list of arrests that in the end came down to a couple of disorderly conduct charges? "No, no, no, no. That's the way the press reported it. What you have here is robbery, attempted robbery, possession of a gun." Convictions? asked a startled Hume. "Yes, convictions and arrests, both." The word "convictions," while technically true (disorderly-conduct violations are convictions in much the same way speeding tickets are convictions; the offender pays a fine), was obviously intended to make it seem as if Dorismond had been a one-man crime wave. The mayor pressed on. "People do act in conformity very often with their prior behavior," he said. Finally, he confirmed to Hume that he himself had authorized the release of Dorismond's juvenile records. Hume was visibly shocked. The mayor was visibly shocking: stern, insistent, hectoring, utterly unapologetic, not at all sympathetic toward Marie Dorismond, whom the news cameras had captured in various states of heartbreak over her son's death. The nation had just seen, for the first time, Local Rudy.

The condemnations were swift. Every Democratic politician in town mauled him. Charlie Rangel wrote Attorney General Janet Reno, asking for a federal monitor of the NYPD. Black leaders, even some who had been careful about their public criticisms of the mayor, like Dennis Walcott of the New York Urban League, jumped in. "He is just creating a bigger wedge between the police and the community," Walcott said. Jesse Jackson said Rudy's problem wasn't just "meanness, it's mental." Al Sharpton said Giuliani "borders on needing therapy." Hillary, always handy with the safest language possible, charged that the mayor was leading a "rush to judgment." The word on talk shows and op-ed pages was unanimous. Giuliani had spent months content to sit back and do very little—to let his team raise millions while he, without ever saying that yes, he was in fact running, stood off to the side and took potshots at Hillary, letting her be the story. Now, for the first time, he was the story. Gail Collins summed it up pithily in her op-ed column in the *Times* on March 24: The mayor's strategy for victory in the

Senate race was "to drive New Yorkers so crazy they'll vote for him just to get him out of town."

His campaign team responded to the criticisms by intensifying a line of attack that had started back in January and that linked his opponent to his worst critics. Hillary, the mayor said, was "an Al Sharpton Democrat." Giuliani said to reporters on March 6: "How is it that Al Gore, Bill Bradley, Hillary Clinton seem to be reading from a script written by Al Sharpton, in which they want to give him a great deal of prominence?" Hillary had had nothing to do with Sharpton since that January appearance, but Giuliani knew how to push white voters' hot buttons, Jewish voters' in particular. This line even made it to the floor of the House, when Florida GOP Congressman Joe Scarborough introduced a resolution to the House condemning Sharpton for various acts of demagoguery. "Al Gore is an Al Sharpton Democrat," Scarborough said (Gore had met with Sharpton, secretly and clumsily, in February). Teitelbaum, after the Dorismond explosion, was telling anyone with a notebook all about "Hillary and her pal Al Sharpton."

The sound bite may have appealed to Giuliani's core Jewish constituency, but as a line of attack against Hillary it sounded overheated and a touch defensive. Normally Giuliani was a master at controlling the debate, making sure it was he, not the opposition, who was on the offensive in the next day's headlines. But his behavior now was inexplicable by any political calculus. Team Hillary had been waiting for Rudy to blow a gasket and look "unsenatorial." Now it had happened. And outside of Hillary's circle, people were starting to wonder whether Giuliani wanted to win this race.

In fact, people were starting to wonder whether Giuliani was even going to *make* this race. Insiders had pondered, throughout the winter, the mayor's light travel schedule. They wondered, too, about his strategy. He had said scarcely a single word about what he might actually do in the Senate. The grumblings about this had become loud enough that the *Times* did a story on it on March 19, which for the political class meant that the situation pole-vaulted from being a matter of idle gossip to one of Official Concern. Adam Nagourney wrote: "The mayor . . . has yet to deliver a full speech discussing what he might do in the Senate. . . . His campaign trips have been irregular. . . . [He] has not even staged the formal announcement that most candidates welcome as a high-profile opportunity to make the case for their candidacy. Mr. Giuliani's aides say that he most likely never will." These aides told Nagourney that Giuliani was content to run what we might call a Carl Schurz Park strategy—that's the park where Gracie Mansion sits, the municipal equivalent of the Rose Garden—the better to avoid missteps, wild utterances, puncturing the ribs of placid upstaters with his sharp city elbows. All that may have been true. But even before his Dorismond outburst, it was weird. After, it was incomprehensible.

Some Passion! Say Amen, Somebody!

The e-mailed press release from the Clinton campaign arrived the morning of Monday, March 20. Hillary was giving another major speech, this time at Bethel A.M.E. Church in Harlem, on West 132nd Street. Surely this one, I thought, would have to be an improvement over the month's previous major speech.

It was.

Hillary entered at 6:35 P.M., in the company of Charlie Rangel, Bill Perkins, the local councilman, and others. The house was packed with about eight hundred people. The pastor thanked the Lord for Hillary Clinton ("Yes! Yes!" answered the congregants), asked him to "bless her and keep her and sustain her." Then Rangel spoke. "Take a good look at who's sitting next to you," he said, "and remember that this may be the most important night of your life."

It was certainly, up to that point, the most important night of Hillary's campaign. The audience, like the one that had gathered in Purchase for her announcement speech, yearned for Hillary to inhabit the moment. For the first five minutes, she dished out the usual platitudes. But then she turned a rhetorical corner and suddenly she was off like a rocket. "The mayor"—she rarely said the words "the mayor," always instead saying "others who" or "those who"—"has hunkered down and taken sides and further divided this city"; "last week, the mayor and I both said that New Yorkers should wait and reserve judgment on this latest case. . . . I am still waiting for a full and fair investigation. Unfortunately, the mayor has not. . . . At just the moment when a real leader would have called for calm and tried to unite the city, he has chosen divisiveness. . . . Many rank-and-file police officers are caught in the middle of the mayor's battle with the [minority] community. . . . New York has a real problem. We all know it. All of us, it seems, except for the mayor of this city. . . . For the sake of the communities, for the sake of police officers, for the sake of our children, for the sake of all New Yorkers, the *mayor must stop dividing this city!"*

It was unbelievable. Bam, bam, bam, bam, bam, like a boxer's combinations. And she delivered the words with real passion. So often her voice just sat there, uninflected and passionless. But this night, it bounced and jumped and carried people up in its rhythms and took them back down again. She had shown no sense previously of being able to feel an audience's mood, and no ability to respond to it and build her cadences around it. This night, though, she did. I was sitting next to Ellen Wulfhorst of Reuters. At the first mention of "the mayor," we looked at each other, eyebrows raised in cautious interest. By the fifth, and sixth mentions, we were staring at each other in disbelief. This was a candidate!

The next day's papers gave the speech glowing coverage. Even the *Post* put her attack on its cover, and the play was all sympathetic; inside, the *Post* ran an editorial blasting Police Commissioner Howard Safir—and, implicitly, Giuliani—for the department's failure to assuage public concern about police shootings of blacks. (Some things never change, though: Dick Morris's column that day ran under the headline HOW HILLARY SECRETLY SOLD OUT SCHOOL REFORM in Arkansas. She had done so, it turned out, by following Morris's polls.) It was the first moment of genuine excitement in Hillary's campaign. Because it raised the stakes of the campaign, and because the speech surely alienated some white suburban voters, it was also her first real risk.

Giuliani responded by accusing her of "projection," arguing that in fact she was the one dividing the city. That might have flown just two weeks before, but after the Dorismond episode, it was dead on the ground. The "Al Sharpton Democrat" line got yet another workout. But every move he made looked bitter, small. The next Sunday's *Post* came out with a poll showing Hillary ahead—barely, but ahead—of Giuliani for the first time in months. Her lead represented a ten-point swing from just three weeks before. Gregg Birnbaum's story declared her "the new comeback kid." Bob McManus, the *Post*'s newly appointed editorial-page editor and one of its columnists, wrote a column on March 23 that tried to defend Rudy for a few paragraphs but concluded, intriguingly, by saying that the mayor had mangled the Dorismond case, harmed his candidacy perhaps irreparably, and should not be looking to the state Republican Party to bail him out: "Now he's truly on his own." When even the *Post* was talking like this, you knew Hillary had it good. Finally, she had risen to an occasion.

Fearless Receives a Visitor

Not everyone, however, was elated by Hillary's speech. The following week, one source of mine—a politically connected person who was sympathetic to the first lady's campaign—hopped aboard the express elevator in the Waldorf-Astoria to meet the president. Or Fearless, as some in Hillary's circle, my friend was amused to learn, called him.

Now, why are you here? Fearless asked my source. "Because your wife's campaign is a disaster," my source said. "It's unfocused. And it's too liberal. The Harlem speech was all well and good, but let's face it, she will not beat Rudy Giuliani in a statewide election by saying he's mean to black people." Fearless, on this point, expressed tactical agreement. "I've told her a hundred times," the president said, "that if she makes this race a referendum on his mayoralty, she'll lose." But more than the president's evident disagreement with his wife's approach, my source noted a certain casualness in Fearless's attitude. Was it possible that he didn't care that much? That was not the case. He was already talking with his wife regularly, and checking with Penn for the numbers. "I think he just felt that, as long she stayed close, he could come in and bail her out at the end," my source says. "He even said at one point, 'Well, she'll be all right as long as she's within five points in October.'"

Al Gore may have wanted Bill Clinton to stay put in the Rose Garden, but evidently the president was resolved to be of use to one campaign.

CHAPTER 8

April 2000:
The Diagnosis

The Campaign in Rudy's Mind

ADAM NAGOURNEY'S *Times* piece from March concerning Rudy's intentions had reopened the debate about what sort of candidate Rudy was, and indeed if he even *was* a candidate. A view was developing, however tentatively, that maybe Rudy was looking for a way out of this race. "Remember," insiders would say, "he never really wanted the job to begin with." Conservative Party chairman Mike Long's occasional remarks to the press, expressing his deepening skepticism about Giuliani, fueled the speculation. Two post-Dorismond polls showing Rudy losing his lead had insiders atwitter. Then, on Sunday, April 2, ABC's *This Week With Sam and Cokie* had Rick Lazio as a guest. Lazio had never really gone away—he was still in regular contact with Long—and now he had decided to make a public move. The state GOP, he said, was "potentially blowing" this race; Giuliani was "dramatically collapsing." "I say I am ready to run," he said on the show. "If I can make a fair case to the public of New York . . . I will be back in this race. And I think that's up to the Republican leadership." It was Lazio's most public declaration since the previous August, when Pataki had endorsed Giuliani, that he was still in the game.

The "Republican leadership" needed three days to respond to

Lazio's awkward challenge. "I don't think it is particularly helpful," the governor told reporters at the Albany Capitol, "for other Republicans to do anything other than get behind the candidacy of Mayor Giuliani." It wasn't that George Pataki had become a fan of Rudy Giuliani—that would never happen—but for the sake of the national party, he had to keep the state GOP working from one set of plans. The same day the governor spoke, *Post* columnist Eric Fettmann roasted Lazio and Long in his op-ed column. When a *Post* columnist did that, it was reasonable to conclude that he might be sending a message from the sanctum that insiders sometimes like to call, investing it with a Whitehall-ish sense of prominence, "the second floor"—that is, the floor of the state Capitol where the governor's offices are located.

For his part, Long was secretly pursuing a Plan C that involved neither the mayor nor Lazio. Since the previous fall, Long had been fishing for a possible candidate, ideally someone who would both accept the Conservative line *and* challenge Rudy in a GOP primary. During the winter, he found such a candidate. Long spent the early months of 2000 persuading his choice to enter the race. By April, his secret weapon had agreed, and was within forty-eight hours of declaring his candidacy. Long had even taken the step of calling Nagourney to tell the *Times* correspondent that he had a candidate who was about to declare. He did not tell Nagourney the candidate's name, but he assured the reporter that he would be granted the first interview. Long had lined up a preliminary campaign team, and the candidate had sat for publicity photos. But it never happened—at the last minute, the candidate backed out.

His name was Bruce Bent. A friend of Long's and a contributor to the Conservative Party for three decades, Bent was a cofounder of an organization called Change New York, a conservative political action group created in the late 1970s that helped finance the campaigns of various conservative candidates. Change New York had assisted George Pataki in his first run for the state senate. But Bent brought a little more to the table than that meager credential. The son of a postal worker, Bent invented, in 1971, the money-market account. Now he ran a $9 billion company. He was prepared, like New Jersey liberal Jon Corzine, to put several of his own millions into the race. He was a strict conservative on most matters, although with a couple of surprising twists—he opposed the death penalty, and he supported gun control (even though he had a rifle range in the basement of his home). He was, in other words, smart, rich, and ideologically interesting—a combination that has put more than one man in the Senate in our time. He loathed Hillary Clinton, and he didn't have much use for Rudy Giuliani.

"I was prepared for a Republican primary," Bent says, "but I didn't think Rudy had the balls to do something like that. My thinking was that he wouldn't get into something he could lose." But after a last-minute conference with his family, Bent decided the time wasn't right.

Giuliani, meanwhile, was still not campaigning so much as carrying on with the small-arms fire that he opened by attacking Billy Joel back in February. There is no Cuban vote to speak of in New York, and there are no odds in a New York pol's acting as though there is, but those facts didn't prevent the Elián González controversy from having its brief moment in the New York sun. The April 1 papers carried Giuliani's announcement that Elián should be given citizenship immediately. Hillary didn't respond right away—unlike the famous "war room" of her husband's campaign, with its well-oiled rapid-response machinery, Hillary's campaign was becoming famous for its anti-rapid responses—but the following day she came out against the mayor's position and for leaving the issue to the courts. Giuliani could not have been invoking Elián for the sake of public opinion in New York, which consistently supported Janet Reno on the issue. Obviously, it was to raise money from Cuban-Americans and others on the Right, and to make the emotional argument that Hillary was pro-Castro.

On Friday, April 7, the *Times* published the results of its first post-Dorismond poll, and the results were a shock. Two previous post-Dorismond polls had shown Rudy tied with Hillary. But this one showed Hillary with her biggest lead since the days when her candidacy was just a pleasant idea. She led the mayor 49 to 41 percent, as close as she'd ever come to the talismanic 50 percent. The mayor still led in the suburbs, but upstate, Hillary had managed to deadlock him, a remarkable feat for a Democrat. In the city, Hillary was now ahead three to one. And, among blacks, Giuliani had achieved a truly rare distinction: "The number of New York City black voters who said they approved of Mr. Giuliani's job rating," wrote Nagourney and Marjorie Connelly, "was so low as to be virtually unmeasurable." Zero percent approved, and 88 percent disapproved. Overall, just 32 percent of New

Yorkers approved of Giuliani's job performance, the lowest approval rating ever, by 10 percent.

Giuliani had a mess on his hands. True, he was still effectively tied, or within shouting distance, depending on which poll you liked. His campaign was still raising money at the speed of light, the total by now approaching $20 million. And he did have reasonably effective commercials on the air, including one featuring John McCain—who, despite losing the New York GOP primary to George W. Bush the previous month, was still a popular figure in the state, especially in the critical Long Island counties.

But the man himself was doing nothing. He was involved in a campaign; that was clear from statements like the one he made about Elián, which he wouldn't have made if he were only the mayor. To be fair, he was answering reporters' questions every day, on any topic that they cared to ask about, which was far more than could be said of Mrs. Clinton. But he wasn't really *running* a campaign at all. He had a payroll and a staff, but his campaign was, in essence, three people: Himself, doing whatever moved him; Teitelbaum, overseeing the fund-raising, talking to reporters, responding to whatever Hillary or Wolfson said that day, lining up support around the state; and Adam Goodman, a Florida-based Republican consultant who was producing the mayor's television ads, as he had in the 1997 mayoral race. There were weekly meetings that began around this time, at which various Giuliani intimates talked strategy and reviewed the week's events. The group included Peter Powers, Randy Mastro, and Randy Levine, who had been high-ranking Giuliani-administration officials; Joe Lhota, Dennison Young, and Tony Carbonetti, who still were; and Ken Caruso, whose relationship with the mayor went back to the Reagan Justice Department. (It was interesting that this working group did *not* include Ray Harding. The Liberal Party leader, who had been so indispensable when Giuliani was running for mayor in heavily Democratic New York City, had become, now that Giuliani needed to shore up his right flank, less crucial.)

But the working group was a loose confederation at best. The campaign was Rudy, Bruce, and Adam. And, if you wanted to peel things down to absolute fundamentals, Teitelbaum and Goodman did not have the authority, finally, to make major decisions. The campaign was in Rudy's head.

So he did as he pleased. He had made a few quick dashes upstate, like the one to Elmira, where he went off the ledge while talking to Brit Hume about Patrick Dorismond. But they were sparse, and fast. Republicans were complaining, and the mayor responded to the complaints on Friday, April 7, when he finally did go to Binghamton, where he mirthfully told his audience that he hadn't been able to travel much because "I have a full-time day job. And, I say this most respectfully, Mrs. Clinton doesn't." At least he was acknowledging, now, that he had a problem; a problem, aides said, that the mayor would attack the next week, when he would undertake a two-day, four-event swing.

April 12 was to find him in Rochester, at a Women for Giuliani lunch. The event, to be held at a Hyatt hotel, had been planned months in advance. Almost seven hundred tickets, at $50 a piece, had been sold, according to Stephen Minarik, the Monroe County Republican leader, whose wife, Renee, had been one of the lead organizers of the lunch. But the day before the event, the mayor said he wasn't going. He was going to the Yankees home opener. "Long before I was a politician, I was a Yankee fan," he told reporters at City Hall. There was only one home opener, he said; "you can raise money any time." Some of the event's organizers learned about the mayor's cancellation from reporters. Rudy was totally unapologetic, and, although the mayor's staff did call Minarik to apologize and reschedule the event for June, he clearly was not appeased. "It was a fairly thin excuse, to go to a ball game," he says. "People held the company line publicly, but privately people groused about it quite a lot." Actually, Minarik did complain publicly about the McCain commercial, which was fine for the city market but which wasn't performing much magic upstate, where Bush romped. The mayor was asked about this. "Oh, everybody complains about everything," he said. Rudy Giuliani, Minarik says with hindsight, "was not a highlight of my life."

Hillary, finally, seemed to be feeling more comfortable and confident on the trail. After learning about Rudy's blow off, she made a little impromptu joke about the mayor's troubles ("He's had a tough couple weeks. It might be good for him to go to a game"). Her campaign proceeded to put together a last-minute event in Rochester for her, where she stopped at a restaurant, chatted with people, and ordered two tuna sandwiches to go (taking care to leave a $20 tip). She was all over the state in April—Buffalo, Rochester, the Finger Lakes, Albany, the Adirondacks, Long Island. On Long Island, speaking to a business group on April 14, she unveiled a plan to pay down the national debt. This would barely have made the papers if Rudy hadn't done two things to ensure that it did. First, it emerged that the group to which Mrs. Clinton spoke had also invited the mayor, the association's president told the papers, but never heard back from him. Second, at his daily City Hall press briefing that day, Giuliani snapped at reporters who kept hitting him with questions about her speech: "Oh, come on, Mrs. Clinton, Mrs. Clinton. You guys are unbelievable. You're like, knee jerk, knee jerk, knee jerk. Thank you." Thank you, as in, this press conference is over. But it wasn't quite. Stomping out, he added: "Why don't you just join the Democratic National Committee?"

Over the years that Giuliani had been mayor, his behavior had from time to time been so unusual, so outside the unimaginative parameters to which most politicians are slaves, that reporters and pundits didn't quite know how to analyze it. Does he know something we don't know? reporters would ask themselves. Is being so needlessly confrontational some sort of strategy we don't get? Often it was. There was the Local Rudy I described in the last chapter, who knew that New Yorkers would generally consider boorish behavior a plus, as long as he was getting the job done. He understood, also, that confounding the media's expectations was more often than not a source of joy to his rank and file. But it was also just who he was. He talked the way he talked because . . . it was the way he talked. And, the more he sensed that responsible political opinion expected him to do A, the more certain it became that he would do Not A, just to mess with people. So the more the city's pundits and pollsters whacked him on Dorismond, the more strongly he stood his ground. The more the state's Republicans keened about his not going upstate, the more you could bet the mortgage that he would keep to his routine—City Hall, fires, cop shootings, speeches, the two or three restaurants he was known to haunt, Elliot Cuker's cigar bar, and then, finally, when the eighteen-hour-a-day mayor had attended to his duties and completed his amusements, Gracie Mansion.

Family Values, Gracie Mansion Style

When Giuliani became mayor in January 1994, the newspapers ran a few light stories about how Gracie Mansion would once again be home to a nice, uncomplicated nuclear family. David and Joyce Dinkins's children were grown by the time the Dinkinses moved into the mansion. Besides that, there were rumors enough about Dinkins's roving eye that, though no one ever printed it, the initiated never assumed complete marital bliss. Before Dinkins, there was Ed Koch, the bachelor. Family-values corn obviously is not the commodity in New York City that it is in some other places. Still, things haven't yet reached the point where it's an active minus. So when Rudy moved in with his adoring wife, Donna Hanover Giuliani, and adorable young children, the chubby little Andrew and the Junebug-cute Caroline, the city had a First Family again.

Donna had campaigned for him. Donna had helped him write speeches. Donna—a television newscaster and actress—had advised him on his electronic image. At the only Gracie Mansion reporters' Christmas Party to which I was invited, in the first year of their mayoralty, Donna was there, shaking hands, wishing everyone Merry Christmas, Happy Hanukkah, giving a speech extolling the city's nascent turnaround, and smiling.

It was shortly thereafter that things took a turn. By mid-1995, the situation was clear enough. Rudy and his top press aide, Cristyne Lategano, were inseparable. He was even spotted helping her pick out a dress. It was hard to infer that the relationship was, as they maintained, strictly professional. In September of that year, my colleague Craig Horowitz did a cover story in *New York* on Lategano. That article was less about the scarlet A allegedly hanging over City Hall than about the surprising degree of political influence Lategano, a person who at the time could claim no high-level experience in government, had with the mayor, but people were somehow less interested in the latter than the former.

The rumors persisted. Both mayor and aide denied them. No one found a smoking gun, and, lacking it, no one was quite rude enough to make an issue of it. There was a piece in *Vanity Fair* in 1997, again discussing the alleged affair, but again offering no proof. But the fact remained: Rudy and Donna, from early 1995 on, were almost never seen together. Ever so often, something would pop up on one of the gossip pages. In February 2000, for example, a *Daily News* photographer snapped a close-up of Rudy gesturing firmly with his left hand—a hand, it was noted, on which he now didn't even bother to wear a wedding band. Donna, throughout, maintained silence, except to say, whenever a new project came out, that she was enjoying her career just as Rudy was enjoying his.

She would drop hints. Hint number one was her makeover. Her hairstyle had always been aggressively unflattering—first, those 70s-style, curling-iron wings, like the girls in my high-school yearbook; later, a short bob that looked a little butch. But sometime in 1997 she switched to a looser, straighter, and more natural style. She wore less makeup. She toned up. She smartened up her wardrobe. She was a dish. Everyone noticed. I remember walking into City Hall for a speech by Rudy not too long after Donna's makeover and seeing Lategano for the first time in a couple of months. Cristyne usually wore her hair pulled back so tight against her scalp that it looked as if it must hurt. But this day she had a new hairstyle, feathery and light, that softened her face's sharp angles rather than accentuating them. I was certain there was a connection.

Beyond the makeover, there were verbal hints. If she sat for a rare interview, and a reporter called her "Donna Hanover Giuliani," she would curtly correct that it was "Donna Hanover." She gave one such interview, on March 25, to Heidi Evans of the *Daily News,* in which she talked briefly about her husband's Senate candidacy, her most revealing (though not, by this time, surprising) comment being that if Rudy won, she did not expect to move to Washington: "I will be an apartment dweller in Manhattan, like I was before."

That caused a little stir. What happened on April 20 caused a bigger one. Donna, said her spokeswoman, was taking a role in a play called *The Vagina Monologues.* The play, by Eve Ensler, featured three actresses, each playing a variety of roles, based on interviews the playwright had done with women about sexuality, relationships, men, women, orgasms, even rape. The play had run to favorable reviews for more than a year, and any number of respected actresses had performed in it. Donna would costar with Kirstie Alley and Hazelle Goodman, and her run would last from May 30 through June 11.

God love New York that this didn't create the immediate moralistic earthquake you'd expect. It was a big story, naturally, and some observers were outraged—the *Post* editorial page wasn't happy, despite the paper's great, playful headline the day the story broke: GYNO-MITE! HANOVER'S GETTING IN ON THE ACT. But most New Yorkers were amused or puzzled. Okay, we're in New York, most people thought, we can deal with this. Still, the press couldn't help pointing out that this *was* kind of a weird thing for a politician's wife to be doing, especially when that politician was smack in the middle of his worst month in this Race of the Century. It emerged from the coverage that one of the three actresses faked an orgasm onstage; would the first lady of the City of New York be playing *that* part? It didn't help, from Rudy's point of view, that Ensler was a huge Hillary supporter, indeed a member of her exploratory committee (vaginas, apparently, were not a matter of controversy for Democrats). Back in the fall of 1999, Donna had been distant but dutiful. On two occasions, she was supposed to appear at the same event as Hillary; she gave one a polite pass and arranged things at the other so that the two would not be there at the same time. That had been Donna's habit for five years now. While she displayed no affection for the man who was still, if only at this point legally, her husband, neither did she do anything to cause him embarrassment. But this was an intervention. Here was at least one white woman voter who seemed to hate Hillary less than she hated Rudy.

Giuliani was starting to unravel. He was even more testy and edgy than usual. On April 22, when U.S. marshals seized Elián from his Florida relatives' home, Giuliani called them "storm troopers." Lots of Republicans talked like that after that raid. But lots of Republicans hadn't been the number three man in the Justice Department, overseeing the U.S. marshals, as Giuliani had in the early 1980s. And lots of Republicans weren't mayors whose police commissioners had been U.S. marshals, as Howard Safir had. It was a bizarre thing for a man with Giuliani's pedigree to say.

Insiders had been saying since the race started that one of these days he'd flip his wig over something and show his ugly side. The Dorismond shooting put that side on display, and he followed up with behavior that was unusual even by his roomy standards. And Hillary? All she had to do was watch. When the opposition is being punched by everyone else, just stand aside. And, though she had no way of knowing it as she went to bed on the night of Wednesday, April 26, the punches were only just starting.

"I Have Prostate Cancer"

Late that night, New York 1 began reporting in its "news-wheel" that the mayor had undergone extensive tests at Mount Sinai Medical Center on the Upper East Side that day. A source was reporting that his PSA levels were abnormally high, but the station drew no conclusions from its reporting, at least none that it aired.

The next morning, the wood on the *Post* was, NO-SHOW RUDY: SOURCES SAY MAYOR WILL SKIP SAUCY SHOW STARRING DONNA. Cover treatment included a photo of the couple in happier times. The page 3 story, by David Seifman and Gregg Birnbaum, noted that the night of Donna's debut conflicted with the state Republican convention, scheduled for May 30 in Buffalo, and quoted "one insider" as saying that "even a Yankee game couldn't keep him away" from that.

Right below the Donna story, though, ran another, on which Seifman also shared the byline, this time with Mark Stamey, which was altogether more intriguing. Seifman had been tipped off about the tests before Giuliani went to Mount Sinai. Stamey showed up at the hospital and chatted the mayor up. "Fine, fine," Giuliani said. "I'm just in for tests. That's all." He joked that he was competitive with Hillary upstate even though he hadn't been campaigning there because "as they see her more, they like me better, and as they see me less they like me more."

The New York 1 report, buttressed by the *Post* story, pointed toward one conclusion, which would be obvious, at least to many men over fifty. High PSA levels meant only one thing. Rudy Giuliani had prostate cancer.

In an interview after the election, the mayor told me that he had been facing the possibility of cancer privately for about two weeks. Doctors had put him on antibiotics for ten days to see if it was just an infection. But his father had died of prostate cancer, so he "wasn't one of those people who was able to say, 'Well, it was probably nothing.'" Then he had a biopsy, the results of which confirmed the diagnosis.

Even then, he says, "I don't think I appreciated what it meant. I think I thought of it like handling another subway crash, or the West Nile virus, or a terrible snowstorm." It would be four or five days until he realized that this wasn't like a subway crash at all.

In the meantime, with City Hall abuzz with speculation, he decided to handle it like a municipal crisis and be up-front about it. "I thought I could probably get a few days by obfuscating," he says, "or I could just say that I had it." So, around ten o'clock on Thursday morning, the mayor came into the Blue Room and told reporters: "I've been diagnosed with . . . well, I have prostate cancer." He said he "kept getting positive and negative mixed up. I kind of think of negative as bad and positive as good. So when he told me it was positive, it took me a second to figure out, 'Oh, gee, that's not good.' " He went on to say that he had "no idea" if he would still run. "I hope that I'll be able to run," he said, "but the choice I'm going to make . . . is the treatment that gives the best opportunity to have a full and complete cure. Then, after I determine that, then I will figure out does it make sense to run this year or doesn't it or whatever."

Well. People had expected that, in this race, the unexpected would happen. But no one could have anticipated anything like this. Rafael Martinez Alequín, a City Hall reporter who published *The Free Press* of Brooklyn, was standing on the City Hall steps shortly after the press conference. Alequín was a constant burden to Giuliani, taking pleasure in asking him the rude questions no one else would dare. He didn't like the mayor, and the mayor had often regarded him with contempt. But Alequín had undergone an operation for stomach cancer the year before, and now even he was shaken and subdued. He told me he and Rudy had had a brief heart-to-heart that morning. Alan Hevesi, the city comptroller, was walking up the steps. Hevesi and Giuliani had in recent weeks been at each other's throats over a city workfare contract that Hevesi charged had been let improperly. The comptroller had recently taken the rare and incautious step of calling the mayor "a liar," on the record. But Hevesi was a prostate cancer survivor himself. They went toward each other, all smiles, and shook hands.

The mayor looked *awfully* calm. Often, his face was scrunched up in anger or petulance. That Thursday, he looked serene and unconcerned. If he runs, I thought—and my hunch from that moment was that he wouldn't, although I would go back and forth in the coming weeks—he will be a much more relaxed and attractive candidate. He'll stop picking all these petty fights. He'll be a little vulnerable. He'll get a sympathy vote.

He'll win.

On Friday, April 28, the *Daily News* front-paged a grim-looking Rudy under the obvious one-word headline. The *Post* went with the kind of front-page that tabloid newspapers usually reserve for declarations of war. It eschewed a picture entirely, as if the news were too grave to be rendered in anything other than stark, black-and-white type: CANCER CLOUDS RUDY RUN. The *Times* gave it two columns across the top, with another two columns occupied by a photograph of the mayor. The mains and sidebars were full of background speculation from insiders—this one swearing that Rudy is a fighter whose resolve would only be strengthened now, that one guessing that his diagnosis gave him a sterling excuse to get out of a race he didn't want to be in anyway. Both scenarios were entirely plausible. The only thing that was crystal clear was that no one really knew what he would do. He directed Teitelbaum and Goodman to soldier on; he told friends, sources say, that he'd still like to run. But nobody knew. His campaign was now completely inside his mind, entirely a function not of polls or money or the upstate strategy but of his mood, his health, and his emotional state. And it would be three weeks—three tumultuous weeks such as even the wizened veterans of New York politics swore they'd never seen—before his mind was made up.

A Courage Born of Convenience

The Independence Party is New York's version of Ross Perot's Reform Party. Just as Perot once did, the party represents the aggrieved center. Voters who were fed up with both parties and could go either way. It also represents a nice chunk of votes. Chuck Schumer had received 172,000 votes on the Independence line in 1998. It was a line worth going after.

The party had scheduled its nominating convention for Saturday, April 29, at an airport hotel in Buffalo. It was just eighty or so people in a conference room. And they wouldn't even vote their endorsement that day—that wouldn't come, they said, until early June. But it was important enough that ABC sent George Stephanopoulos to cover it and do his *This Week* segment live from there. It was important enough that Rudy, who canceled a few commitments after his diagnosis, kept this one.

Which was all kind of amusing, because the party was in the throes of a comic crisis. There were two factions fighting for control: The people who were loyal to Tom Golisano, who had helped found the party and was its more or less respectable gubernatorial candidate in 1994; and people from the New Alliance Party, a parasitic left-wing movement whose leader, Lenora Fulani, had spent years trying to inveigle herself into a position of prominence somewhere. It was the New Alliance habit, going back to the early 1980s, to try and "join" one political grouping or another in order to take it over. Fulani's Marxist politics had not prevented her from endorsing Perot in 1992. Stranger still, they had not prevented her from endorsing presidential candidate Pat Buchanan, whom the Golisano forces opposed vigorously, in 2000. Buchanan happily accepted her endorsement. Each loathed the other's politics. But in terms of their fulminating outsiderish psychology, they were made for each other.

The two factions fought their battle over control of the party in the courts, and a court decision just before the convention had given the Fulani side temporary control, and thus the power to handpick a Senate candidate. Who wanted to be associated with her? Among other things, she had a history of rising to the defense of Louis Farrakhan and Khalid Muhammad whenever the "Zionist media" persecuted them. But more pressingly, who wanted to be associated with Buchanan? The Senate candidate who won the Independence Party's endorsement would be sharing a ballot line with America's General Franco.

Still, 170,000 votes is 170,000 votes. The party may have been a joke, but only insiders knew that. Regular, centrist, anti–big-party voters walking into the booth on election day would notice which candidate had this line and would vote accordingly.

Hillary's people believed, initially, that she should go for this endorsement. Hillary and even the president himself, along with a handful of leading New York Democrats, had placed calls to Frank McKay, the party's state chairman, who was not himself a New Alliance member but who had thrown in his lot with Fulani in the party's internal struggle. Giuliani's people just wanted as many ballot lines as possible. "We weren't worried about Buchanan," a Giuliani source told me. "With Rudy's record on the Jews, and on Israel, he was going to worry about Hillary Clinton, who kissed Suha Arafat, trying to call him an anti-Semite?"

It was the first and only time Hillary and Rudy appeared on the same stage (albeit not together), a sight very much worth seeing. McKay, making introductory remarks, outlined the litmus-test issues to which candidates seeking the Independence Party's backing were meant to pay deference, which had to do with "opening up the democratic process": same-day voter registration, less onerous ballot-qualification laws, looser rules for putting initiatives and referenda on the ballot. McKay finished and said we'd have a five-minute break; thirty seconds later, in walked Rudy. He delivered a speech saying that absolutely, he was for all these things—which in nearly seven years as mayor he'd never mentioned once that I could remember. He said he was for term limits, confident that no one there would remember that he had fought a term limits referendum that passed while he was mayor, and had even sought, after its passage, to have it undone. He took a question from Fulani about how perhaps, as senator instead of mayor, he could reach out to the black community as he hadn't before. "I hadn't thought of it that way," Rudy said. "But the answer is yes."

It was one of his all-time worst performances—pure pandering, made all the stranger because he was pandering to a woman for whom he had previously shown nothing but contempt. That's how important these minor-party lines can be. But two days after the man had been diagnosed with cancer, no one dared write that.

And, wouldn't you know it, it was one of Hillary's best performances. Rudy, Bruce, Adam Goodman, and company were long gone when she hit the stage shortly after two o'clock. She was there to say what she stood for, she said, "and, as importantly, what I stand against." That was all the tip-off the experienced Hillary-watcher needed—she was going to do something unusual here. She talked up the McCain-Feingold bill and laundry-listed a few good-government items. But she didn't tailor her speech to them. Then came the hammer: "The internal battles have cast a terrible shadow over this party," she said. "This party must stay true to mainstream principles. If, however, it succumbs to the anti-Semitism and the extremism of a few shrill voices of the extreme Right and the extreme Left, you will be doing yourselves and this state a disservice. I will not embrace or excuse those with extreme positions. And I will not run on a line with Pat Buchanan on the top of the ticket."

In truth, her saying this was not a big political risk. Given her troubles with Jewish voters, she couldn't afford to get within ten miles of Buchanan. And, given the fact that she and her husband had courted the party's leader, it was obvious that she'd summoned this courage only after it was evident to her that she wasn't going to get their line. Courage born of convenience is not courage at all. Still, she went before a hostile crowd and told them something they didn't want to hear. And she did it coolly, with poise and toughness. I flew back to the city that evening thinking that, even though she had blown whatever slim chance she had at winning their endorsement, she had won the day. It would have made a fantastic commercial, if Team Hillary had been airing commercials. But so stalled was the team by its internal arguments that no Hillary commercials had yet aired.

Fortunately for Hillary, people would spend May talking far more about her opponent.

CHAPTER 9

May 2000: The Spin-Out

"He's, Like, on a Date or Something"

THE SAME FRIDAY that Giuliani's cancer diagnosis was on the front pages, his schedule featured a dinner in Saratoga Springs. He had already announced that he was canceling some local events the following week, along with a trip to California to raise money. But to send a message to voters (and journalists) that he was still in the hunt, he decided to go to the Saratoga Springs event.

It was one of the most successful of his entire campaign. He drew an overflow crowd of fifteen hundred admirers. He gave his standard speech, and then, toward the end, he addressed his cancer diagnosis, and promised his audience he would reach a decision soon. His ovations, before and after the speech, were thunderous. His illness may have made the Republican Party pooh-bahs nervous about his candidacy, but on the party's rank and file, it seemed to have precisely the opposite effect. People wanted him to run now more than ever. And what a story line! The brave and noble Giuliani, now doing battle against not one but two malignancies.

Saratoga Springs is a little north of Albany. The next morning, the mayor had to be in Buffalo for the Independence Party event. A man less set in his ways might have decided, since he was already upstate, to bed down somewhere in the vicinity of Saratoga or Albany, perhaps at the home of a contributor or local pol, as Hillary often did when she was on the stump. From there, he could easily fly to Buffalo in the morning. But Giuliani was not such a man. The Rochester event didn't end until after nine o'clock, but even so, the mayor wanted nothing more than to come back to the city.

Wrong decision.

That night, Roger Friedman, a gossip columnist for Fox News Online, was having dinner at Elaine's with John Connally, a former NYPD detective and a freelance journalist. Elaine's is one of New York's most famous watering holes, a roost for journalists and authors and politicians and a few real celebrities, like Woody Allen. This particular night was quieter than usual, and the only person Friedman and Connally recognized was Sid Zion, then a *Daily News* columnist and an Elaine's habitué for years.

Shortly after eleven P.M., a friend of Friedman's walked in. "Get this," the friend said. He had just walked over to Elaine's from a place across the street, and who was in there but the mayor. With a woman: "He was, like, on a date or something." Well, Friedman thought, I'd better check this out.

As he approached the place and sized it up, he didn't recognize it as any place where the smart set went (although it turned out, perhaps predictably, that it was a Yankees hangout). He noted the name— Cronies. He walked in. There was a long bar on the left and a dining room on the right. "But then," Friedman says, "sort of behind the bar, there was this little alcove or banquette." And there, sure enough, sat Rudy Giuliani with a woman who very clearly was not Donna Hanover.

Friedman watched them for a few moments. They sat close to each other, though they engaged in no overt public displays of affection. As luck would have it, another friend of Friedman's was at the bar, a happenstance that gave Friedman an excuse to linger a bit longer than he might have. He talked to the owner. Yes, that's the mayor. Yeah, he comes here a lot. Sometimes with her, sometimes with his son. "That's nice," Friedman thought. "He brings his son to the same place he brings his girlfriend."

Friedman returned to Elaine's, where Connally and Zion were waiting with bated breath. He gave them the skinny. Zion decided he'd try his luck, which would raise the stakes considerably, because while the mayor may not have known Friedman's face, he was certain to know Sid's. But Zion returned empty-handed. Evidently, the owner had tipped the mayor that someone at the bar was being a little nosy, so he left.

In journalism seminars, they might debate the ethics of Friedman's situation. But to him it was pretty clear-cut—he was a gossip columnist, and if the mayor of the City of New York being spotted on the town with a woman other than his wife wasn't gossip, then it was hard to say what was. "The only question," he says, "was how to break it."

Friedman called around to other gossip columnists who were friends of his. He first called Richard Johnson, the editor of the *Post's* widely read Page Six column. Johnson already knew about the romance. And so did others at his paper. Johnson had mentioned it at an editorial meeting before Friedman's sighting, and editors at the meeting said we know that already; in fact, we have pictures. Johnson had a name, too—Judith Nathan. But he didn't know for sure that the woman in the pictures his editors had *was* Judith Nathan. Johnson says the *Post* was going to run the photo on Page Six, without knowing the woman's identity, but held off at the last minute. "I think it was just a feeling that it wasn't the proudest day in journalism, just to run a picture of the mystery woman," he says.

On Monday, Friedman says, he and Johnson agreed that Friedman would post an item for Fox online that evening, and Johnson's page would prepare an item for the next day's *Post*. Friedman's editor at Fox gave him the green light. Friedman understood that he worked for a Murdoch property, and an item like this one might have to jump a few extra hoops. At the top of the Fox News food chain sat Roger Ailes, the former GOP consultant who was a friend of the mayor's and had managed Giuliani's first mayoral run, in 1989. But Friedman was moving ahead with his item until late in the day Monday, when Johnson called him to say the *Post* wasn't prepared to go with it. Johnson was still trying to confirm that the woman in the pictures the *Post* had was indeed Judith Nathan. Friedman backed off printing his item and decided to turn the story over to another friend, Mitchell Fink, a gossip columnist at the *Daily News,* whom he had also told about the sighting.

On Tuesday, May 2, Fink's column led with an item about Jerry

Seinfeld celebrating his forty-sixth birthday. The second item concerned some models lobbing ice at each other at a nightclub. Then,
under the headline RUDY & FRIEND DINE & DINE, Fink wrote that the
mayor had been spotted last Friday dining "with a friend at Cronies on
Second Ave." He had returned with "the same friend" Sunday night,
"this time sitting in a more open section of the eatery." It wasn't until
the penultimate paragraph that Fink introduced the salient fact about
this friend: "One restaurant staffer opined that the mayor was with his
wife, but shown a picture of Donna Hanover, he said it wasn't her."

The next day, the *Post* supplied both the woman's name and picture. On page 7, the page the paper reserves for late-breaking news, the
Post ran a short story by Johnson and Linda Massarella under the headline RUDY'S MYSTERY BRUNCH PAL IS UPPER EAST SIDE DIVORCEE. The
story identified her as Judith Nathan—Johnson had confirmed her
identity through a friend whose daughter attended the same East Side
private school that Nathan's daughter attended—and said the mayor
and Nathan "have been seen togther at restaurants and functions over
the past several months." The story was accompanied by two pictures,
one of Giuliani and Nathan and her daughter strolling down the sidewalk after a recent Sunday brunch, and the other a closer shot of
Nathan herself from the same day. It turned out the *Post* had been
tipped to the couple two Sundays before.

It was amazing enough that the story of the mayor's extramarital
habits was finally, after all the years of rumor-mongering and rude
jokes behind his back, breaking. But that it was breaking *now*—in the
middle of this campaign and just five days after the man announced he
had cancer—was mind-bending. In fact, though, there was a logic behind the timing of these improbable developments. For years, several
factors had conspired to keep the lid on this particular bottle: New
Yorkers' blasé attitude toward the Giuliani/Hanover union; the fact
that no one had ever caught the mayor out alone with another woman;
the mayor's firm insistence on his zone of privacy; his general image of
righteousness and rectitude, which the media had helped cultivate and
was hesitant to undermine; the fact that the one paper most likely to
print such a story, the *Post,* was firmly in his corner.

New Yorkers' blasé attitude may not have changed, but each of
the other conditions had. Now, of course, the mayor *was* out on the
town with another woman. Second, the mayor seemed to have relaxed

his zone of privacy: what other conclusion could possibly be drawn from his taking his girlfriend to a place right across the street from Elaine's? It seemed clear that, on some level, he wanted to get caught. Third, the reporters who covered Giuliani were finally anxious to nail him on something. The mayor and his administration had spent the better part of seven years calling reporters jerks, withholding information that had been considered public under previous administrations, and leaking stories to the few reporters it considered friendly. The relationship between Giuliani's City Hall and the city's political press had always been tense. But political reporters had never found anything on him. And, among the papers' editors and executives, there had never been much enthusiasm for interfering with the New-York-Is-Back story line. But now the New-York-Is-Back story was aging, and the Senate race offered a new narrative context. The time had come, prostate cancer or not, for the screw to turn. That it was the *Post* that busted him was a striking irony, given how fiercely the paper had defended him over the years.

The episode was emblematic of a change that was going on at the *Post*. In the last two or three months, a close reader of the paper could have noticed that its coverage of Hillary was very different from its coverage of her back during the Listening Tour. February's "Tipgate" notwithstanding, the paper was throwing far fewer punches her way. The editorial section, Dick Morris excepted, had turned the heat down on Hillary a notch or two. John Podhoretz had been the editorial-page editor when the campaign began. But he had left that position in December. His successor, Bob McManus, was every bit as conservative as Podhoretz, but less perpetually apoplectic. The paper had even given favorable coverage to her March 21 speech at that Harlem church, when she lit into Giuliani for the first time. And it had taken a couple of whacks at Giuliani. For example, it played the post-Dorismond poll that showed Rudy tanking on its front page, on a Sunday, under the surprisingly aggressive headline WAKE-UP CALL.

None of this is to say the *Post* was suddenly pro-Hillary. That wasn't going to happen. Undoubtedly, once the race heated up again, the paper would return to form. But it was evident that the *Post* wasn't so keen on Rudy these days either. A source close to the paper told me that some of the *Post*'s higher-ups had come to resent the mayor's attempts to steer its coverage, his assumption that it was his sheet.

"They'd tell me how he'd read the bulldog," this source says, referring to the edition of the paper that hits the stands the night before the issue date, "and he'd call up and say, 'Can't you change this word in this headline? This lede [lead paragraph in a story] isn't accurate.' There was a lot of that."

There was also the question of Rupert Murdoch's feelings toward Giuliani. It had been an open secret in 1993 that the paper was about to endorse George Marlin, the Conservative Party candidate, for mayor over Rudy that year. The paper supported Rudy in the end, but the hesitation was a sign that Murdoch wasn't really a great Giuliani fan. The paper may indeed have sat on the photos of Judith Nathan for a while. But when the time came, it published them.

It was a stunning day. In the wake of the cancer announcement, there had been a lot of talk about how the mayor might look more sympathetic and human, might become kinder and gentler. More than that, the conventional wisdom was unshakable in its conviction that, for a while at least, everyone was going to have to be nice to him. This was a very New York idea of nice.

Feeding Time

In the early afternoon, everyone I was talking to was saying things like: Just wait until tomorrow's papers. The *Post* has the whole story. The *News* has twelve people on it. They met through their kids. They met through Elliot Cuker. They've been together since last summer. Donna's fit to be tied. Even *The Times* is doing a piece. And obviously the Judith story would be on the covers of both tabloids. What could possibly knock it off?

A few hours later, Cardinal John O'Connor, the archbishop of New York, was dying.

The New York Archdiocese announced that the cardinal, who'd been stricken with cancer the year before and whose public appearances had grown more and more infrequent, was receiving his last rites. It was a matter of hours, at most.

He died around eight that night. The moment was surreal. O'Connor and Giuliani had followed such similar arcs. Giuliani became the U.S. Attorney for the Southern District in 1983. O'Connor came to New York the following year. The cardinal supported many charitable and liberal causes, preaching on alleviation of poverty and the importance of labor unions. But he devoted his most energetic political parries to the conservative causes for which the Roman Catholic Church is best known—opposition to abortion and gay rights. Giuliani actually disagreed with him on these two issues, and Giuliani's Catholicism was very much of the lapsed variety. Nevertheless, the two had been public allies, occupying similar turf in the city's ongoing battle between those who defend the traditional moral order and those who challenge it. O'Connor had criticized pro-choice Catholic Democrats like Mario Cuomo and Geraldine Ferraro very publicly and insistently. He had not done the same apropos the mayor. From time to time, as during the flap over the Puerto Rican nationalists the previous September, he would interject himself into the debate on the mayor's side. And now, at exactly the moment of the mayor's moral crisis, the one man who might have been willing and able to weave a cocoon of sympathy and forgiveness around him lay dying.

Or maybe in death the cardinal had done the mayor one final favor. The papers and the local newscasts would be filled with tributes to O'Connor for days—certainly until his funeral service, which would be a full week away. Could the papers simultaneously cover this most somber of stories *and* keep the ball bouncing on this most salacious of stories? It seemed that Giuliani might have bought a break, albeit under tragic circumstances. In Hillaryland, certainly, no one was gloating about the mayor's troubles. Clinton staffers operated on the assumption, during the mayor's crises, that press and public sympathy was not a zero-sum game—that is, they knew that whatever good will Giuliani might have lost would not be automatically transferred to their candidate. And it was Hillary's attitude, staffers said, that for obvious reasons she would not go anywhere near the mayor's marital problems. She would keep her head down and keep working.

Meanwhile, down at Giuliani's campaign headquarters in lower Manhattan, they were thinking that the Nathan story had maybe four or five days' worth of legs. When *Vanity Fair* did its piece in 1997 about the mayor and Cristyne Lategano, that's how long the hubbub lasted: five days. Then everything went back to normal. There's no reason, they thought, why things should be any different this time.

It turned out there was room enough for both stories. The *Post* ran just one piece on Rudy and Judi. But the *Daily News,* reclaiming ownership of the story from its competitor, ran four pages of articles. "She's a good friend, a very good friend," the mayor told reporters at his daily City Hall press briefing (that he even *had* his daily City Hall press briefing was testament to his admirable trait of dealing with things as they hit him, and also to the fact that he was no longer in the mood to hide the relationship). Speaking on background, "mayoral aides" and "mayoral confidants" dribbled out details of the relationship, and it was hard to imagine that those details, too, were being shared without the mayor's okay. They're "an item," one said. It's an "open secret," said another. It turned out that Nathan had been at his side at the huge Times Square–New Year's Eve celebration. It even emerged that he had taken her to the Inner Circle dinner back in March—in other words, he took her out on a date in the presence of every political reporter and gossip in town! No one noticed, save one *Times* reporter, but the *Times* didn't cover those kinds of things.

It did now. Tastefully, and in proportion, but it covered them. The next several days were feeding time, and they provided a case study in how the newspapers, especially the tabloids, can keep a story alive by pushing new angles and dreaming up creative packages. There were columns considering Nathan's impact on his campaign (the *News*'s Michael Kramer spoke to five mayoral confidants, and "none . . . professes to know the mayor's thinking about the Senate race"). There were stories about Nathan, "a business manager for a Fortune 500 drug company [who] split up with her husband eight years ago and lives with her teenage daughter in a luxury apartment building on E. 94th St."; "a doting mom and a fitness buff who loves chess, backgammon, and bridge." There were interviews with her most recent beau, Manos Zacharioudakis, who called her "one in a million." In the *News* for Friday, May 5, a story detailed the mayor's assignations with Nathan the previous summer at her condo in the Hamptons, complete with a map showing the condo's location. (A mere condo! The papers did not have to spell out the social-climbing aspect of that.) The papers dispatched reporters to Hazelton, Pennsylvania, where Nathan had grown up, to fetch details like the fact that young Judith Stish, Hazelton High School Class of 1972, was "a member of the Cadets, the Diggers, the Ecology Club, the Library Club, the Literary Society and the Spirit

Club." The *Daily News* took Judi's "style temperature," showcasing her $4,900 Hermes handbag, but declaring her overall temperature "tepid." It also was revealed, in the *Post,* that though Rudy may have won her heart, "he's never had her vote"—though an enrolled Republican, Nathan had rarely exercised her franchise.

Day after panting day, the press demonstrated that this one would *not* go away in five days as the Lategano story had. And the two paramours seemed happy to let the story bleed out. From Giuliani's end, there were the leaks from aides casually confirming details about the relationship. And, judging from a series of pictures of Nathan outside that East 94th Street apartment building, Nathan didn't seem to mind the invasion. The mayor had pleaded with reporters to grant her, if not him, some degree of privacy, but there was to be no Yoko-style hiding under large hats and sunglasses for her. She was all smiles, and right at the lenses. She seemed, with her designer blazers and neat coif, to have primped for an hour in preparation for walking that little dog of hers, and she seemed to be walking that little dog several times a day ("the smallest canine bladder in town," one insider joked to me).

And, finally, of course, there were polls, which found that voters didn't care. A *Daily News*/New York 1 poll on Saturday, May 6, found that 77 percent of respondents said the news of the relationship wouldn't affect their vote. This astonished many insiders and pundits, though I could never see why. The 45 percent who backed Rudy supported him in no small part because they hated Hillary, and obviously they weren't going to switch allegiances just because he was fooling around outside a marriage that was widely recognized as hollow already. As we learned during the Lewinsky matter, the public's tolerance for such moral lapses is far greater than the press imagines it to be.

On the record, most Republicans stood by him. Off the record, though, they were aghast, not so much morally as strategically. Just what was going on with this man? They—Pataki, D'Amato, Joe Bruno, Bill Powers—had come to his aid last year and shooed Lazio out of the race. And for this—so they could watch as he managed to make Hillary Clinton's marriage look healthy? He was increasingly isolated. At Cardinal O'Connor's funeral, held on Monday, May 8, at St. Patrick's Cathedral on Fifth Avenue, a photograph was snapped that summed up what was happening better than any column or news story could. There, in the front pews, were Bill and Hillary Clinton; Al and Tipper

Gore; George W. and Laura Bush; George and Libby Pataki; and, by himself, Rudy Giuliani, surrounded by these men and their wives.

Some conservative columnists turned on him. The *Post*'s Eric Fettmann wrote, on Wednesday, May 10, that the mayor had always willfully challenged "the notion that lowering the standards of acceptable public behavior is something to be tolerated," but that the existence of his "very good friend" had rendered that posture null and void. That day's papers also carried news that State Senate Majority Leader Joe Bruno, speaking from Albany, urged Giuliani to patch things up with his wife and pull himself together: WORK IT OUT! screamed the *Post*'s wood. The mayor would work it out, all right, though not in quite the way Bruno suggested.

The Separation

That same Wednesday, I was having lunch with Juleanna Glover Weiss, the recently hired Giuliani campaign press secretary. We met around 12:30 and were still exchanging pleasantries when suddenly her cell phone rang. She rolled her eyes, reached into her purse, and turned it off. "If I don't just do this now," she said, "this thing will never stop." That's awfully polite of her, I thought.

I got back to my desk around 2:15 and was surprised to find a voice-mail message from Glover Weiss. She wanted to make sure I'd been comfortable picking up the check, and then she said: "Oh, and I think I've learned a lesson about turning off my cell phone. Go check your TV."

As we were lunching, the mayor had been finishing up a routine event in Bryant Park, behind the New York Public Library. He was surrounded by more aides and friends than usual. At the same time, says one reporter who was there, there were fewer reporters tagging along than usual, and the mood was strangely subdued. The floor was opened to questions. Elizabeth Bumiller of the *Times* asked, "Do you have any reaction to Mr. Bruno's comments yesterday on Fred Dicker's radio show about your marriage?"

"I do," the mayor said. "It was very, very painful. For quite some time, it's probably been apparent that Donna and I lead, in many ways, independent and separate lives. It's been a very painful road and I'm hopeful that we'll be able to formalize that in an agreement that protects our children. . . ." He had not hired an attorney, he said. Donna was not moving out of the mansion, for now. It was all very difficult. He wasn't thinking about politics right now. "My emotional state," he said in response to a question, "is I'm very sad. I feel terrible."

The press conference, replayed in its entirety on New York 1, was without precedent in recent American politics. Most politicians would make such an announcement by issuing a statement, ducking out of town for a few days, and leaving the dirty work to their aides. But, as he had with his prostate-cancer announcement, Giuliani did the exact opposite. He stood up there and told the world everything, or an amount of information that, for a politician, was astonishingly close to everything. There will be people who agree with what I'm doing, Giuliani said, and there will be people who disagree, but "I have to try to do what I think is right for me." It was hard to imagine any other politician laying himself bare like that. Maybe there was a strategy to it—maybe he knew that his honesty in such situations would disarm critics. But he was sailing on uncharted seas here. You had to respect it.

There was one aspect to his announcement that was rather more difficult to respect, though. It seemed he had forgotten to tell his wife that he was announcing their separation. Donna Hanover had, at the beginning of the month, canceled her turn in *The Vagina Monologues* after the news of her husband's cancer. She had attended the cardinal's wake, alone, after the Nathan story broke, and said she still hoped to save her marriage. But on this day, about two hours after the mayor announced their separation, Donna emerged from Gracie Mansion and read a brief statement to reporters. Holding back tears, voice aquiver, perfectly on the edge of control, she said she "had hoped that we could keep this marriage together. For several years, it was difficult to participate in Rudy's public life because of his relationship with one staff member." She said she and Rudy would discuss separation, but that for the time being she and the children would remain at Gracie.

Apparently not telling her first hadn't been such a grand idea. If he had, maybe she would have refrained from that obvious reference to Cristyne Lategano. Take that sentence out of her statement, which spoke in general terms of her sadness and about an attempt at reconciliation the previous summer, and her words carried no particular charge. But the mention of "one staff member"—that was war. That gave the press an excuse to revisit the whole Lategano history. (Lategano and the mayor continued to deny an affair.) Every chapter of the mayor's relationship with her would be reopened—in the context of a Senate campaign, and not just in the local media, but on *Hardball* and *Crossfire* and you name it. If divorce proceedings were to move forward during the campaign, Lategano would undoubtedly be deposed, and the deposition undoubtedly leaked. It was a pretty strong return of serve.

The next day, Thursday, found the mayor doing an event about a food drive in the East Village. Again, he took questions. Reporters now were shouting at him—about which woman he was really seeing the previous summer, when Donna thought they were reconciling but he was hopping out to Judi's Hamptons condo, and about Lategano. "Don't you guys have any decency?" he wailed. *"Hey!* HEY! Can't you see how you're embarrassing yourselves?" He had a point. And, in his eagerness to bat questions back and forth with the press, he was even kind of funny. Comedy was where we were now. We'd left the standard arena of politics and entered some zone usually reserved for events like Michael Jackson's marriage to Lisa Marie Presley. And weirdest of all: He was continuing to say he might run, and he was still—because of his record and his money and the animus toward Hillary—undeniably in a position to win.

Things got weirder still on Friday night, when Giuliani and Nathan and three mayoral aides had dinner at an Upper East Side restaurant and then strolled up Second Avenue, walking Judi home. He even gave her a little buss on the cheek before she retreated to her building's lobby. This was possibly the strangest thing any politician has done, ever. Imagine Bill Clinton strolling with Monica up Wisconsin Avenue in February 1998. But it didn't hurt him. In fact it helped him. Some people gleefully yelled "Rudy! Rudy!" as they walked. The tabloids put the stroll on their covers, naturally, but by now they were playing the Rudy-Judi story for kicks, not as if he were mayor and Senate candidate but as if he were Donald Trump or Marv Albert. So sure was he of the pulse of the New York news cycle that he knew bringing his girlfriend out in the open would convert him, in the pages of the tabloids that had been smacking him, from run-of-the-mill philanderer and emotional basket case into swashbuckling bon vivant. It would make him look, to many voters, interesting, devil-may-care, entertaining.

When I saw the next day's papers, though, I couldn't help but think of another audience. Donna and the children had flown out to Los Angeles, where her parents lived, to get away from everything—and to celebrate, if that's the word, Mother's Day, which would arrive on Sunday. Obviously, Rudy knew the picture would be on the front pages of both tabloids. And, obviously, he knew that anyone in Los Angeles who really wanted to, including his in-laws, his wife, and the two children he had vowed solemnly just two days before to protect above all else, could find the *Daily News* and the *Post*.

The Laundry Lady

Hillary, whenever she was asked about the mayor, either had nothing to say or wished him and his wife and his children strength at this difficult time. She had a big moment of her own approaching: On Tuesday, May 16, she would formally accept the nomination of the Democratic Party of New York for United States Senator.

The nomination was a foregone conclusion; what mattered was the event, and whether it could give her a lift during the mayor's tailspin. At the beginning of the month, in Fred Dicker's *Post* column, four thousand Democrats were said to be preparing to gather in Albany's Pepsi Arena, home of the city's arena football team. The next week, in Joel Siegel's politics roundup in the *News,* it was eight thousand. By the night itself, the actual number was 11,500—mostly rank-and-file Democrats and union members who were bussed in from all over the state. The previous state nominating convention, held in a hotel ballroom in a suburban town called Rye, consisted of perhaps four hundred people. Hillary's campaign may have had trouble converting people beyond the most loyal foot soldiers, but those loyal soldiers were willing to take a bayonet for her, or at least a five-hour bus ride to Albany.

The event was rather short on ambience. Assembly Speaker Sheldon Silver hosted a reception—with no booze—in one of the arena's lower concourses. "Early basement," wrote the *Post*'s Cindy Adams of the decor. At one point Cindy and Ken Sunshine and I were chatting about the rumor that was whipping through the reception, that Giuliani would, that night, announce either that he was running or that he was getting out. Either announcement would have stolen headlines from Hillary, and the thought that Giuliani would choose that moment made perfect sense to anyone who knew him.

About eighty-five Democrats spoke before Hillary, so, as often happened at these mega-events, the crowd had pretty much run out of gas by the time the climactic moment arrived. People tried gamely to whip themselves into a new frenzy, but it felt a little forced. Hillary gave them good, populist, Democratic red meat. But her speech was essentially a laundry list—she patted every interest group on the head and, wishing no demographic group or remote corner of the state to feel left behind, threw in something for everyone. So the speech was well received, but it was uninspiring.

This laundry-list style was partly a result of excessive polling. Bill Clinton, the master laundry-lister, would take the fifteen items that Mark Penn's polls showed were popular and plow through them, on the stump and, especially, in his State of the Union addresses. Clinton could pull it off with some panache. In less supple hands, the laundry-list approach could leave a listener numb. By contrast, Mario Cuomo and Jesse Jackson and Ronald Reagan were anti-laundry-listers. Their speeches tended to be built around one or two basic themes, and they rose to a crescendo. If you asked a listener, right after a Cuomo or Jackson or Reagan speech, "What was that speech about?" he or she could probably tell you in one clear sentence. The laundry-list speech is less likely to produce such thematic clarity. Ergo, the central problem of the laundry list, especially for a candidate trying to define herself to a skeptical electorate: A laundry list tells listeners the various measures a candidate supports, but it leaves listeners with no firm grasp of what the candidate truly believes.

In her speech, Hillary mentioned no fewer than twenty-four issues: higher education; health insurance; the environment; the economy; the national debt; Social Security; Medicare; public schools; tuition deduction; care for disabled family members; increased minimum wage; gun control, or "gun safety" as New Democrats had taken to calling it; mental health; prescription drugs; broadband Internet service; et cetera, et cetera. Unobjectionable things, and solid New

Democrat–populist fusion. The ovation was rousing. Bill, again silent behind her on the stage, beamed with pride. (He had decided to fly up only at the last minute and had, one source told me, fiddled with her speech almost up to the moment of delivery.) Moynihan and Schumer and various others joined her onstage. There was much cheer, and even, finally, a little whiskey, at the receptions afterward. But the one thing that didn't happen after her speech is the one thing that's supposed to happen: bounce. She had preached with brio to the converted, but nothing more.

The Exit . . .

On Sunday, Donna Hanover stepped out on her parents' porch to inform the press that her husband had called to wish her a happy Mother's Day. Saturday evening, she and her parents and the children had attended Mass at Our Lady of Perpetual Help in Santa Clarita, where the Reverend Patrick Powers, during offertory prayers, added a prayer that "this springtime will be a time of renewal, especially for those under stress."

The stress, meanwhile, was building at Gracie Mansion. That Sunday, the next week's *Newsweek* went out to media insiders, and it carried a report that the mayor had decided on a course of treatment for his cancer (surgery followed by radiation therapy). It also said that he had decided two weeks before to drop out of the Senate race but had delayed announcing his decision after the Nathan story broke.

The *Newsweek* story sent City Hall and the mayor's campaign into a whirl; several Mother's Day brunches were intruded upon as aides spent the day on their cell phones doing damage control. Giuliani emerged from the mansion on Sunday to blast the story as "malicious" and "totally inaccurate." It was inaccurate insofar as the mayor had made no decision about his course of treatment. And he had not yet, sources say, decided to quit the race. But the state Republican convention was now getting quite close (May 30), and the state GOP wanted an answer out of Rudy sooner rather than later. The next week would bring matters to a head.

That Monday, he was scheduled to hold his usual press briefing at

City Hall. Because of the *Newsweek* piece, and because it just seemed to be about time, everyone expected that Rudy would announce his decision that day. But as soon as I walked into City Hall's Blue Room and saw twenty-five television cameras, I knew this wasn't going to be the day. There was no way Rudy was going to give the press the satisfaction of making his announcement when we expected it. That night, he told an audience at a fund-raiser in Westchester County that he remained "very much inclined" to run. His aides, who wanted him to run, were already talking up a strategy by which he would flood the airwaves with commercials and limit his travel to occasional strategic upstate forays. There's no reason to believe this strategy wouldn't have worked. Remember that joke he made to the *Post* reporter as he was walking into Mount Sinai hospital, about upstaters liking him more the less they saw of him? Maybe there was more than a little truth in it.

Tuesday brought a scorching op-ed column by Fred Dicker in the *Post*. Dicker was a reporter, and he wrote a weekly inside-dope column for the paper. But I could not remember him ever writing an opinion piece. He felt moved to do so this day, excoriating Giuliani, whose withdrawal from the race (which Dicker expected now) "could cost the New York Republican Party a U.S. Senate seat, control of the state Senate, two congressional seats, and a shot at helping elect a President Bush." His closing shot—"Judas Giuliani indeed!"—invoked the old Joe Bruno quote from 1994.

Wednesday, Donna and the kids returned from the coast. Wedding and engagement rings still affixed to her finger, she told reporters she'd "dropped the kids off to school this morning and it's nice to be back at Gracie." We were in a calm-before-the-storm sort of moment. Things were getting back to normal. It was starting to seem that Rudy had weathered the Nathan tempest. Sources I was talking to, people who had thought he wasn't running, were reconsidering now.

Thursday night, he sat for an interview with Andrea Mitchell at the 92nd Street Y for national broadcast on MSNBC. The hall was packed with Rudy partisans, and the appearance marked the triumphal return of National Rudy. He was calm. He was funny, and sensible, and charming, and even remorseful, for the first time, about his handling of the Dorismond matter, admitting that the leak of the man's juvenile record was "a mistake." He looked good, and he looked every inch a candidate. I remember leaving the hall thinking, well, he may run after all—but knowing Rudy, he could change his mind in five minutes.

That night, a source says, a group of about fifteen Giuliani confidants went out for dinner after the Mitchell interview to an Italian restaurant on the East Side. Tony Carbonetti was there, and Denny Young, and Joe Lhota, and Bruce Teitelbaum, and even Ray Harding and his son, Robert, who worked for the administration. Rudy having just hit a tape-measure home run on national television, the mood was joyous. Maybe he was running after all. The group talked of politics and sports; eventually they lit on the topic of a coup that certain state Democrats had recently hatched against Sheldon Silver, the speaker of the state Assembly. An unusually high level of intraparty acrimony had made its way to the papers and was the subject of intense political gossip. There was a pause in the conversation, which the mayor broke by saying: "You know, there's too much fighting in politics." An odd comment from a man who'd spent his mayoralty in search of fights. My source knew right then that Rudy was not running.

Giuliani knew it too. He had gone back and forth often during the previous three weeks, but a couple of days before the Mitchell interview, he says, he had basically made up his mind. He did not want to spend another weekend going through the same emotional contortions. He would do the interview, sleep on it, and make his final decision the next morning. After dinner, he went back to the mansion with a smaller group of friends and talked it over. He bade them goodnight and "got a very bad night's sleep."

In the end, every thought pushed him toward the conclusion he'd been leaning toward anyway. He was facing a life-and-death question that had to be dealt with in the coming six months; he loved his current job; he didn't want to embark on a campaign he might not be able to finish. "Whenever you deal with these things, somebody will say to you, 'When you have seeds put in, 70 percent react this way, 20 percent react this way, and 10 percent react this way,' " the mayor told me. "You don't know, 'Am I the 70, am I the 20, or am I the 10?' Suppose I'm the 10—the worst possible reaction? And it's September, and I'm in the middle of an election, and now for two weeks I can't do anything." He woke up on Friday, May 19, comfortable with his decision, and he went to City Hall and told his people the news.

Just before one o'clock, New York 1's David Lewis broke the

news. Rudy was out. In short order, the mayor was again before the microphones at City Hall, explaining his decision. Again, he left a powerful impression. He was relaxed and funny. His words and demeanor said: So I'm not running for Senate, it's not the most important thing in the world. The papers seized on the fact that he mentioned "love"— as in, love of family, children, and friends, which was more important than politics—a dozen times. Of the race itself, he said, "Sometimes I think yes, and sometimes I think no, and it isn't right to take on that commitment if you don't feel a strong sense of certitude that you can complete it."

Hillary seemed more thrown by the announcement than Giuliani himself. She was doing an event at a union hall later that Friday afternoon. Reading carefully from a prepared statement (which was all of three sentences), Hillary said she'd called Giuliani to wish him well. Her face was stony and emotionless, her eyes blank. It made a striking contrast to the mayor, who was alive and engaged and personable.

Republicans were furious. Democrats were gleeful, though careful to be tasteful about it. And Dick Morris, true to form, wrote a column speculating that Clinton henchmen had dug up the dirt on Rudy and Judi and fed it to the papers, even though he acknowledged that "I have no confirmed information" for this explosive allegation. He had "knowledge of how my former clients operate," but apparently couldn't trouble himself to make one call—to the editors of his own paper, no less—to learn that the *Post*'s original source on the Nathan story was not a Clinton person (Richard Johnson confirmed to me it was not). It was a new low, even for Morris.

Sources say that virtually everyone around the mayor wanted him to run, except Peter Powers, the mayor's oldest political confidant, and Elliot Cuker, who had been pressing the mayor especially hard to drop out. People speculate that Cuker's motives were selfish—that he liked being the mayor's buddy and wanted it to last as long as possible. Whatever the case, Cuker and Giuliani were extremely close—they had met back in the 1970s, when Cuker had a little tax problem and Giuliani helped him sort it out—and had become very close in late 1995. Some of the mayor's political advisers came to believe Cuker held a sway over the mayor that was unusual and maybe a little eerie.

"People said, 'You can campaign half time,' " the major recalls. "But I couldn't do it. And it seemed to me that the advice of people who cared about me the most, rather than the senate, the Republican party, the mayoralty, or anything else—the people who cared about me the most, very, very old friends, came to me and said, 'You're crazy. Cure this first.' "

But it defies everything known about the man to think that anyone made up Rudy's mind except Rudy. His clock ticked in singular time. True, he wanted to beat Hillary Clinton in an election. But he clearly didn't want to be a U.S. senator. He had the classic New Yorker's attitude toward Washington, in spades. He would find little to entice him at The Monocle, the Capitol Hill watering hole that senators frequented. The playground he knew, the one where he felt at home, was on the East Side—Cronies and Hanratty's and Elliot Cuker's cigar bar. His allegiance was to cops and firefighters and the Yankees and the Metropolitan Opera and genuine thin-crust New York pizza. The man whose passions hadn't changed since he was fifteen or even five had a need to stay close to those passions, and no urge to charge into an environment over which he had no control, especially with cancer and radiation or surgery looming. It was in his nature to invite the world into his personal psychodrama for three weeks in a way no other prominent politician in America would have dared. But to embrace a change that was uncertain and unknowable proved beyond him. And there, at his emotional comfort point, with his municipal crises and his faithful buddies and his cocker-spaniel-walking new sweetheart, we leave him.

. . . and the Entrance

It took all of one day for Rick Lazio to gather his family and friends and supporters at West Islip High School, from which he graduated in 1976, to announce that he was launching his candidacy for the Senate.

The newspapers formed a quick consensus around the new candidate. LAZIO OPENS RACE WITH AN ATTACK ON MRS. CLINTON, ran the headline above Adam Nagourney's *Times* piece for Sunday, May 21. The play in the other papers also emphasized his attacks. In his speech, and in an interview with Nagourney, Lazio "jumped at almost every opportunity to criticize Mrs. Clinton" as a "far left" candidate supported by "every possible liberal group from outside our state." Of himself, he said, "I'm the real thing. I don't have to try to be someone else. I was born here. I went to school here. I fished in these waters. I clammed in its bays. . . . There will be no question of my commitment to this state."

The state's Republicans had lost their strongest candidate and been forced to send in the back-up, but on balance they were happy to be through with the soap opera and back to politics. Pataki brought up his own 1994 race as proof that the right David could topple a vulnerable Goliath. Lazio hit six Sunday shows on May 21 (Hillary had never done those shows) and immediately set off on a four-city upstate swing, making sixteen stops in his first twenty-four hours as the candidate. Howard Wolfson dubbed it Lazio's "Statewide Insult Tour," and Harold Ickes wasted no time in slamming Lazio, a deputy whip in the House, as a pawn of Newt Gingrich. But Lazio, for now, seemed immune to attack. He was handsome, with a handsome family. He was young. He was politically moderate. The political reporters, despondent at the mayor's withdrawal and fearful of their stories landing on page 24 now, still wanted a race. A poll taken just days into Lazio's candidacy showed it instantly close—Hillary 46, Lazio 44. It appeared that as long as he wasn't Hillary Clinton and could define himself in a way that was even reasonably compelling, he actually could win.

Several pundits seemed to think so. Mary Matalin, on CNN: "In under a week . . . he is winning in the suburbs, he's winning independents, he's winning in all the demographic groups." David Broder, in *The Washington Post:* "The realization is beginning to sink in that Clinton may have a tough time against Rep. Rick Lazio." Rod Dreher, in the *New York Post:* "If Lazio can seize the initiative, defining his own public image while making the election a referendum on Hillary, he will win." These were not, at that point, unreasonable sentiments.

Certainly Team Hillary was worried. "We had to run a whole new race," Mark Penn says. No longer did they have an opponent who was just as controversial and polarizing as their candidate. A certain number of white liberals could be counted on to vote for Hillary, however unenthusiastically, because they couldn't bear the thought of helping to put Rudy in the Senate. If Lazio ran the right kind of campaign, these same white liberals might now be in play. And what of the African-American vote? One million black voters did not hate Rick

Lazio. Would they be as motivated to vote now, with Giuliani out of the race? True, the Clinton people had Newt Gingrich to use against Lazio. But even that was a bit of a reach—Lazio's voting record was far more moderate. The Clinton people feared having to run against someone who seemed genuine and likeable, whose profile was so pleasant and unthreatening.

That profile took a literal beating on Memorial Day, when, during a parade in Babylon, Long Island, Lazio was running to catch up with other marchers and fell splat on the pavement, unwisely cushioning his blow with his upper lip. Lazio, wrote the *Post,* "spent most of the hour-long Long Island parade wiping streams of blood from his face and holding ice to his swollen lip." The cut required nine stitches.

The lineaments of the figurative beating were sketched the next day at the state Republican nominating convention. The mood in the ballroom of the Hyatt hotel in downtown Buffalo where the nominee spoke was the combination of relief and good cheer you would expect to find at such an event. But what exactly about the new candidate should produce that cheer was another question. There were the minor amateurish touches, like the fact that the copies of the speech that were handed out to the press were labeled "DRAFT 13" across the top. There were the tropes about how the candidate wanted "to bring New Yorkers together" and reject "the politics of division" and would "unite all New Yorkers behind a positive vision for our great state." Partly the problem was that these bland phrases were, almost to a word, Hillary's phrases. And, partly, it was the fact that, a few paragraphs before he'd promised this campaign of unity, he'd already attacked Hillary Clinton, who "comes to New York with the support of every left-wing special interest, from Washington insiders to the Hollywood elite." Strange, also, were the issues he talked up—the environment, schools, the disabled, the upstate economy. These were Hillary's issues, core New-Democrat issues. I had to stop myself from time to time and wonder which party's convention I was attending. This wasn't my reaction alone. In the *News,* Joel Siegel wrote that the speech "was studded with the kind of lines the First Lady might deliver as both seek to grab the political center."

Political conventions, humble state ones no less than national ones, are supposed to answer questions. But this one served mainly to raise a question. Just who was Rick Lazio, anyway?

CHAPTER 10

June 2000: The Shift

The Occam's Razor Candidate

WHEN RICK LAZIO became the Republican nominee, the obligatory profiles appeared in the press. The Associated Press reported that his full given name was Enrico. *The Washington Post* had it as Ricardo. After a couple of days, reporters noticed the discrepancy and asked his campaign aides which was correct. They didn't know.

It was a small matter, but a telling one. No one—Hillary's team, the press, even the Republicans who were relieved to have him as their candidate—had much of a sense of the man. The basic biographical elements were soon enough supplied. He was forty-two, married to a nurse, the former Patricia Moriarty, with two cute little girls. His father had been an immigrant who settled in Long Island's Suffolk County, opened an auto-parts shop, and played a supporting role in local Republican politics that included chores like meeting Richard Nixon at the airport. Enrico/Ricardo had enrolled at Vassar, an unusual choice for a man in 1976, so shortly after Vassar had gone coed, and earned his law degree from American University. He returned to Suffolk County and became an assistant prosecutor. He won a seat in the Suffolk County legislature.

He made his political mark in 1992, when he ran for Congress and toppled Democratic incumbent Tom Downey, who'd been named as a culprit in the House banking scandal and had grown susceptible to the charge, a favorite of challengers of longtime incumbents, that he had become "too Washington" and "lost touch" with the good people back home. In the House, Lazio had been careful to create an uncontroversial and moderate image. His voting record was conservative, but far from radically so. The issue with which he was most closely associated was housing. This was most unusual for a Republican. And working alongside his friendly smile and easy bearing, which suggested a person who was delighted and not a little surprised to find others actually taking him seriously, it was quite enough to convey the message that he was a *nice* Republican.

The package was an appealing one, and Lazio entered the race exploiting it. He made the rounds of the television shows, and he invited reporters onto his bus, the "Mainstream Express," for brief interviews. He cheerily repeated the mantra of his homespun, born-and-bred-here virtues. He proclaimed himself to be "an average middle-class guy" (that "average," of course, could cut two ways). His wife made it clear that she cleaned her own house and said plainly, "We're decent people." The menacing Giuliani with his baroque romantic life and the haughty and inscrutable Clinton with her endless series of mysteries unrevealed were both so . . . complicated. Here, by comparison—and to everyone's relief—was the Occam's Razor candidate: For Rick Lazio, it seemed, the simplest explanations sufficed.

Or did they? In fact, the question of what made him tick was far more interesting than that, and serious explorations of the matter tended toward rather darker conclusions about the man than the sunny paint job on his exterior suggested. For example, if voters heard only the "moderate" label that journalistic shorthand applied to him, they would conclude that, for a Republican in Newt Gingrich's House of Representatives, he seemed reasonable enough. But upon examination, his moderation was of a strange variety.

Jack Newfield, a longtime journalist in New York and the *Post*'s token liberal columnist, wrote two columns about Lazio, one on May 23 and one on June 6, that poked devastating holes in Lazio's moderation. Lazio, he wrote, did possess a centrist voting record covering the years 1993 and 1994, his first two in Congress, which coincided with

the beginning of the Clinton era and a more liberal mood in the country. But come 1995, after the GOP takeover of the House, he followed
the new mood, tacked to the right, and was rewarded by Gingrich and
Dick Armey with a deputy-whip post and appointment to two key
committees. Lazio cast many pro-choice votes, and called himself
"pro-choice." But he also cast votes against federal funding for abortion, which meant his position really was that abortions were all right
for women who could afford them. In the early 1990s, he had defended the National Endowment for the Arts against attacks from its
hard-shell conservative critics. But he had later sponsored a grand-
standing and obviously unconstitutional resolution, with Armey and
Tom DeLay, stating that the Brooklyn Museum "should not receive
federal funds" until it closed the "Sensation" exhibit. He voted for the
Brady Bill. He later opposed handgun-licensing measures. He voted,
once, to raise the minimum wage to $5.15. Later, he came out against a
further increase unless it was tied to tax cuts. Lazio, Newfield wrote,
"votes in order to be all things to all people, to be able to cite one good
vote as the explanation for each bad vote, without having to defend the
substance of the bad vote. . . . Lazio's moderation is a myth."

Newfield was a liberal, but he was not a Clinton fan. He had opposed Hillary's candidacy, so he could not be accused of playing the
shill. A similarly disinterested party could be found in James Traub of
The New York Times Magazine. Traub was a moderate liberal who had
once written more favorably than not about George Pataki in *The New
Yorker.* As a journalist, Traub was known more for the quality of his
analysis than the heat of his invective. But sent by the *Times Magazine*
to profile Lazio, he came away completely unimpressed. He talked to
Lazio's classmates at West Islip High School, who could remember
nothing about him. He asked Christopher Shays, a Connecticut Republican and a big Lazio supporter, to name a time when Lazio had put
himself on the line. "I'll get back to you," Shays told Traub, but he
didn't—this from a fellow Republican, on the record, in the heat of a
Senate race. My colleague at *New York,* Chris Smith, a features writer
on many topics who grinds no particular political ax, asked Lazio a
similar question. The best Lazio could come up with was a vote he cast
against a half-cent county tax increase in 1992. The Suffolk County
executive at the time, a Republican, pushed the increase, so Lazio ar-

gued that his vote cost him some party backing. Maybe. But opposing a tax increase in a mostly Republican district while you're running for Congress does not exactly call to mind Montgomery at El Alamein. Smith concluded that "even Lazio's friends cite his amiability as his foremost quality, and then struggle to come up with a second distinguishing characteristic."

His friends might not have said it, but that second characteristic was clearly ambition. No consistency of principle could explain this patchwork quilt of votes—for something one year, and against the same thing two years later. Lazio never did a convincing job of explaining it himself. Absent an explanation from him, only one conclusion could be drawn. Lazio had voted as he had over the years to cover himself politically and make himself appear attractive when the time came to take the next step. Even Republican colleagues of his, when talking off the record, would chuckle as they described the way Lazio would often wait until the House voting clock was winding down to cast his votes.

If anything, Rick Lazio was *more* ambitious than Hillary Clinton. At least with Hillary, you knew that, however vaguely she might have expressed them or inconsistently she might have lived them, she believed in certain ideals about a nurturing communalism that were firmly grounded in both her nineteenth-century habit of mind and her 1960s consciousness. She was ambitious, to be sure, in a way that many people found threatening, and she was indifferent to all criticism. But at least there was a philosophical core in there somewhere, which even her enemies granted (indeed it was what they despised about her most). And she had been willing to take it on the chin when she thought she was right about something. Lazio, beyond the homiletic tribute he paid to values like faith and family and a common-sense approach to issues, revealed no philosophical core whatsoever. There seemed to be nothing that he was finally and fundamentally and unalterably *for,* beyond the idea of Rick Lazio becoming a senator.

But Lazio's ambition was not an idea that could be peddled, and so the Clinton campaign had a difficult time trying to figure out how to attack him. When he entered the race, the first line of attack was that he was "a foot soldier in the Gingrich revolution." Harold Ickes had delivered this broadside unsparingly the day Lazio got in the race. But by mid-June, the word Gingrich had vanished from the Clinton vocabulary. On June 20, Adam Nagourney wrote in the *Times* that "even Mrs. Clinton's advisers now acknowledge that Mr. Lazio is no Newt Gingrich." Penn and Grunwald say that the temporary disappearance of the Gingrich argument was intentional. They felt Ickes had jumped the gun and painted Lazio with broad strokes, whereas they wanted to string out a series of commercials that tied Lazio to Gingrich on five or six very specific votes. For the first month Lazio was in the race, though, that didn't happen.

Hillary tried, instead, to hit him on certain votes concerning abortion and gun control and Medicare, arguing that her opponent had "a pattern of changing positions, trying to figure out which way the political winds are blowing." This line of attack had the benefit of being true, but making it sound alarming wouldn't prove easy.

Nevertheless, the race did assume a new character during June. No longer a battle of the titans, the campaign reverted to a more traditional Democrat-versus-Republican form. Lazio may have been a moving target, but at least he was more closely identified with the national Republican Party than Giuliani was. For Lazio's part, he immediately hired Mike Murphy, who had just come off a career-making run with John McCain in the GOP presidential primaries. Murphy had actually begun his career in New York, with two congressional races in the 1980s. But he had also worked for Oliver North in Virginia and a variety of other hard-Right conservatives, and he had a track record in those races of making stark ideological arguments with his ads.

On another front, the Byzantine calculations that had governed the minor parties when Giuliani was in the race sorted themselves out now. To his great relief, Liberal Party leader Ray Harding was able to back Hillary and set himself right with the state's Democrats—and with Al Gore, whose campaign had been getting pressure from New York Democrats to refuse the Liberal endorsement for the presidency if the party backed Rudy in the Senate race. Gore refusing his line would have left Harding looking powerless. At a midtown Manhattan hotel on a June Saturday morning, Harding ladled praise on Hillary so generously, reeling off the roster of New York's great senators and remarking on what a natural addition she was to that list, that a person who didn't know better never would have thought that two weeks before, Harding had been virtually certain to endorse her opponent.

Mike Long's Conservative Party, no longer mud-wrestling the mayor, and having lost his secret candidate, had finally settled on a former congressman from Westchester County in May. But after Rudy left the race, the party threw its weight quickly and enthusiastically behind Lazio.

Long was still bitter about the way many GOP leaders had lined up behind Giuliani without concern for his position. "Republican leaders rolled me," Long says. "I take it that way. I don't forget that. They were willing to take the train and lead the charge without the Conservative Party. They were willing to make the first break [between the two parties] in twenty-five years. And they didn't care. So that's something I still have in the back of my head. The governor didn't roll me. It was all the other Republican leaders who were forcing the governor to make his decision. And you know, you name it. Bill Powers. Joe Bruno. Every elected official." If Giuliani had run and won, Long believes, "then they were gonna make a move to take me out. So I'm supposed to just forget about that?" That's a battle that will be fought another day. For the purposes of the Senate race, Long and the Republicans were, for now, allies.

Most important, the race was no longer a referendum on two people. It was a referendum on one. It would emerge over the next several weeks that some people who showed up at Rick Lazio's campaign events couldn't pronounce his name—"Lay-zio" and "Lonzio" were among the versions reporters heard (they privately took to calling him "Dick Lonzo"). His many quickly accumulated fans knew almost nothing about him. But they sure knew the person he was running against.

Hillary's *Other* Woman Problem

Hillary's advisers were not only having some trouble settling on the best way to define Lazio. They remained at odds over what to do with their candidate. Giuliani's departure only heightened the internal tension over whether she should address voters' distrust or ignore it. Since she could no longer rely on a certain percentage of votes from people who didn't like her opponent, she now had to do a little more thinking about how to get people to like *her.*

Hillary's television ad campaign started in May, serviceably but unspectacularly, with a handful of ads that tried to promote her thirty years of doing battle for women and children. The tag line was "more than a first lady," and if the ads didn't give her a boost in the polls, maybe that was due less to their quality than to the fact that the record itself was somewhat nebulous. Late May brought the first ad with Hillary talking into the camera. As was her exasperating custom, going back to the *Talk* interview, she addressed a situation by only half-addressing it. "I didn't know what to expect when I started this campaign," she said. "I'm sure you didn't either." For many voters, even many Democrats, the question was hardly one of not knowing what to expect. The question was what she was doing in New York in the first place.

In June, in the *Times Magazine,* James Bennett profiled Mark Penn, "The Guru of Small Things," as the headline put it. Bennett briefly mentioned the internal fight in the campaign, between those who wanted Hillary to "address why it is that so many people can't stand her," and those, Penn chief among them, who wanted her to talk issues, issues, issues. Bennett procured some internal poll numbers, leaked to him "by someone unhappy about Penn's sway over the first lady." Inside the campaign, this leak was devastating. There were several meetings about it, one source told me not long thereafter. It forced restrictions on which people had access to what information, and created an atmosphere of spectacular mistrust between the warring camps.

The argument over the campaign's direction had just kicked into a new gear. In late May, Hillary had finally authorized that $87,000 check to Dwight Jewson. (Half the Jewson fee was paid through the state Democratic committee. The *Times* discovered this in July, although Jewson's name, and the work he did, never made the papers.) And so, finally, Jewson would conduct his focus groups, which were designed to probe the dark question of Hillary's candidacy, the one that Penn and Grunwald and the candidate herself had hoped to avoid: Why did so many people hate her so? Why did suburban women, in particular, seem to detest her? In 1998, when Hillary visited the state on Chuck Schumer's behalf, Schumer wanted to be seen with her in the suburbs. She was considered an asset there. When New York Democrats started thinking seriously about Hillary's run, they assumed, originally, that suburban women would be among the least of her problems. The main tactical reason, in fact, that she unveiled herself upstate was the assumption that she would be fine in the city and hold her own in the suburbs, and that she therefore needed to introduce herself to the voters who were presumed to be most resistant to her.

But by the summer, polling showed clearly that upstaters had taken something of a shine to Hillary. Her endless sojourns across their unglamourous plains had paid off. In the city, she was fine, as expected. In the suburbs, however, she was getting mauled. Suburbanites had loved Rudy for making their Saturday night outings to Sardi's and *Phantom* more pleasant, and Lazio was a suburbanite down to the soles of his shoes. But even putting aside her opponents' popularity, there was a tremendous suburban animus against Hillary, one that was somewhat mysterious. Urban baby-boomer women may have felt that Hillary failed them as a role model, but the campaign always hoped that they would ultimately vote for her (they couldn't vote Republican, and they couldn't not vote). Suburban women, however, were entirely capable of voting Republican or not voting. And there were enough of them that if Hillary didn't make some headway with them, they could decide the election. So, after two months' hesitation, Hillary finally decided to let Jewson see if he could get to the bottom of it.

Jewson and his associate, Shira Nayman, conducted four focus groups in Westchester County—two on Wednesday, June 21, and two more on Friday, June 23. I obtained audio tapes of the two June 23 sessions, each of which consisted of two-hour interview sessions with ten suburban women. The first lady herself was spared from hearing them. This was, if not for the campaign then at least for her ego, a very good thing.

The audio tapes were labeled Group 1 and Group 2. In Group 2, actually, she didn't fare quite so badly. Five of the ten women professed varying degrees of admiration for her. When I heard, toward the beginning of the tape, Nayman ask the women what woman in public life they admired, and one said Rosie O'Donnell, another said Madonna, and a third said Chelsea Clinton, I knew she was relatively safe (although among even this "good" group, only half liked her). Group 1, however, was another story.

When we in the press and the chattering class talked about Hillary's Woman Problem, we tended to fixate on the sort of women we knew, the sort of women who interested us most, and whose dislike of Hillary made for interesting copy: urban, white, professional women. But it turned out that Hillary had another Woman Problem, with a different demographic. The women on these tapes were housewives, second-income earners, single mothers, students, or young low-wage workers still living at home; mothers, grandmothers, widows. Suburban women. Nayman eased them into Hillary, asking them first to describe their lives by writing three adjectives on a piece of paper, then to name a famous woman they admired and why, then a woman in their personal experience they admired and why, and then, finally, questions about Hillary. Here are some of the things they said about her:

> "She's smart, savvy, cold, pushy. Fights for what she wants, very focused. Back stabbing. Concentrates on winning no matter what. Determined, this is her place. This is her spot in the sun now."

> "Very controlling."

> "Self-serving. She's very cunning, independent."

> "She's cold."

> "All I can remember is a clip that happened right after he won the election is that they woke up in bed the next morning and they looked at each other and this is what they said, 'We did it.' And it was almost like, 'We put one over on the American public.' You know, I took it as a negative, I don't know why, but I just took it that way."

> "I remember her being on the *Today* show and her saying that they were framing them, and that really sticks in my head because she thought that everyone was out to get them . . . and when something bad happens they have to blame it on somebody else instead of looking within."

"You can't judge people by the cover but when I look at her, I see nothing. I see someone who is very self-serving and she could be the nicest person in the world if I knew her personally but first impressions are lasting impressions."

"She doesn't represent me as a woman, you know. . . . The incident with her husband, I think, 'God, at least Giuliani's wife made a statement.' She's a woman. She's ticked and she let us know, and she's on the radio today with a dog show and she's living her life. [Donna Hanover was guest-hosting a radio program at the time.] She doesn't give me a message. I'm upset at her for not taking a stand as a human being and a woman that she was publicly ridiculed."

"She's not a stoic like Jackie Kennedy, who was a quiet, reserved type of woman who you'd look at and admire. Hillary has accomplished a lot, but she's a professional. She wants a career. She has wanted a career. She wants the power Bill has. She's not maybe going to attain it in her lifetime, but she wants to start the ball rolling, and she wants as much as she can."

"You get the sense that she doesn't think like a woman. She thinks like a man."

That's just the first twenty minutes.

What's fascinating is the extent to which these women seemed to equate intelligence and toughness with rank ambition and hunger for power in Hillary (one woman used the following adjectives in succession: "gutsy," "smart," "strong," "cutthroat," "calculating," "evasive"). Indeed intelligence and strength, usually not seen as pejoratives, became, as these women saw them in Hillary, negative qualities. Later, Nayman asked them to compare Hillary to a woman they knew. One woman, sure enough, selected her mother-in-law:

"She's self-centered, and I think Hillary is extremely self-centered. I felt tense in a sense that I didn't want to say anything wrong to send her off into whatever it was that she was thinking because she tended to think that whatever she says was the right thing. She was always right. . . . I have the feeling that that is how Hillary Clinton is also, that if you differ, you asked for it. If you differ with Hillary Clinton, she is going to nail you and squash you."

Another compared Hillary to a nun in Catholic school she was afraid of, "a very scary lady." A third speaker likened her to a casual friend who thought nothing of embarrassing her in front of others. One woman, when asked what she would like and not like about herself if she suddenly became Hillary, averred that she might "put a bullet to my head or start drinking."

What did these women want from Hillary? Nayman asked. What hadn't they seen in her that they would like to see, that might stand a chance of cracking open sympathy's door? In their various ways, they all said the same thing:

> "The human side of Hillary Clinton. We really don't know who Hillary Clinton is."

> "Like, you never really hear her talk about personal things like herself, everything about what she's trying to do or what she's already done."

> "We don't know her human side."

> "It seems to make her more controlling in a sense."

> "She's afraid of showing a weakness to us. That if she does say, 'Oh, well, I'm so upset with Bill, he's done this to me,' we will not look at her as a political candidate, we're going to look at her as a woman, as a wife and as a woman."

> "I couldn't imagine going through what she's gone through, and I feel for her. But if she's not going to ask for it, show us that she's sad, then why should I give it to her? It's

almost like I'm angry at her for that. . . . All of us have been through crap and all of us have been through things, and people cheating on people or whatever, we've all been through it. Sort of share it with us—not get into detail, I don't mean in that sense share—I mean share it with us that she's a part of us also. And yes, I admire people who can be strong, but people who can be strong can also be emotional."

Nayman showed them a clip of Hillary talking to Charlie Rose at the 92nd Street Y, a magnet for high-toned celebrity lecturers, the previous fall. In that appearance, Hillary gave her fullest accounting of why she was running for senator—that she had had many opportunities presented to her, among them joining a foundation or returning to the law, but that she decided she could make more difference on the issues she cared about in the Senate. Hillary then talked about her gratitude to the American people for the last eight years. I was at that event, and I remember thinking at the time that, though the spiel sounded too rehearsed to be convincing, it was about as open and conversational as Hillary was capable of getting. The focus-group women were only partially persuaded. "She started out a little bit smug," one woman said, "and I wrote down cocky and arrogant, and as the interview went on I felt that she was a little bit more human."

Finally, Nayman tested an idea for a possible television ad. "What she would tell you in that advertisement," Nayman told the women, "is, 'I'm very proud of my enemies. I'm not going to get one vote from the big conglomerate health-insurance agencies, and I'm proud of that because I fought for what I believe in, and I take a stand against those kinds of bodies.' What's your reaction to that as an advertisement?" After an hour and forty-five minutes of tearing her flesh, nine out of the ten women in this group said they'd respond positively to such an ad. "That's a strong person," said one. "She stands up for what she believes. She doesn't care what somebody else believes. This is her."

For months, pundits had been puzzling over why women seemed not to like Hillary. But no one could really say why. The tapes said why, in ways that revealed things about Hillary—and about the women doing the talking. Much of what they said about Hillary was true—she did not reveal her personal feelings about anything, she could not publicly acknowledge any sort of frailty. But the women on these tapes were clearly caught in some sort of inner, emotional tug of war over feminism and its legacies. They admired tough, smart, successful women. But they also wanted women to be softer than men—vulnerable, and, most of all, nurturing. And these qualities seemed on balance more important to them than strength and determination. When Nayman asked them about women in their own lives whom they admired, almost to a person they mentioned women who were both successful (or had overcome a difficulty such as a bad marriage) and who gracefully accepted their duties as women, which feminism, from their perspective, had done little to change. They liked humble women. And women who made sacrifices. One admired her mother, who "was pretty much to herself, quiet." Another admired her daughter, who had passed away, and who "was just a go-getter and asked for nothing." Another admired a ninety-seven-year-old friend who "does her own cooking, cleaning, and she doesn't take from anybody." Another liked her boyfriend's mother, who'll "do anything for anyone."

Hillary had often been described, and had described herself, as a "Rorschach test." To women like these, the Hillary ink blot looked threatening and unwomanly. Hillary was not quiet. She did not ask for nothing. She obviously had never done her own cooking and cleaning, and she certainly didn't seem like the kind of person who would do anything for anyone. The feminist-era phenomenon of men fearing tough women was well enough understood. Evidently there were also more than a few women who feared, or distrusted, tough women.

This was an entirely different Woman Problem from Hillary's trouble with boomer women. Boomer women might have felt that Hillary had let them down as a role model; that in not leaving Bill, she had caved in to some ancient and oppressive ritual of womanhood. But for suburban women, Hillary had never been a role model. To them, Hillary was complicit in the disruption of some ancient and valuable ritual of womanhood. There was no way to please both groups. And yet, in the end, these suburban women did respond to that potential ad that Nayman laid out for them. And maybe that positive response meant the campaign could find a way to wear down these women's resistance to Hillary and deal, finally, with the negatives.

The Meeting

The next Friday night, June 30, a meeting was called at the White House for Jewson to discuss his findings and recommendations. Bill Clinton was there, and Hillary, as well as Penn, Grunwald, Bill DeBlasio, and Howard Wolfson, among others.

Jewson, a source says, presented two basic findings: First, that Hillary's approach to issues was too laundry-listy and that she should pare her message down to four or five basic issues—health care, education, taxes, one or two others—and become firmly associated in New Yorkers' minds with those issues; second, and more crucially, that the campaign should find a way to convert her perceived coldness into independence and strength, after the fashion of the theoretical ad Nayman had presented to the focus-group women. The president, one source says, was enthusiastic about Jewson's recommendations and said Jewson should have a role in the campaign, coming up with themes and possible ads that would confront Hillary's negatives in the way Jewson described. Hillary followed his lead. Penn and Grunwald were willing to go along, if without much enthusiasm. But if the president himself said something was going to happen, it was going to happen. Jewson would be brought on board, not with an official role but as an adviser to Penn and Grunwald on these matters. The campaign would not abandon Penn's focus on issues, but it would supplement that approach with an attempt to deal with the question of Hillary's image.

The process had already begun, however tentatively, in the candidate's speeches. From the time he joined the campaign, Ellis Verdi had wanted Hillary to address these elephant-in-the-living-room questions, in a humorous way. Verdi had even proposed a commercial that would show viewers a carpetbag; then the carpetbag would open up, and emerging from it would be items labeled to reflect Hillary's plans for the state—a stronger upstate economy, more access to health care, lower prescription drug prices, more and better schools, et cetera. That was rejected, but another idea of Verdi's did find its way into Hillary's stump speech. One common criticism of Hillary centered on the word "agenda"—that is, on the idea that her candidacy was a part of a larger (meaning secret and nefarious) agenda. At Verdi's suggestion, Hillary began opening her speeches with a sentence that went, roughly: "You know, people say that in running for the Senate, I have an agenda. Well, I do—it's an agenda that includes more jobs for upstate New York and lower prescription drug prices" and so on. Not bad; she was trying. But to work, the line needed to be delivered as a joke, and it required timing and delivery for people to get the joke. And the joke, of course, would have to be on herself. I always felt it had the potential to be endearing—acknowledging a criticism, making light of it, turning it around so it became something for her to brag about. But she just couldn't do it. I watched her deliver this line in Ithaca and Binghamton and Rochester and Utica and a few other places in upstate New York in early July. Each time, she raced through the line as if she were hoping that no one noticed it.

Could a woman like this take the kinds of risks that Jewson would recommend? Would Penn and Grunwald go along? They didn't want to go Jewson's route; it wasn't their strong suit. Their belief was that to acknowledge that some people didn't like her, or to acknowledge the existence of *any* problems, in the overheated media climate of this race, especially with the *Post* around, would mean that people would remember only the problems, and not Hillary's attempts to deal with them. They wanted to defeat the resistance by dint of simple hard work and keep the focus on what Hillary would do in the Senate.

Penn and Grunwald's strategy was not a great hit with the press, who wanted nothing more than for Hillary to open up about something, anything. By June, frankly, reporters were getting really bored with her—the amount of coverage of the campaign slipped noticeably, mostly because it was no longer a Hillary-Rudy race, but also because a reporter can write the "Hillary makes learned and earnest plea for more jobs upstate" story only so many times. But the Clinton campaign was quite happy to get less media attention.

Maybe Penn and Grunwald did know better. The press may have found her evasive and stultifying. But it's the voters who matter. Maybe Hillary's best strategy was to draw as little attention to herself as possible, to stick to the issues and hope that in the end the issues were what motivated voters when they drew the voting booth's curtain. The strategy was debatable, but this much wasn't: Penn and Grunwald were the ones who knew the candidate better than anyone else. They knew what Hillary could and could not do, and what she would and would not do. Making self-deprecating jokes and acknowledging weaknesses and taking risks were not in Hillary Clinton's character. But the president and the candidate had agreed at the June 30 White House meeting that the campaign would, somehow or other, try. Thus began the wrestling match over the soul of the campaign.

CHAPTER 11

July 2000:
The Showdown

Secrets of the Rope Line

COME JULY, both candidates hit the road upstate. Lazio, still the beneficiary of an encouraging measure of good will from the press, hopped
his "Mainstream Express," the Long Island answer to John McCain's
"Straight-Talk Express," on July 3 for a five-day swing. Hillary spent
the Fourth in the city with Bill, surveying the annual parade of the tall
ships up the Hudson River, and began her five-day trip on July 6. It was
billed as Hillary's "Upstate Economic Tour," during which she would
unveil her plan for upstate revitalization and try to drive home the idea
that she would be the reliable servant of the state's far-flung and forgotten corners.

I went along on Hillary's tour. One embarks on these trips with
high hopes, thinking that five days in the candidate's presence will yield
world-shaking insights into the campaign's most closely held secrets
and the candidate's mind. In fact you learn little, at least until a campaign's final weeks, when you can judge momentum by the size of the
crowds and observe the candidate at crunch time. Until then, not
much happens. You get on the bus. You start in on the day's ceaseless
stream of junk food. You get off the bus. You stand around and wait for
the event. You listen to the speech. The candidate holds a press confer-

ence, under a tree in a park in Elmira, or in the garage of an ambulance service in Rochester. The "avail," short for press availability, happens early enough in the day so that the daily reporters can file their copy in time for the early editions. Then you go to an evening event—on this trip, usually a county Democratic picnic—and hear the speech again. Often there's a third event, and even a fourth, so you hear the speech again. Finally, you pull into a hotel in a small town around ten o'clock, after all the restaurants have closed.

Reporters, invited to witness only the superficial manifestations of the campaign's workings, quickly grow restive and resentful. The candidate, delivering the same speech over and over, soon finds it difficult to keep alive any passion. The crowds can sometimes inject energy into the routine, but even they have usually been kept waiting so long that the enthusiasm with which they arrived has long since dissipated. I was often surprised to talk to an audience member and be told that the crowd had been instructed to assemble at five o'clock, although, according to the schedule the campaign gave the press, Hillary wasn't even supposed to show up until 7:45.

When she finally appeared at her events, she did so in a black Ford van that looked more suited to carting around a traveling NASCAR official than a first lady. Its raised roof and very 1970s paint job, with detailing along the sides in three or four tones of gray, helped lead reporters to dub it the "HRC Speedwagon." (The name also arose from the fact that, one night while campaigning in Albany, she shared a hotel with 1970s rock monsters ZZ Top.) You could never get too close to it, what with the Secret Service detail always hovering around, but it did not look especially luxurious. She sat behind the driver in a standard-issue captain's chair. The Secret Service detail both led and followed her, in a Cadillac and an SUV. It was an oddly unprepossessing little motorcade. All the same, when New Yorkers saw it pull in, there was little question about who was inside.

On day two of this trip, for the first time, Hillary got on the reporters' bus. It was a year to the day from the Moynihan farm appearance, a fact that naturally (and this was not, of course, unplanned) invited news stories about her reflections on her first year and about how much she had improved as a candidate. And she had. She was quicker on her feet and more willing to give and take with the press, even kibbitz with us a little, even if most of her answers remained tight and scripted. Access to her, while still a long distance from normal, had improved since the Listening Tour. So the on-the-bus press conference represented a kind of campaign *glasnost,* notwithstanding the fact that her hand had been forced by Lazio, who had gone on his reporters' bus the week before.

It was chiefly a "visual," done for the benefit of television, in particular CNN, and there was an air of forced spontaneity about the event—as if a large and quarrelsome family, accustomed to convening in the den, had decided to gather in the living room, expecting that the change of scenery would bring fresh excitement. But the press conference ended up being about the same old frustrating topic—why she said so little about herself. And Hillary responded to the questions by saying, in essence, tough luck. " 'Who are you?' and all of that," she said quietly. "I don't know if that is the right question. Even people you think you know extremely well, do you know their entire personality? Do they, at every point that you're with them, reveal totally who they are? Of course not. We now expect people in the public arena to somehow do that. I don't understand the need behind that."

Journalists continued to find her infuriating and opaque. Voters, it became apparent on this trip, were arriving at a very different conclusion. The woman who a year before tended to enter and leave rooms through private doors was now charging into crowds and establishing a rapport with her audiences. Everywhere she went, she worked every rope line and shook every hand and posed for every picture. Nearly three hours each day—to the dismay of her Secret Service detail, which had not been used to seeing the first lady get so close to so many people—were devoted to rope-line time. By the second day, I had learned to follow close behind Hillary so I could study the people who waited for her, especially mothers who brought their young daughters to meet her. They had looks of rapture on their faces when she spoke with them. Some people were shy and overwhelmed. Others were unselfconsciously gabby. Hillary focused on them all, with that grandiose nod of hers, and obligingly posed for every picture, probably two or three hundred a day. The Hillary haters, who were far more vocal in their disapproval, got more ink. But evidently, her admirers, while they made for less exciting copy, were a force as well.

Something else happened on those rope lines, and in her many meetings with local union members and business leaders and health-care providers. Hillary quizzed people about local problems, and took mental notes, and retained a tremendous amount of the information they passed on to her. Neera Tanden, Hillary's issues person, described the process like this: Hillary would be working a rope line, say, in Watertown, near the Canadian border, and a person would complain to her about the slow flow of traffic across the border and its crippling effect on the local economy. Or she would meet with someone in a program at Cornell University that gave local farmers access to the school's expertise and wonder why there was no similar arrangement between the university and local high-technology firms. Tanden would be asked to delve into such matters.

Tanden was a smart and disciplined adviser who had played a crucial role in briefing Hillary for the Listening Tour sessions. Her calm and cheerful manner made her a popular figure within the campaign. She had worked on the White House domestic policy staff when the Lewinsky story broke, and later in the first lady's office, so very little could happen in this campaign to shock or unsettle her. As the campaign evolved, Tanden sat down with Hillary every other week for a lengthy meeting in which Hillary would go over the many issues people had mentioned to her in her travels. At one point, Hillary did a child-care event in Westchester County where she spoke with a woman who worked at a community health center, who had suggestions about improving services for uninsured people. Tanden followed up, and the woman's suggestions worked their way into speeches and policy papers. Tanden recalls getting ready to leave the office in Manhattan one Friday night at 9:45. Then Hillary called. "Do you have a minute?" Hillary asked her. For the next forty-five minutes, they talked about power plants. "She became kind of obsessed with power plants," Tanden says.

The dichotomy between how Hillary behaved with the press and with voters was not so much a matter of conscious strategy as it was a natural extension of the candidate's personality. But it was a pivotal, perhaps *the* pivotal, development in this campaign. This degree of on-the-stump intelligence gathering was rare among political candidates. To be sure, it reflected the fact that Hillary had a lot more to learn about New York than someone who was actually from the state and already enmeshed in its politics. But it also reflected her earnest approach to campaigning and her insistent focus on issues. She didn't have much patience with reporters, and she showed no signs of caring very much about courting the press. As far as she was concerned, that way lay danger. In talking to citizens about power plants and the traffic flow across bridges, though, there was no danger whatsoever. There were only opportunities—to educate and improve and reform and be seen by regular citizens as their tireless warrior who was interested in absolutely everything. The Secret Service may not have liked those rope lines and the opportunities they presented for the local crazies. But Hillary felt far safer on them than she did on the press bus, and the people on the rope lines felt a much richer connection to her than journalists ever did.

And by the Way, Who Was He?

By early July, this had become, at $49.3 million, the most expensive Senate campaign in the country's history. Lazio announced that he had taken in $4.5 million in donations in the six weeks since he had entered the race. Add to this to the $3.5 million he already had, in an old congressional reelection account, and he was doing rather well.

A few days later, the technique behind that success was revealed. Lazio had signed off on a fund-raising letter declaring that the president and Mrs. Clinton "have embarrassed our country and disgraced their powerful posts." Hillary, it continued, "covets power and control and thinks she should be dictating how other people run their lives." It was pretty strong stuff. There were other letters, too, that spoke of Hillary's "ultra-left agenda." Lazio, when asked by reporters, didn't have the gumption to stand by them. "Frankly, these letters are not written by me," he said at a stop in Watertown. "[But] I'm not disowning it." The Lazio missives were nothing compared to one that state GOP chair Bill Powers released the following week. Among the twenty-three adjectives used to describe Mrs. Clinton were: "cold-blooded," "hot-headed," "abrasive," "annoying," "brash," "bitter," "calculating," "scheming," "distant," "deceitful," "polarizing," and "power-hungry." Later in the month, when Powers summoned reporters to his office to announce the release of a second, similar letter, they noticed on his desk a bumper sticker that read "Kiss my N.Y. ass, Hillary."

This sort of hyperbole about Hillary never aroused lasting controversy. The letters did, however, serve as an early-warning sign of what would become Lazio's central problem: Beyond being Not Hillary Clinton, who was he? He tried to insist that he was the one with the positive message. But his stump speech, which he had perfected by now, was full of little slaps at Mrs. Clinton, about her left-wing agenda and the Hollywood interests backing her—more slaps, in fact, than specifics about what he planned to accomplish in the Senate. Then came news of something like his fund-raising letters, which made it hard to avoid concluding that he wanted it both ways, knowing that he could rely on his nice-guy persona and the public perception of Hillary as a devious cutthroat. By mid-July, the candidate who had been so media friendly when he jumped in the race, doing six Sunday shows and inviting reporters on his bus, was now avoiding the press. In Washington, he ducked reporters seeking his comment on the Supreme Court's decision regarding Nebraska's partial-birth-abortion law. To reporters who followed him into an elevator at the Waldorf-Astoria, he said not a word. He was suddenly less available for the talking-head shows. Then again, reporters sometimes ducked him. On July 5, Lazio, after marching in a Fourth of July parade in Ticonderoga, called a news conference. But after two questions, reporters couldn't think of anything else to ask.

Lazio could rely on getting 42, maybe 45 percent of the vote just by being on the ballot against Hillary. But to get the other 6 to 9 percent, to make 51, he'd need to tell people something about who he was beyond the eternally sunny and humble image of the immigrant's son who now headed the decent middle-class Long Island family that kept its own house. By mid-July, eight weeks into the campaign, he had of course talked about issues on the stump. But he had not given a major policy speech, and he had displayed no character traits beyond the most general and inoffensive. If he didn't define himself Hillary, whose campaign was now running ads attacking him on abortion rights and other questions, would be happy to do it for him.

"The Fate of Our Campaign Is in Your Hands"

The Clinton campaign was doing just that, and confidently, for the first two weeks of July. But everything changed in an instant late on the afternoon of Friday, July 14.

The *Post* had bought serialization rights for yet another anti-Clinton book, *The State of a Union,* by a former *National Enquirer* reporter named Jerry Oppenheimer, published by HarperCollins (like the *Post,* a Rupert Murdoch property). An advance copy had been sitting on the desk of a *Post* features editor for a couple of days, unread. The book was embargoed, meaning that it couldn't be written about until a certain date specified by the publisher. That date was the following week, when serialization was to begin.

Then, that Friday afternoon, someone at the paper happened to look at Matt Drudge's Web site. The site trumpeted a "world exclusive": Oppenheimer's book was to reveal that in 1974, during a famously acrimonious conversation just after Bill Clinton lost his first congressional race, Hillary had allegedly called campaign aide Paul Fray a "fucking Jew bastard." From the way the item was written, it seemed clear that Drudge hadn't actually seen the book, but that this episode had been described to him by someone who had.

A *Post* editor went over to Robert Hardt, Jr., and Gregg Birnbaum, the paper's two chief reporters on the Senate race. Hardt said he'd look into it, and he logged on to Drudge's site. The item certainly seemed interesting, but there was a problem: because of the embargo, the paper couldn't quote from the book. Hardt told his metro editor he didn't feel comfortable writing a story based on Drudge's reporting without being able to cite the book himself. Then the paper's library came up with a phone number for Mary Lee Fray, Paul's wife, who had corroborated her husband's charges in the Oppenheimer book. Hardt talked to Mary Lee Fray for an hour. He now had quotes of his own he could use, without having to rely on the book. He had questions about the allegation, but he felt that now that he had the charges on the record from a source who claimed to have heard the slur directly, he could go with it.

He called Howard Wolfson for comment. Wolfson had seen the Drudge page, so he was already in damage-control mode, calling around to ascertain whether the allegation could possibly be true, and to find ammunition that could be used to puncture the Frays' credibility. When Hardt called, Wolfson went ballistic. "I feel like the fate of our campaign is in your hands," Wolfson told Hardt. (Wolfson says he doesn't remember saying that.) Hardt tried to assure him that he'd write the story in a balanced way. Wolfson responded by telling Hardt that "if you go ahead with this, this is totally going to change our relationship with your paper. I don't know if we're gonna communicate with you anymore or send you advisories anymore." Hardt didn't appreciate the threat, and when he hung up his phone he threw it against the wall, smashing it into pieces.

Later that night, the Clinton campaign issued a statement to the paper calling the allegation an "outrageous lie." Hardt's piece, which made the wood the next day—under a headline citing the "furor" that had not yet ensued, but was now about to—was not unfair under the circumstances: He cited the charge, he included the campaign's denial, he had quotes from Mrs. Fray indicating that she didn't really hold the remark against Hillary, and he noted that three other aides from that 1974 race had never heard of the explosive charge.

It's not surprising that it was the *Post* that broke this story, but the fact that it was Hardt who wrote it was a little ironic. He was not one of the *Post*'s ideological crusaders, and he enjoyed a reputation among insiders as one who tried hard to be balanced. He had made a defensible journalistic decision—he had on-the-record quotes, and besides, the charge was going to hit the paper the next week anyway, when the book was released. Whether it was reasonable that a candidate should have to answer for one sentence that may or may not have been uttered twenty-six years previously was another question. This question would have its day in court over the next week, as would two others. First, there was the fact that, while his paternal great-grandmother was Jewish, Paul Fray was a Baptist, and Hillary may not even have known of his roots. Second, Fray had been interviewed by at least five news organizations previously about the argument and had never mentioned the slur.

The story was leaking out late Friday, and by Saturday, it was all over the television, and every media outlet in New York and Washington was playing it big. On Sunday, the *Daily News* ran with quotes from Neil McDonald, a Dallas businessman who had also worked on the campaign, who confirmed that he had heard the slur, albeit from the next room. McDonald said he still supported the Clintons, portraying the comment as just a "heat-of-the-battle" kind of thing and arguing that Hillary was no anti-Semite. Interestingly, the Frays said the same thing in subsequent interviews and emphasized that they supported Hillary's candidacy.

These assurances did little to halt the story's momentum, and inside the Clinton campaign it was panic time. A tense argument ensued between those who wanted Hillary to respond to the allegation forcefully and those who wanted to ignore it and hope the story would die in a few days. Ickes, DeBlasio, Wolfson, and Ann Lewis wanted Hillary to respond. Penn and especially Grunwald wanted her to stay away from it.

On Sunday morning, July 16, Hillary woke up to a blistering editorial in the *Daily News* (the very paper whose endorsement the Clinton team considered critical to Hillary's chances). Under the headline HILLARY'S CANDOR ON TRIAL, and taking up the full left-hand column, a space usually devoted to three different topics, the editorial excoriated Hillary over the Suha Arafat kiss, which Hillary had addressed, again, two days before the Fray story broke, in response to a question from a woman at a Jewish senior center in Queens. The woman had pronounced herself satisfied with the candidate's answer, but the *News* savaged Hillary, accusing her of "doublespeak on top of doublespeak" and saying "it is no wonder that voters may have some difficulty deciding whether Clinton is telling the truth about the 1974 incident."

The Sunday shows, too, were full of the story. In a late-morning conference call with advisers, Hillary decided she had to respond. She called a press conference in front her Chappaqua home. Her "face taut, her voice trembling and her eyes welling with tears," as Adam Nagourney put it in the *Times,* Mrs. Clinton strongly denied the charge. "It did not happen," she said. "I have never said anything like that. Ever. Ever."

Meanwhile, of his own volition, Bill Clinton placed two calls to the *News*—one to columnist and political editor Michael Kramer, and the other to publisher Mort Zuckerman, vacationing in Italy at the time. "In twenty-nine years," he told the *News,* "my wife has never, ever uttered an ethnic or racial slur against anybody, ever. She's so straight on this, she squeaks." It was unusual for the president to involve himself openly in his wife's race, all the more so because he was in the midst of the Camp David peace negotiations, and because he made the calls without telling anyone at the campaign.

This story could have been a mortal wound for Hillary with Jewish voters. It stayed in the news cycle for six days, and the damage soon registered in Penn's internal polls. Penn says he measured a seven-point drop "that took us two weeks to make up." It was precious lost ground among a key voting bloc with whom she had very recently been gaining a little ground. As the story subsided, an intense debate swirled among Clinton insiders about whether the campaign's handling of the matter had helped or hurt. Hillary's statement had seemed, to commentators, an overreaction—not only did she say that she not called Fray the name in question, she claimed never to have said anything like that in her life, not even once. At her press conference, she said she didn't even remember the argument. That last statement really seemed to strain credulity. After all, the argument, without the slur, had been reported so many times that it had become a piece of Clinton folklore. Some of the daily reporters covering her felt it was the first time they'd heard her tell a straight-out lie on the trail. And finally, there was the matter of the president's intervention, which infuriated Hillary's entire camp. Her advisers felt, and most voters would surely agree, that one could ask for a better character witness than Bill Clinton.

To the campaign's relief, the allegation faded away. Unlike the Suha Arafat kiss, it was not a topic to which commentators and Hillary-haters would return (fresh material aplenty on Jewish issues would appear late in the race anyway). She may not have been kosher on Israel, but in the end, most political leaders and newspapers didn't quite buy the idea that this politically correct Sixties girl was capable of coarse ethnic language. New York politics had not cut Hillary many breaks, but it was doing so now. The *Times* ran an exculpatory editorial on July 18, headlined MRS. CLINTON'S CREDIBLE RESPONSE, and the next day, Mayor Giuliani said he found the charge hard to believe. Even George W. Bush jumped in, declaring it irrelevant on *Larry King Live*. The *Daily News* sent reporters out to ask Jewish voters around the city if they believed the charge, and only 18 percent did. The next month in a scientific poll Quinnipiac University found voters, somewhat surprisingly, evenly split on whether they believed she'd said it. But even among the 40 percent who believed the charge, nine out of ten said it would have no effect on their vote. The Frays drifted away. In August, Paul Fray did pass a lie-detector test—arranged and paid for by the *Post*—but by then, people were no longer that interested, and it was a one-day story.

Inside the campaign, though, the episode had an impact that was lasting and transformative. The campaign higher-ups, and Hillary herself, concluded from Penn's polling that they had been wrong to answer the charge, or at least that they had only helped to keep the controversy alive by answering it so publicly. But it's hard to see how Hillary could have simply ducked the allegation. Silence would surely have been interpreted as guilt, and she would have been hectored at every stop until she did respond. It seems clear that if she hadn't confronted the charge, that *Times* editorial would have been headlined something like MRS. CLINTON'S EVASIONS. And one doubts that Rudy Giuliani and George W. Bush would have come to her defense. Nevertheless, her handlers decided they'd botched it. This conclusion hurt the position of some who had argued for responding, and it strengthened the hand of those, notably Grunwald, who had argued against it. "This was Mandy's moment of strength," one source says. "And a lot of the arguments about how the campaign should proceed started to go in her direction from that point on." The timing, from Grunwald's point of view, could scarcely have been better, because that same week those arguments were coming to a head.

Showdown at Chappaqua

Dwight Jewson's agreement with the campaign called for four more focus-group sessions. The first group of sessions, in June, had been designed to find out what people thought of Hillary. The four July sessions were intended to test possible messages that might change those perceptions. The first two were planned for Syracuse on Wednesday, July 19, and the second pair for Westchester County the next day.

By now, the lines between the dueling camps were firmly drawn. On one side were Penn and Grunwald, arguing the no-risk, stick-to-the-issues strategy. On the other were Jewson and Ellis Verdi, arguing that the campaign should also try to deal with Hillary's negatives. The point of these sessions was to test Grunwald's ads, most of which were already up and running on the air, against Verdi's ads, some of which had been based on Jewson's findings and had never been given the green light. It was showdown time.

There were two sessions in Syracuse, in which groups of ten voters were shown a variety of ads. The first group included men and women, and the second group, women only. The Syracuse groups saw about fifteen ads, most of them Verdi's and a few of them Grunwald's. One Grunwald ad had just started airing that week. It showed footage of Hillary from the upstate swing earlier in the month, touting her economic plan. Strictly on the issues.

The Verdi ads tried very directly to use some of the negative buzzwords about Hillary and, per Jewson's advice, convert them into strengths. One opened with shots of a broken-down school, an unemployment line, and abandoned factories and farms. The voice-over said that these depressing sights presented opportunities for the candidate who was willing to roll up her sleeves and try to change things. "Her critics call her an opportunist," the narrator said, "and they're absolutely right." Another opened with footage of Hillary and then cut to shots of criminals, child abusers, and anti-choice protesters. "With your help," the narrator said, "these New Yorkers will go from merely disliking her to hating her." The carpetbag ad, which began with a shot of a carpetbag that opened up to reveal such items as modernized schools and long-term health care and more cops on the beat, ended with the tag line: "It's a pretty heavy bag, and it can only be carried by someone strong. Hillary." A fourth opened with shots of kids outside a school, their backpacks clearly visible. The narrator talked about kids bringing guns to school and made the case that dramatic action was needed. "So don't be afraid of a senator who comes on strong," the narrator said. "Be afraid of one who doesn't."

The results, according to one source, were clear. The Verdi ads "blew Mandy's commercials away. It was a home-run situation. Mandy and Mark were totally freaked out." Penn argues that none of the ads on either side tested terribly well.

Penn and Grunwald had been with Hillary since her campaign was just an idea. Now there existed the chance that Hillary would decide to change gears at the behest of a latecomer—that she might move away from Penn's cherished issues-only strategy, or at least augment it with another approach that tried to deal more directly with voters' various reservations about her. Penn and Grunwald had known about the Syracuse focus groups, but they hadn't attended. Now, however, they decided that they needed to be in Westchester the next night, to ensure that more of Grunwald's ads would be shown to those voters. That was done, but in Westchester, neither set of ads wowed the groups, so neither side could claim a clean advantage.

When the focus groups ended late that Thursday night, an exhausted candidate and her advisers made their way to the adopted Clinton homestead in Chappaqua for a tense powwow. There were Hillary, Penn, Grunwald, Jewson, Verdi, Susan Thomases, and Patty Solis Doyle, a longtime Hillary confidante who had been one of her very first hires as the first lady and who had been helping out with the campaign. Howard Wolfson was supposed to be there, but he had the misfortune to ingest a nut that night; he's severely allergic to them and had to be rushed to the hospital. He joined the others later by telephone. "She said it was the first time she'd had guests in her house," said one participant, laughing. "She made coffee." The conversation was a spirited exchange about the campaign's direction. Until 2:30 in the morning, each side argued its case with force. Hillary made no definitive statement at the conclusion of the meeting, but everyone left with the same feeling. Penn and Grunwald had won the day.

Penn maintains that he was not against bringing Jewson in—he himself had hired Jewson to do focus groups for Al Gore early in the vice president's campaign, when Gore was fretting about Clinton fatigue. He says he believes Jewson provided a good analysis of the problems that various groups, especially suburban women, had with Hillary. But he argued that trying to find the very best way to deal with people's emotional responses to Hillary was futile. "It was a useful exercise to look at the problem," he says. "But it also was sort of a search for a magic bullet, and the magic bullet didn't exist." Another campaign source who had been sympathetic to Jewson's involvement concurred, saying, "Dwight's analysis was sharper than his solutions were."

In the wake of this meeting, Penn's control over the campaign's message, which had been solid when the campaign started but had loosened during the months of Jewson's involvement, reasserted itself; he vetted the speeches now, and he and Grunwald ran the ad campaign. Hillary went with the people she knew best, and with the strategy that was more comfortable for her. Just as Rudy Giuliani was comfortable in his city, and uncomfortable about a race that had too many imponderables, so Hillary was comfortable sticking with the issues. It was not in her nature to try to deal with people's emotional reactions to her. " 'Who are you?' and all of that"—as she had put it to us on her campaign bus two weeks before—was not a door the campaign was going to fling open.

It had been her trial-by-fire week, and quite possibly the most important week of the campaign. Publicly, she had dealt with a charge she couldn't possibly have anticipated, a charge that threatened for a few heated days to turn this historic candidacy into a losing proposition. And privately, she had made a crucial decision about strategy that touched the core of who she was. The woman who had always campaigned efficiently for her husband, and who had burned up the campaign trail in behalf of Chuck Schumer and others in 1998, was discovering that being, rather than supporting, the candidate was pretty different after all.

CHAPTER 12

August 2000: Positioning

The Race Moves to TV

HILLARY'S CAMPAIGN, as August opened, was entering its second year. Lazio's was in its third month. Yet both campaigns had arrived at a similar point. Activity on the ground had decreased somewhat as both sides geared up for the post-Labor Day push. The battle, for the time being, moved to the television screen.

The ad wars had actually begun earlier in the summer, with Team Hillary airing its first attack ads in mid-June, when Lazio had been in the race barely three weeks. The idea, of course, was to define him before he had a chance to define himself. Ever since, the stream of attacks had been, if not overwhelming, then at least steady. The ads were not nasty in the personal sense; they were always aimed at his votes on issues like a patient's bill of rights and Medicare funding, and they were usually, by the elastic standards of the political consulting business, reasonably truthful. The Clinton team's pro-Hillary ads were rarely memorable—dry and humorless assurances that Hillary would be "on your side" on this or that issue. But the anti-Lazio ads were much sharper. Newt Gingrich, after a brief hibernation, had reappeared by early August with a vengeance. Lazio voted with Gingrich, one ad proclaimed, to cut $270 million from Medicare. ("Cut" was a bit of a stretch, as what Lazio actually voted for was a cut in the program's projected increase; but every Democratic candidate in America calls those cuts, while every Republican calls them responsible increases.) Another said he voted with Gingrich to shut down the federal government in 1995. In another, he voted to abolish the Department of Education, and in another, against Medicaid funding for abortions. And in these attack ads Team Hillary did something it never managed to do for its own candidate—it came up with an effective tag line: "The more you know, the more you wonder." All this was enough, in a state as heavily Democratic as New York, to make even Democrats who were lukewarm on Hillary begin to feel uneasy about the Republican.

Lazio responded with ads defending himself against this barrage, looking into the camera and saying Hillary was running these ads "because it's a lot easier for Mrs. Clinton to attack me than to name a single thing she has ever done for New York." This, too, was truthful. But where were the ads bragging about his record, trying to link him in the public mind with issues, like housing and assistance for the disabled, on which he could legitimately claim to have helped people? It would be late September before such ads would appear, about his tax-cut plan and about work opportunities for disabled people. But even those weren't very strong, and the latter, as we'll see, produced considerable trouble for him.

One ad in particular, made on behalf of Lazio by an outside group, stirred the pot for several days. A soft-money group supporting Lazio had produced an ad trying to position Lazio as a legislative ally of Pat Moynihan—and therefore as his logical successor. The ad began with President Clinton thanking Lazio for his legislative work during a White House bill-signing ceremony. It then spliced shots of Lazio and Moynihan walking down different halls in such a way that the casual viewer might have thought they were walking together. It was amateurish sleight-of-hand. Moynihan's Senate office immediately released to the press a letter he wrote to Lazio asking him to withdraw the ad and saying that "we have never, to my belief, been photographed together." This was a golden opportunity for the Clinton team to haul out Moynihan and have him make the same complaint in an ad. It never happened. Instead, the Clinton team—after letting six days pass—put up a response ad that featured stock footage of Hillary and Moynihan together.

Lazio was skating by because of slow responses like that. Certainly, his mini-bounce after the "Jew bastard" flap didn't have much to do with anything he was doing. His campaign, too, lacked focus. There were days throughout August when Lazio had no public schedule at all, devoting his time instead to fund-raising trips to California, Nevada, Alabama, and other states. Given his late start, raising money was, to be sure, a pressing concern—more pressing, the campaign decided, than Lazio's being on the stump. His only "campaigning," on those days, typically consisted of one interview with an upstate radio station during drive time.

Meanwhile, Hillary's March of the Micro-Issues continued apace. In early August, she—with Chelsea in tow—visited her opponent's home turf and unveiled her "Long Island Livability Plan," in an effort to do something about her dismal Long Island numbers. (Her opponent's provenance, combined with the island's natural tilt toward the brand of Republicanism that comes naturally to middle-class people who've fled the city, made Long Island by far her worst major area of the state.) "It bothers me that the lobsters have died off," she said after dining with lobster fishermen. "What does that mean not only to the lobsters but to children and the rest of us?" She did not elucidate this lobster–children link.

The Squanderer

The Lazio campaign was a sailing ship that couldn't quite catch the wind. As August opened he'd been in the race for a little more than nine weeks. He had not, in that time, managed to identify himself strongly with a single issue. He had stuck to the script laid out in his convention speech—Hillary was not a New Yorker and could not be trusted, and he was a New Yorker and could be trusted. That was pretty much the argument.

How do unknowns topple giants in elections? The best recent model, for New York purposes, was to be found in George Pataki's upset of Mario Cuomo in 1994. At the time, Cuomo—like Hillary, a universally known figure about whom minds were already made up—suffered from the perception of having overstayed his welcome.

(Cuomo, incidentally, was one major New York Democrat with whom, a Clinton aide told me, Hillary's campaign sought no association, because his name was still thought to be poison among the upstate swing voters Hillary was working so relentlessly to impress.) And so Pataki's first argument was, I'm not Mario Cuomo. But he then went on to make two more arguments. First, that he would cut taxes, and, second, that he would reinstate the death penalty. So he told people about two specific ways in which he wasn't Mario Cuomo. The issues he chose reminded voters of two widely perceived Cuomo weaknesses—lower taxes and the death penalty both had broad support in polls—and, through them, Pataki told voters exactly how he, and the post-Cuomo era, would be different. The Pataki campaign, in other words, didn't just simply say "I'm not Mario"; it said "I'm not Mario, and here are two clear examples of why I'm different." Pataki and his handlers understood that the charge against the opponent had little meaning for people if it wasn't backed up by a specific promise or two.

Lazio himself had done this very thing well in 1992, when he knocked off Tom Downey. He hammered away at Downey over the House banking scandal, but he also managed to say that he would stay in touch with the district, he wouldn't accept outside income, he wouldn't become just another Washington insider. The positive argument about himself, combined with the negative one about Downey, worked.

But now he was making a positive argument that really appealed only to people who hated Hillary Clinton already. Over the course of the summer, he took to saying on the stump that this election was "the most important of my generation," trying to invest the election with a measure of world-historical importance, as if he were a latter-day John Kennedy. This election, he would continue, "will determine whether or not character still counts in public service, whether or not integrity matters, and whether or not the rule of law applies to all or just a privileged few." One doubts that he really meant to complain that the Clintons were among the "privileged few" to whom the rule of law applied; even so, these were not arguments that were likely to make headway with undecided voters.

His staff, like his stump speech, was a bit of a hodgepodge. Lazio had brought in Mike Murphy, the slash-and-burn conservative operative, to give his campaign national stature and a McCain-like aura. Then he had hired as his campaign manager a fellow Long Islander, Bill Dal Col, whom he had known for many years and who had managed Steve Forbes's New York effort until it fizzled. At the same time, parts of the Pataki machine were involved, and other parts were not. Some Pataki associates, such as Michael Marr, Eileen Long, and Patrick Mc-Carthy, who worked in the governor's press office, were part of the Lazio effort. But other Pataki people were privately miffed that Lazio hired Murphy instead of Arthur Finkelstein and Keiran Mahoney, who had worked on the Pataki and D'Amato campaigns. And, in hiring Dal Col, Lazio had passed over Rob Ryan, a Republican operative who had worked on the governor's campaigns. Ryan, a source says, was in intensive negotiations with Lazio for three weeks; they ultimately collapsed because Lazio felt Ryan's hiring might send a signal that it was Pataki, not Lazio, who was running this show.

Among the Pataki people, Mike Murphy had few admirers. During the presidential primary campaign, when Murphy was with McCain and Pataki was backing Bush, Murphy had complained about the New York Republican Party's ballot-access rules for presidential candidates, which for a time threatened to keep McCain off the ballot in the New York primary altogether. Murphy had held a press conference in front of the Russian consulate to drive home the point that New York Republican politics stank of totalitarianism, and he referred to the governor as "Comrade Pataki."

Neither side really trusted the other, and the result was a near constant low-level tension between the Lazio campaign and the state Republican machinery. The friction abated only in the race's final weeks as Republicans joined forces under duress. One GOP source notes that the Lazio team often didn't do much to coordinate its events with local party operatives, and thus did not exploit the party's resources to the fullest extent. "They thought of their upstate swings more as hitting media markets," this source says, "which is fine if you're John McCain and you've got a thousand reporters following you. But in this kind of campaign, you can't just blow into town, get off the bus, have people throw confetti for fifteen minutes, and then get back on the bus." And inside the Lazio camp, some felt that the state party was doing too much second-guessing of Murphy to let the campaign run the kind of race it wanted to.

So, like Hillary's campaign, Lazio's was a beast with too many heads. And the factions had different priorities. The priority of Murphy and the national wing of the team that he represented was to stop Hillary. On June 25, Murphy had told *The Boston Globe*'s Fred Kaplan that stopping Hillary was his "patriotic duty." Others, such as Dal Col and a few operatives who had worked for Lazio over the years, were more interested in promoting their man. The Lazio campaign was caught in a constant tug-of-war between those who thought their man could win by demonizing Hillary and those who wanted to win by promoting their candidate with a more positive message.

Lazio had good days, such as August 4, when he campaigned on Long Island with John McCain at his side, saying he would refuse to accept soft-money donations if Hillary did the same. Hillary had raised about $4 million in soft money, the unregulated contributions that go, in theory at least, to "non-candidate committees" and that are not bound by the $1,000 limit imposed upon so-called hard money. Lazio had not raised such money himself, but he had taken advantage of soft money raised by others. The fake Moynihan ad, for example, was produced and paid for by a group called the Republican Leadership Council, which counted Pataki and D'Amato among its board members. Offstage, there were fourteen groups promising to spend $32 million to stop Hillary. So there was an element of trickery to Lazio's proposal, insofar as he knew very well that he didn't have to raise soft money because plenty of other people were planning to do it for him. But being on Long Island with McCain, where the Arizonan was enormously popular, and hitting Mrs. Clinton where she was ethically vulnerable gave Lazio, for the time being, the moral high ground on the issue.

And there were bad days, such as August 1, when it became clear that he would play no role in that week's Republican National Convention in Philadelphia. Lazio and his advisors had decided that he should not identify himself too closely with a pro-life, pro-Second Amendment presidential candidate who was, at the time, 10 to 15 points behind Al Gore in New York. And yet—a prime-time speech on national television is not the kind of opportunity that comes the way of a little-known congressman very often. The press, not to mention the Clinton people, found it strange that Lazio would be spending only part of one day at the convention and would not make a convention speech.

There were also days, as August progressed, when his failure to release his tax returns when he got into the race was the main story. Candidates do this as a matter of course. Hillary and Rudy had. But Lazio refused. He kept saying, somewhat mysteriously, that he would release his returns "by the end of the summer." Naturally, the press assumed that there must be dynamite in those returns. The state's Democrats took to having a young operative named Eric Schultz dress up in an Uncle Sam costume and follow Lazio around on the trail. Naturally, speculation grew as the delay continued that he must be hiding something. But when he released them on August 28 and apparently had nothing to hide—modest yearly incomes (for a Senate candidate, anyway) of around $150,000, a respectable level of charitable donation—the delay seemed unfathomable.

In late August, he made his first big play at becoming more than Not Hillary. Before the Chamber of Commerce in Amherst, a Buffalo suburb, he laid out a tax-cut proposal that he said would save the average New York family $3,000 a year. He expected the plan, which included eliminating the inheritance tax and the marriage penalty, to cost $776 billion over ten years.

The very day Lazio was announcing this plan, August 24, editorial writers at the *Daily News* were preparing an editorial, CLOCK TICKS ON RICK'S SHTICK, which argued that he had to be more than "the not–Hillary Clinton candidate." Lazio might have been entitled to think, then, that the paper would welcome a few specifics from him. Instead the *News*'s Joel Siegel and Joe Mahoney wrote a piece, under the unambiguous headline LAZIO TAX PACKAGE DOESN'T ADD UP, showing that the real cost of the plan was $1.1 trillion. Aides acknowledged to the *News* that the plan had calculated the cost of ending the marriage penalty over only five years instead of the ten years on which the plan's other assumptions were based. The proposal was consonant with everything that had been learned about Lazio's method and voting record in the preceding weeks—he was trying to split the difference between Bush's proposed tax cut ($1.4 trillion) and Gore's ($500 billion), to be neither too liberal nor too conservative. But when the numbers didn't check out, he just looked silly. He had sent up his first more-than-not-Hillary flare, and it fell to earth a dud.

Al and Joe

Hillary, meanwhile, had her own convention problem. It had started on July 11, when *The Washington Post* reported on its front page that the Clinton and Gore camps were sparring over the schedule of the Democratic convention in Los Angeles. The Gore people wanted to follow what they called "the Reagan model," referring to the 1988 Republican convention, when the retiring President and Mrs. Reagan were paid tribute on Monday night and left New Orleans the next morning so as to hand the remainder of the convention over to George Bush. *The Washington Post's* John Harris reported that Hillary was pushing for a Tuesday speech, and that the Gore people were livid.

Hillary was in Niagara Falls the day that story broke, speaking at a Best Western to the Niagara County Democrats. She gave her speech in an upstairs ballrom and then, sitting alongside an indoor pool on the lower concourse, gave a series of ten- or fifteen-minute interviews to the daily and wire-service reporters for Sunday analysis pieces. It was a strange circumstance: Here she was being accessible—yet getting a reaction out of the campaign to *The Washington Post* story was next to impossible. With a normal candidate, say Chuck Schumer, this would have taken three minutes. Schumer would have known that reporters needed a reaction for the next day's stories and strolled over and said, "Okay, off the record, the situation is this. For the record, I'll say this." But Hillary was not in the habit of strolling over to reporters to help them meet deadlines, and Howard Wolfson had to check in with Ickes, Penn, and Grunwald before he could speak to the question.

Hillary, Mark Penn insists, didn't really care when her convention slot would be. "She said, 'I'll take five minutes, whatever, it should be Al and Tipper's show,' " he recalls. He and Grunwald concede, though, that they cared rather more than Hillary did. "Staffs tend to get caught up in these things," Grunwald says. So there was a great deal of tension between the two campaigns over the matter—enough so the Gore people assumed that Penn leaked the story to *The Washington Post* (Penn says he did not) and effectively froze him out of their campaign from that point on.

The national press was fairly obsessed, at this point, with the question of Al Gore's "separation" from Bill Clinton. Anything, therefore, that either Clinton did to suggest that they wanted any part of the spotlight—for example, Bill's confession in the run-up to the convention that his relationship with Monica Lewinsky had been a "terrible mistake," which reminded voters of the scandal at the very moment Gore wanted them to forget it—was interpreted as theft of vice-presidential thunder. Gore aides were grousing in the papers, on background, about Hillary's high Los Angeles profile. She made an appearance on *The Tonight Show* the Friday before the convention, and the next night was the guest of honor at a huge fund-raising concert at the Malibu home of Stan Lee, the creator of Spiderman, featuring a list of entertainers that would be the envy of many a presidential candidate (Whoopi Goldberg, Stevie Wonder, Patti LaBelle, Cher).

In the end, the Gore people won—Hillary was given a Monday night slot for her speech, right before her husband. She spoke briefly, mostly about children. The speech was nothing special—a pastiche of lines from her stump speeches, with very little fresh language commemorating the special occasion—and she rushed through it as if she were in a hurry to get off the stage. In fact she probably was: Bill was speaking after her and the president's staff was keen on his finishing by eleven o'clock (it didn't happen, of course, but he was so good it didn't matter). It seemed like another missed opportunity. Penn maintains, though, that polling he did in the days immediately after her speech (and before Gore's, so as to be sure respondents were reacting to Hillary's speech alone) revealed that it went over well—which goes to show what a prime-time speech on national television can do, even if it's not very good.

Gore's people may have been angry with Hillary, but the candidate himself had, without intending to, done her a favor that helped change the course of her campaign. A week before the convention, he chose Joseph Lieberman as his running mate. The first Jewish vice-presidential nominee came along at a very handy time for Hillary, who just three weeks before was fending off charges that she'd used an anti-Semitic slur and who'd had trouble appealing to Jewish voters since she got into the race. It was an additional stroke of luck for Hillary that she could claim to have known Lieberman for thirty years, ever since she and Bill were law students at Yale, and Bill had volunteered on Lieberman's first campaign for the Connecticut state senate. The awkward fact that Lieberman had called Bill's behavior with Monica

Lewinsky "immoral" on the Senate floor was a hurdle, but a small one, which Hillary jumped by noting that Lieberman "was expressing what many people felt at the time." There were far more positive words than negative, with Hillary expressing the hope that Lieberman would campaign with her, and him responding, "I sure will." Wolfson was lying in bed watching the *Today* show the morning the choice was leaked. It's no wonder that he jumped out of bed and started "dancing around the living room for five minutes, yelling and screaming." He refrained from dancing with reporters, but he made little effort to conceal his glee as he fielded calls.

Lieberman's presence on the Democratic ticket was a plus for Hillary in two ways. First, it ensured that Gore would steamroll Bush by an even bigger margin than expected in New York—that the small percentage of Jewish voters leaning toward Bush would probably be chopped in half. Gore, now, would almost certainly win the state by a million votes, or perhaps more. With around 6.5 million people expected to vote, this meant that Gore would beat Bush by at least 3.75 million to 2.75 million, which in turn meant that, for Lazio to overcome that top-of-the-ticket deficit, about one out of every six Gore voters would have to switch lines to Lazio. Much ticket-splitting was expected, but not that much.

Second, the Lieberman choice meant that, because New York was now a done deal, the national Republican Party would spend no time or money in the state. Indeed, seen from New York, this presidential campaign looked like an event that was happening somewhere else. No television ads, no appearances by the candidates (in the end, Gore made one campaign stop in the state, and Lieberman two). This was true of both parties, of course, but the impact was far worse for Lazio, because he was more in need than Hillary of the kind of big events that build excitement. If Bush had campaigned in New York, he would have done so in the upstate cities or exurban communities where his conservative positions weren't liabilities, the very regions that Lazio needed to carry by large margins to offset the fact that Hillary would club him in the city. But the selection of Lieberman meant that Bush wasn't even going to bother.

Of course, Hillary had nothing to do with Lieberman's selection. The trick would be in using this happy accident to full advantage without looking as if she was trying too hard. An early commercial fea-

turing Lieberman offering Hillary a testimonial was discussed, and rejected as a little too obvious. The feeling inside the campaign was that
it would probably be best to hold Lieberman in reserve and use him to
respond to the inevitable Suha Arafat attack ad, which would probably
come very late in the race. So it would be five weeks after the announcement before Hillary's people finally brought Lieberman to
New York to campaign with her. Some Democrats privately second-
guessed this delay, and saw it as evidence of a continued lack of organization. But, by late August, it was getting harder and harder for anyone
to make the case that this campaign was disorganized.

The Machine Comes Together

Though no benefits were yet visible, the Clinton campaign was, by the
time of the Democratic National Convention, reorganizing itself to get
ready for the post-Labor Day stretch. The process had begun in the
wake of the crucial third week of July, when the Clinton team was
publicly dealing with the "Jew bastard" story and privately sorting out
the question of Jewson's role and how the campaign should best present its candidate. After the meeting at Hillary's house in Chappaqua,
the candidate—and her husband, who by now was playing a far more
active role in his wife's campaign than he had been in the spring—
made a series of decisions that would pay off dramatically down the
stretch.

First, Hillary decided that Jewson had not found the "magic bullet" of which Penn spoke, and concluded that she should just go with
the team and the strategy that had brought her this far. Earlier in the
year, dealing with people's negative emotions about her would have
been a good idea. At that point there was plenty of time to try to
change people's perceptions of her. But as Labor Day approached, the
time required for such a massive reconstruction project was getting
short. To have changed strategy at that point—to try to take on
Hillary's negatives, or try to deal directly with her suburban-women
problem—would only have muddied the message and made it appear
that the campaign was overhauling itself in a panic. And internally, a
war of egos would surely have broken out if the campaign had had

Penn and Grunwald putting out one message and Ickes, Verdi, and Jewson putting out another. So Hillary was going to succeed or fail on the basis of her issues arguments.

Second, Hillary determined around this time that, as one aide put it to me, "everyone should just do what they do best and leave other things to others." This meant that Ickes would devote most of his energies to fund-raising, which he had done so prodigiously (and controversially) for the president. It also meant that Bill DeBlasio, with the assistance of political aide Ramon Martinez, would now devote the bulk of his time to coordinating events and endorsements from New York pols, working with the unions, lining up phone banks, and seeing to it that everyone was following the same script. DeBlasio had vast New York campaign experience, and he knew exactly which politicians Hillary needed to stroke. Most conspicuously, there was Dov Hikind, an Orthodox Jewish state assemblyman from Brooklyn's Borough Park section. Hikind was not New York's most influential politician. But he had no equal in making it appear that one word from him would send thousands of Jews charging to the ballot box to do his bidding. A statement from Hikind that Hillary just didn't get it on Israel, or something along those lines, would have made enough headlines to cause the Clinton team considerable grief. Only DeBlasio had the experience with Hikind and the state's many other local grandees to know how best to get them on board, or at least prevent them from going with Lazio or otherwise making trouble.

Third, the Hillary team solidified its "coordinated campaign"—that is, the coordinated efforts of Hillary's campaign, the Gore New York effort, and the state Democratic Party. This was the province of Gigi Georges, who had moved up from Washington in May at Hillary's request. Georges had worked at the American Federation of Teachers, and, before that, on the White House Economic Council. Now she worked with DeBlasio in reaching out to elected officials and labor leaders. She oversaw the massive volunteer operation and made crucial decisions about where the campaign should spend resources. She opened headquarters and placed staff people in counties that Democrats had never won, such as Onondaga and St. Lawrence (Hillary would go on to win them). She also was, in effect, the Gore campaign in New York. Finally, she was in charge of mailings, phone banks, and, in the campaign's final weeks, the get-out-the-vote operation, for which it brought in two young and knowledgeable operatives—Kevin Wardally, who had worked for New York City Council Speaker Peter Vallone, and Patrick Gaspard, who worked at Dennis Rivera's health and hospital workers' union.

The coordinated campaign also included a separate ad campaign, financed by the state party and overseen by David Axelrod, a Chicago-based consultant who had grown up in New York and who had a great deal of experience in the state. Axelrod's personal loyalty to Hillary was intense. He and his wife have an epileptic child, and early in the Clinton adminstration they had asked Hillary to help raise awareness about the disorder. She had responded by doing, Axelrod says, far more than they'd asked, helping them raise money for a foundation they had established and organizing a national conference on epilepsy. In August and September, he made a series of effective man-in-the-street ads that attacked Lazio's votes on education and nursing-home standards.

Fourth, and probably most important, the campaign established a war room, modeled on Bill Clinton's 1992 operation, to try to react to events and damaging news stories more quickly than it had. The war room, on the third floor, five floors below the campaign's official headquarters in a garment-district office building, was mainly the province of Howard Wolfson. He had spent a year at Hillary's side at nearly every public event. Now he left the trail and stayed in the war room, monitoring the papers and the cable channels and the Web. He was joined there by Neera Tanden, Hillary's issues advisor, and by Glenn Weiner, who headed the opposition-research operation. Another war-room specialty was lining up surrogates, from celebrities to upstate legislators, to spread the gospel of Hillary. This was the province of campaign aide Sean Sweeney and Peter Kaufmann, who worked for the state Democratic committee.

Finally, a key third-floor operative was Patty Solis Doyle, a long-time aide to Mrs. Clinton, who very quietly (her name never appeared in the New York papers) moved up to New York from Washington in mid-August. Solis Doyle was, like Hillary, from Chicago. She was the sister of a Chicago alderman, and she was one of those people who, having stuck with Hillary through everything, had earned the first lady's intense loyalty. She had the last word on Hillary's schedule, sorting through the invitations from civic groups and petitions from the campaign's various community-outreach people and deciding where

Hillary did, and did not, appear. But she also was central to the campaign's broader strategic decision-making process, as was the establishment of the war room itself: From its inception up through election day, at 7:30 every morning, the campaign's central decision-makers—Penn, Grunwald, Ickes, Wolfson, DeBlasio, and Solis Doyle—were linked in a conference call, during which they reviewed the morning's papers, decided how Hillary should respond to negative stories, and crafted her message for the day.

The team was now in place. It mixed experienced first-lady staffers, whom Mrs. Clinton knew and trusted, and New York Democratic operatives with knowledge of the state and experience in high-pressure campaigns. DeBlasio was working the pols and the unions. Grunwald had taken control of the advertising, with Verdi tossing ideas at her and creating ads at her request, and Axelrod making his ads. (All was hardly hearts and flowers among these three—Verdi felt Grunwald's approach was far too cautious; she considered him a little green; and Axelrod found that his suggestions often died once Team Hillary got hold of them. But neither did they detest one another, or work at cross purposes, which for a campaign is usually good enough.) Ann Lewis was coordinating efforts among women and Jewish voters. In the latter pursuit she was aided by Matthew Hiltzik, who many months before had studied a map of upstate New York with Judith Hope to plot out the Listening Tour. He had then gone to work at Miramax, but now he took a leave from that job and joined the campaign to expand the Jewish outreach. Taking over Wolfson's old duties of traveling with the candidate, alongside the two Karens, Finney and Dunn, was Cathie Levine, who took a leave from her job as Chuck Schumer's press secretary (Levine had worked on Schumer's 1998 race, traveling throughout the state with him). Overseeing it all, and doing the polling, was Mark Penn.

It took a year, and a lot of fights, but the campaign was finally a smoothly functioning machine. Next month, this newfound efficiency would begin to show.

13

September 2000:
The Advantage

The Handshake

EVER SINCE that very first interview Hillary gave to New York reporters, in Cooperstown just after the Listening Tour started, she had
frequently been asked whether her husband planned to campaign for
her. I'm sure he will, she said; we'll cross that bridge when we come
to it.

We came to it on the morning of Monday, September 11, at a synagogue in Scarsdale, a wealthy suburb in Westchester County. This was
shortly after Labor Day weekend—the time when, by tradition, campaigns kick it up a notch. The e-mail I received from the campaign
over the holiday weekend, announcing that Hillary would be appearing with the president, naturally had me envisioning a large rally and
bunting and a fervent plea from the leader of the free world on his
wife's behalf.

Instead, I arrived at the synagogue to find a gathering of no more
than three hundred people in a cramped basement room. And, far from
being a boisterous, you-go-girl celebration, the event was oddly subdued. Its theme, based on an FCC report that appeared on the front
page of the *Times* that day, was violence in the media—a safe, soccer-
mom topic. The only interesting moment came when Bill relayed two

pieces of advice he said he regularly gave to young people considering a career in public service. "I tell them, number one, you've got to have a reason to run that's bigger than yourself," he told the crowd. "And number two, you've got to hear the music of people's lives. Because everybody has a story." I wondered if he'd given that first piece of advice to his wife, who still stood accused by many New Yorkers of running only for her own selfish purposes.

From the start, according to her team of advisers, Hillary Clinton's Senate campaign had been built on two premises. The first was that the "issue landscape," as Mandy Grunwald put it, was favorable to Hillary. The matters most on American voters' minds this election, education and health care, were opportune ones for Hillary—something that would not have been true if the chief issues of the day had been crime and the size of the federal government. The issue landscape was made friendlier still by the fact that heavily Democratic New York was a particularly amenable marketplace in which to sell her positions on these issues—especially, as Harold Ickes had told Hillary those many months ago, during a presidential election year. This first premise was fairly obvious, and, because polling and a simple glance at the state's voter registration figures and turnout patterns supported it, bankable.

The second premise, though, was far from bankable. It was that people would get used to her; that the months she spent traveling the state, pulling her motorcade up in small towns that rarely saw a Senate candidate, let alone one who was also the first lady, would help her in two ways. First, they hoped she could achieve a sort of normalcy—that by the time she hit Buffalo for the sixteenth time, the reaction would be one less of wonderment at the presence of this mega-celebrity than a simple, "Oh, here comes Hillary again." By the time it was all over, in fact, she had made twenty-six visits to Buffalo, the Lake Erie city that had lost nearly half its population in the last fifty years, where the citizenry was desperate for anyone from the outside world who would just pay the city a little attention.

The Clinton team's other hope was that her constant presence would help to establish a rationale for her candidacy. Hillary couldn't articulate a compelling one in a sound bite, and even if she'd been able to, most New Yorkers wouldn't have believed it. So she would have to build a rationale over time—meet with thousands of voters; become an expert on every topic under the New York sun, no matter how parochial; and eventually persuade enough people that she actually cared about speeding the flow of traffic across the Peace Bridge in Buffalo or cleaning up the pollutants in Onondaga Lake. "It was a theory that she could get from celebrity to candidate, and that she could make that leap just through hard work, through doing," Mark Penn says.

In the fall of 1999, few close observers of this race would have argued that Hillary Clinton could ever become a normal candidate with a defensible rationale. Her parade of errors and the white-hot intensity of the press coverage strongly suggested otherwise. But a year later, there were tentative signs that things were cooling down. On one front, the New York media were no longer salivating over the kinds of minor embarrassments that had whipped them into such a frenzy the year before. This was made clear in early September, when the Clintons vacationed at the Finger Lakes home of Thomas McDonald, a friend and contributor. The Associated Press discovered that McDonald had been the subject, the previous year, of a warrant issued by the state tax department, which claimed that he owed nearly $1 million in back taxes and penalties. A year before, the fact that the Clintons were accepting the largesse of a man in the gunsights of the revenuers might have grown into a three- or four-day controversy. Now it breezed through the news cycle in a day—not only because the Clintons cut the vacation short (they explained that Chelsea was in Washington suffering from a bad cold), but also because the media's appetite for such stories had been sated. Hillary would face her share of harsh news stories in the next nine weeks, but they would arrive on the wings of more substantive matters.

Also, Hillary was, finally, getting the hang of the high-stakes ethnic-group poker game that is New York politics. Certain Jewish groups and politicians—chiefly Dov Hikind, who was not supporting her, but also Assembly Speaker Sheldon Silver, who was—had been leaning on Hillary publicly and privately to call for clemency for Jonathan Pollard, an American who had been convicted of spying for Israel. She was hesitant to make such a dramatic break with her husband's administration on a national security issue. But on September 1 the *Post* reported that, the week before, she had quietly intervened with the White House to save Pollard from a transfer to a more dangerous section of the prison where he was serving a life sentence. This small intervention, undertaken at Silver's and Hikind's behest, was enough to keep Hikind quiet for the time being. Throughout September and October, Bill DeBlasio and Matthew Hiltzik would stay in close touch with Hikind.

One could sense some momentum developing around her campaign. The talk among insiders throughout the summer had been that Lazio, despite all his missteps, was still well positioned to win the race. After Labor Day, that talk began to change. Her campaign was clearly the more focused of the two. She was starting to line up endorsements—on September 5, she got the Sierra Club; Lazio had wanted that endorsement badly, the better to burnish his image as a good environmentalist, for a Republican. The next day, she appeared with Robert F. Kennedy, Jr., to accept his backing. Kennedy represented another environmental endorsement, as he headed a highly regarded group called River Keepers devoted to cleaning up the Hudson River. Symbolically, of course, this son of a beloved, carpetbagging liberal senator represented much more than that, and, as he stood with Hillary at the West Side's 79th Street Boat Basin, he used the occasion to make light of the charge that had swirled around his father's 1964 run and that dogged Hillary: "New Yorkers come from everywhere. We have the most cosmopolitan community in North America."

In the meantime, Lazio was still doing little to define himself to voters. His press entourage was decidedly unimpressed by now with what "Dick Lonzo" had shown them. Snide remarks worked their way into stories, about his khakis-and-blazer outfit, for example, which made him look like a young man reporting for his first job. The papers had fun with a photograph of Lazio going down a slide at an upstate fair, his tie askew. More seriously, Republicans were starting to grouse, on background, about the state of his campaign. On September 3, the *Daily News* reported deep Republican concern about Lazio's light schedule. For the four days preceding Labor Day, he made no public appearances. "It's fair to say," one unnamed operative told the paper, "that a lot of us . . . would love to see him do more events." It was an ill-timed holiday for a candidate who still needed to tell voters who he was and what kind of senator he planned to be.

Instead, he was still splashing around in the same anti-Hillary waters. "You just can't trust her" was the tag line on a series of commercials the Lazio team unveiled in the late summer and early fall; one of them was titled "Positive" and argued that Lazio had the positive message and Hillary did not, even though it was an attack ad. He needled her in his stump speech; when he got to the topic of New York not getting its fair share from Washington, he would note that Southern states got more than their share, and then say, "let's take a Southern state, oh, I don't know, one like . . ." On cue his audience would yell "Arkansas!" This always drew appreciative hoots from crowds that didn't stop to consider that the long-standing imbalance was caused not by Bill Clinton but by the Southern-dominated Republican Party leadership to which Lazio had wedded himself. And he attacked her on Israel, and even, on one occasion that he would come to rue, went after her husband.

Right after Labor Day, world leaders gathered in New York City for a millennial celebration of the United Nations. Fidel Castro was among those who attended the festivities. On Wednesday, September 6, at a small private luncheon, the Cuban leader approached the president of the United States and initiated a handshake that Clinton reciprocated. There were no cameras present to record the moment. But naturally word of the fateful handclasp leaked out. Lazio was at a campaign stop in Mount Vernon, in Westchester County, when he took ungrammatical hold of the issue. "I would not have shook Fidel Castro's hand," he said. "I think we send the wrong message when we embrace—whether it's Mrs. Arafat or Fidel Castro."

Lazio's comments appeared in the papers on Saturday. The next day presented what may have been the race's most ironic media moment. There, in Sunday's *New York Post,* was a photograph of Rick Lazio shaking hands with none other than Yasir Arafat. The picture had been snapped by an official White House photographer in December 1998. President Clinton had scheduled a Middle East trip shortly before the House's vote on the articles of impeachment, and he had invited along a few wavering House members to impress them with Air Force One and jawbone them on the flights over and back. Lazio was one such waverer (in his typical, let's-please-everyone fashion, he finally voted for two of the four articles). Lazio, California Democrat Tom Lantos, and other members of Congress joined the president as he made his diplomatic rounds. It was Lantos, a close ally of the Clintons, who had contacted the *Post,* telling the paper that he remembered the picture being taken, and that he was sure it existed in the White House files. The *Post* called the White House, and the photograph was transmitted to the paper with dispatch.

And what a picture it was! This was no reluctant, Yitzhak Rabin, "all right, if I have to" shake. It was one of those 1970s, "hey, bro" shakes, with the thumbs interlocked and fingers clasped tightly together. Lazio's free hand had settled firmly on the chairman's shoulder, in a quasi-bear hug, the smile on his face as full of happy wattage as the smile of a twelve-year-old Yankee fan meeting Derek Jeter. And that it appeared in the *Post,* of all places, was a stroke of tactical genius. The *Post* may have hated Hillary, but it still knew a story when one fell into its lap. Lantos's spokesman never said that his boss's memory had been prodded by either the campaign or the White House, and Howard Wolfson would not comment. But surely the war room, and the White House, wanted to make certain that readers of America's most Jewish mainstream newspaper saw that photo.

Lazio and Mike Murphy tried to whip the White House's involvement into a controversy. White House spokesman Joe Lockhart had to field a few questions on the photo's release and the propriety of the White House involving itself in the first lady's campaign. Lockhart said that once Lazio criticized the president for shaking Fidel's hand, the flap became White House business. "This wasn't a terribly difficult decision," he told reporters. "It seemed like a pretty straightforward issue to me." And the controversy pretty much died right there. The photo existed, and it was fair game. Releasing it was just politics. As Hillary had learned the previous November with regard to Suha Arafat, a powerful image tends to nullify explanations after the fact.

It was just one picture. No one concluded, because of its appearance, that Rick Lazio was soft on terrorism. But many observers of the race did wonder how he could have carried on so about Mrs. Clinton and Mrs. Arafat, and then about the president and Castro, while knowing that he had glad-handed the Palestinian chairman and that a photograph capturing the moment surely existed. And more to the point: the inevitable, late-October ad featuring Hillary kissing Suha, an ad the Clinton team had anticipated with dread since the moment the photo appeared, suddenly seemed a little less inevitable.

The Space Invaders

The picture of Lazio and Arafat was much discussed. All the downstate papers ran editorials (the upstate papers, as a rule, paid little attention to the aspects of the campaign that sometimes made it seem that this was a race for the Knesset) and it appeared that it would linger as a defining image of the campaign. Three days later, though, voters were presented with another image of Lazio that would do him considerably more damage.

The first of three scheduled Clinton–Lazio debates was slated for Wednesday, September 13, at the studios of Buffalo's public television station. The sense of anticipation was intense. The campaign had been, for a few weeks up to this point, somewhat desultory. Mrs. Clinton held the same four-point edge in the polls that she had maintained more or less since Lazio entered the race, with the exception of her post-"Jew bastard" slippage. In the *Times,* news of the race had largely receded to middle pages of the B (Metro) section. With a few exceptions the tabloids had been relatively quiet—quieter, in fact, than the previous fall.

Debates are about conventional wisdom, and, at 6:50 P.M. that night, when moderator and Buffalo native Tim Russert entered the studio to schmooze the audience for a few minutes before the debate started, the tripartite conventional wisdom was as follows. First, that Hillary still needed to make the case for her candidacy. Second, that Lazio needed to show stature, to demonstrate that he could hold his place on the stage next to this supernova and not seem like a school-boy. These "stature" expectation games always work to the advantage of the lesser figure; the question of whether Lazio could "hold his own" with Hillary was repeated so often that, by the time of the debate, it was almost inevitable that the conclusion would be that he had "held his own" as long as he refrained from blithering like a fool, or getting caught by the split screen picking his nose. And third, the conventional wisdom held that the race had grown a little stale just lately, and everyone who had invested more than a year in this carnival hoped the debate would be spirited enough to wake things up again.

Russert's presence seemed to offer some potential for sparks. He was well known for his tough Sunday morning interviews, leaning his slightly-too-large head across the table as he confronted guests with some old quote that he was bringing back to bite them. He was considered, by many New York liberals at least, to have been intensely anti-Clinton during the Lewinsky scandal. Hillary was a little afraid of him. Since the campaign began, she had avoided appearing on *Meet the Press,* not to mention New York 1 and every other political talk show in America. It was an evasion for which she had rightly been criticized. But her advisers had settled on the position many months before, and she stuck to her course. Maybe five hundred people care whether she does those shows, Howard Wolfson would say; besides, those shows are generally about making news through asking Gotcha! questions, and with Hillary there were plenty of those to ask. No good, and maybe lots of bad, could come from her being on them.

This was the first debate of her life as a candidate, and Hillary had taken part in many prep sessions. She was coached by Michael Sheehan, a longtime image consultant who had helped many Democratic candidates with their debate preparation. Washington lawyer Bob Barnett, an old hand at playing Republicans for Democratic candidates' practice sessions, took the part of Lazio. James Carville sat in to offer suggestions. And, of course, the president was at some of the sessions, although one source says that his presence was less than helpful. At a Sunday night session with Sheehan and Carville, Hillary was great— relaxed, and reasonably proficient at making her points in sixty seconds' time (one skill for which she had shown little talent on the stump). At a later session, when Bill came, Hillary "was worse," this source says. He made her nervous, and "every time she tried to start in on an answer, he'd say, 'No, no, no, do it this way.' It's really just that he wanted to do it himself." The president had ached to come to the first debate, but Hillary didn't want him there, because his presence would be too distracting both to her and to the media. It was left to Penn and Grunwald to break the news to Bill that he had to stay in Washington, where he watched with aide Bruce Lindsey and old Arkansas friend Jim Blair.

What the president, and the rest of us, watched began as a cautious dance of wills. The first question went to Hillary. It was a tough but fair inquiry into the health-care debacle, with specific attention to the way her 1994 proposal would have changed—that is, virtually eliminated— the funding stream for teaching hospitals, of which New York has many. She hemmed and hawed, saying that "we did propose a funding stream that would have provided additional funds," without saying what it was. Russert turned to Lazio for his rebuttal, and he said, simply and directly, that "a New Yorker would never have made that proposal." It was a rehearsed line, but no one could say he wasn't right.

She tried, with nearly every answer, to invoke the name of Gingrich. He tried to throw it back at her: "Mrs. Clinton. You of all people should not try to make guilt by association." She scored points on the upstate economy by telling people how bad things were. He—no doubt because his champion, Governor Pataki, was sensitive to charges that the upstate economy was in bad shape—tried to say things weren't so bad. The psychology of depressed areas being such that people want nothing more than to hear how miserable things are, Hillary won that round cleanly. She took no position on casino gaming in Niagara Falls, which some local mandarins had evidently been pushing. He, to his credit, said he was against it. She, somewhat surprisingly given her backing by the teachers' unions, declared the then-current Buffalo teachers' strike "illegal and inappropriate" under the state's Taylor Law, which proscribes strikes by certain public employees. (When one of the panelists threw the Taylor Law at her, there was a momentary frisson in the press filing room, with people wondering whether she would know what the Taylor Law was. By this time, Good Student Hillary probably knew its provisions far better than the rest of us.) He mocked her work on education in Arkansas, saying, "I don't think we need that Little Rock record in the Big Apple."

Lazio *was* holding his own. Hillary had worked through an early case of butterflies and was fine, if unexceptional. We seemed to be heading toward no firm conclusion. Then, at 7:24 P.M., things changed.

In their debate-prep sessions, Hillary's advisers had readied their charge for some kind of Monica question. They thought Russert might throw her "vast right-wing conspiracy" comment back at her. They guessed he might force her to acknowledge, as she never had, that her husband bore responsibility for the national trauma. What they absolutely did not expect was that Russert would use extensive footage from her January 27, 1998 *Today* interview with Matt Lauer. But there, on the monitors, she was: The old, Washington Hillary at her most unappealing. She looked, as everyone with a memory of that interview knows, terrible—heavy bags under her eyes, and panic in them. The

Hillary that New York had grown used to hadn't looked like that in months. Even the old, less flattering hairstyle was a reminder of everything Hillary had tried to leave behind in Washington. The audience for this debate, both in the hall and at home, watched as the 1998 Hillary denounced the right-wing conspiracy, and it heard her confess that yes, if the charges against her husband were proved true, that would be a serious thing, but they would not be. Russert then turned to her and asked: Did she regret "misleading the American people" that morning, and would she now apologize to those she had branded part of the vast right-wing conspiracy?

It is worth stepping back to remark how little the Lewinsky scandal had figured in this election. As subtext, Monica was present—in Hillary's problems with women, and in the very fact of her candidacy, which was surely a search for redemption after her national humiliation. Spectators along parade routes would taunt her with shouts of "Where's Monica?" and women who met with her would occasionally ask her why she hadn't left the louse. But since that first sit-down interview in Cooperstown, when only one of twenty-six questions had been about her past, and since the flare-up over the *Talk* interview, the New York press corps had largely spared her from having to talk about it. It was old news. It was a Washington story, pursued by a press corps that saw itself—especially at the level of high punditry—as the guardian of the nation's morals. It was not a New York story, and the New York media lacked the Washington media's consuming obsession—and, by the way, its sources—about the subject. Many journalists, even those who had no great love for the Clintons, thought it in poor taste to bring it up to her. The question, at bottom, was, why have you tolerated your husband's relentless cheating? Even reporters who had little use for her had trouble screwing up the courage and locating the right euphemisms by which to ask the first lady of the United States *that*. (Just in case, her handlers kept her miles away from the few who might have asked.) Besides, she wouldn't answer questions about the Lewinsky scandal even when they were put to her, so after a while reporters concluded there wasn't much point in asking.

Russert, however, represented the Washington media. The Lewinsky scandal was *their* story. And since Hillary had never been called to account for her role in it, he was bound to hit her with it. Half of Russert's query, about the right-wing conspiracy, didn't come as a surprise. The other half, however, about misleading the American people, *was* a surprise. Most of America had been willing to give her the benefit of the doubt on this point. At that early juncture, most Americans believed, she was being misled herself. There were any number of legitimate tough questions Russert could have asked Hillary about her role in the scandal. But this wasn't one of them.

Hillary's face froze, as it always did when she received a question she didn't want to have to deal with. She paused and stuttered. "Well, you know, Tim, that was a very, very painful time for me, for my family, and for our country," she said. "It is something that I regret deeply that anyone had to go through. I've tried to be as forthcoming as I could, given the circumstances that I faced. Obviously, I didn't mislead anyone. I didn't know the truth. And there's a great deal of pain associated with that, and my husband has certainly acknowledged that and made it clear that he did mislead the country as well as his family." Those sentences, as she actually spoke them, contained twenty-three "um's."

Russert turned to Lazio. You, Congressman, sent out a mailing saying that Hillary Clinton had "embarrassed our country." Did she? "I stand by that letter," Lazio responded. "I stand by that statement." Russert then ran a clip from the spliced Moynihan commercial of July, asking Lazio if he thought it had been a fair use of the senator's image and if he would not, now, denounce that ad. He didn't. It seemed an attempt at balance: We'll use this footage against Hillary, so we'll use that footage against Lazio. The emotional impact of the two clips, though, was hardly equivalent.

The conversation returned to the mundane—more on the upstate economy, a question on education. Lazio continued to hit hard, with phrases like "beyond shameless" and "positively Clintonesque." Hillary kept harping on Gingrich. Finally, Russert asked Lazio if he would abide by an agreement to ban the use of soft-money advertising, produced by non-candidate committees and paid for by unregulated "soft-money" contributions (to either state party, or to liberal or conservative advocacy groups). Both candidates had proposed such a ban, and Lazio had recently been talking it up quite a lot along the trail. It was Lazio's attempt to McCain-ize his struggling candidacy, and indeed, he had often made the pitch with the Arizona senator at his side. Hillary had said she would go along with such a ban provided Lazio obtained signed agreements from the fourteen outside groups—one called itself the Emergency Committee to Stop Hillary Rodham Clinton—that had pledged to spend $32 million to block her election.

Lazio began by mentioning his votes in favor of the House version of the McCain-Feingold soft-money ban. Then, he reached into the inner breast pocket of his jacket. "I have right here a pledge," he announced, suggesting that they both sign it on the spot, immediately. Hillary mentioned the fourteen groups. Russert asked Lazio if he would promise to procure agreements from them. Then—it was now 7:50—Lazio said, "I want to get this done now." He charged over to Hillary's podium, held the document inches from her face and bayed at her: "Let's sign it! Let's get it done now. Let's not get any more wiggle room!"

Hillary's face gave away nothing as she pushed the pledge away: "You know, I admire that. That was a wonderful performance, and I—"

"Well, why don't you just sign it?"

"And you, you did it very well."

"I'm not asking you to admire it. I'm asking you to sign it."

"Well, I would be happy to, when you give me the signed letters . . ."

"Well, right here. Right here."

"When you give me—"

"Right here, sign it right now!"

"Well—well, we'll shake . . . we'll shake on this—"

"No, no, I want your signature. Because I think everybody wants to see you signing something that you said you were for. I'm for it. I haven't done it. You've been violating it . . ."

"And, and this new radio ad from the Republican Party using soft money is not part of your campaign?"

"Oh, well, what are we talking about here? No, let's just put things in perspective."

At which point Russert interjected: "We are out of time."

After closing statements, reporters charged into the spin room, next to the filing center. Lazio came out with his wife, announced himself the winner, saying he "did what had to be done" tonight and taking only a few questions to which he gave brief answers. That was generous in comparison to Hillary, who wouldn't go near an environment as hectic and uncontrollable as a post-debate spin room. For her side, Ann Lewis and Mark Penn handled the spin. Lewis, trying to portray Lazio as a bully, pressed the point that he "spent much of the time being personally insulting." Penn added that Hillary had "bared her pain."

The post-debate conventional wisdom was clear: Lazio had won. While by no means universal, the majority view was that he had held his own (and, while discussing his record, he had), and that he had pulled off a masterful coup with the pledge trick. The next day's papers handed down the verdict: LAZIO PROVES TO BE A FORMIDABLE FOE was the headline above Gregg Birnbaum's analysis in the *Post.* Jack Newfield, also in the *Post,* wrote that Hillary "should have signed [the pledge] right on camera. Instead, she ducked." He declared it her "weasel moment." The *Daily News* outdid the *Post,* with a wood that shouted IN HER FACE, over a photo of Lazio in mid-march on his way to Hillary's podium.

But the next day's papers also carried another interpretation, albeit under quieter headlines. In the *Daily News,* an instant poll of 274 voters statewide declared Hillary the winner by 49 to 36 percent. A survey of a handpicked group of swing voters in *The Buffalo News* yielded an even more strongly pro-Clinton result. *USA Today* had asked eight voters in Westchester County to watch the debate. Every one thought Hillary won. These numbers matched Mark Penn's. Penn had asked two hundred New York voters to watch and participate in an instant-response survey. Barely an hour after the debate ended, only one hundred had responded, but their verdict was clear enough, Penn says, that "I was able to tell her it was a home run."

In fact it was less a home run than a sort of quadruple intentional beaning that got her around the base path. Over the years pundits had never tired of noting that Hillary's reputation always shot up when she was seen as the victim. On this night, both moderator and opponent combined to make Hillary more sympathetic than she had ever managed to make herself during this campaign. Such is the male-dominated discourse of New York that this interpretation did not immediately sink in. Lars-Erik Nelson in the *Daily News* was one of the few male commentators to read the debate as the voters did, calling Lazio's podium march "a childish, contrived stunt." Then Gail Collins, writing in her *Times* column two days after the debate, noted that Lazio had "invaded her space"—a term that would appear again and again over the next couple of weeks—and asked rhetorically, "How many times do we have to point out that women do not like men who yell?" On some of the radio talk shows, one could hear women beginning to take a somewhat less judgmental tone toward Hillary. Instead they turned their sights on Lazio, the physical space invader, and Russert, the emotional space invader. The press sized up the mood and, within two or three days, adjusted the conventional wisdom to say that Lazio had overdone it.

There would be other pivotal moments in the contest's final days, but, in a broader sense, the advantage shifted toward Hillary the night of that first debate and never really shifted back. And, oh yes, the night before the debate, she became the official nominee of the Democratic Party, defeating a Manhattan surgeon named Mark McMahon in the primary with 82 percent of the vote. McMahon had resented the way the party rolled over for Hillary, sacrificing the open-primary principle that Charlie Rangel had belittled in January ("Ain't nobody going to run against the first lady!"). The primary had carried some risk—not that Hillary would lose but that if she finished under, say, 70 percent, she would look vulnerable. But McMahon had no political instincts, and he did not know how to reach the Reagan Democrats who might have brought him some votes. History will record him as the third most important male adversary Mrs. Clinton stared down that week.

The Wrath of the Editorialists

Hillary was feeling pretty good. She told audiences, in the days right after the debate, that "having two younger brothers" had served to prepare her for things like Lazio's gambit. He, meanwhile, was trying to act energized. His people felt he had dominated Hillary in the debate and, during a quick post-debate swing through upstate cities that was designed to create momentum around his performance, crowds were larger than usual. Still, the candidate hit turbulence at a Rochester charter school, where a second-grader asked him, "Why did you fight with Mrs. Clinton?"

He continued to press the soft-money issue while on the stump, repeatedly saying that he would refuse to allow outside groups to give financial support to his campaign provided Mrs. Clinton did the same. His argument was slightly undercut by the appearance, in the week after the debate, of two soft-money ads attacking his opponent, one paid for by the Conservative Party, the other by the American Conservative Union. These ads permitted Hillary to argue that Lazio wasn't really serious about the ban. (Soft-money ads, made by David Axelrod, were still running on her behalf, too.) Until he gets those agreements from those fourteen groups, she would say, confident that the groups would never agree to pass up their chance to smear her, this is a shell game.

Then, on Wednesday, September 20, during an afternoon speech to a state journalists' association in Albany, Lazio announced that he had the agreements from the fourteen groups.

To say this surprised the Clinton team would be the understatement of the campaign. "It's fair to say we were pretty shocked by that," says one aide. Hillary showed up in Albany shortly after Lazio's announcement to speak to the same group. She tried to put on a calm public face, saying she was "very encouraged" by what she'd heard. But in fact the campaign had been thrown into a panic. First, Lazio now clearly had an issue, for the first time since he got into the race. Second, it was an issue that played into trust and integrity and all the other concerns that constituted Hillary's greatest weakness. Third—and from the Clinton team's perspective, most important—the campaign had come to rely heavily on soft money. Lazio had not needed to—he was raising, on average, more than $1 million a week in *hard* money from Hillary-haters around the country. But Hillary, running an endless campaign with a large staff, had decided long before that she needed to raise money in chunks considerably larger than the $1,000 hard-money limit. Her campaign had raised soft money since its inception. The money was funneled to the state Democratic committee and other soft-money organizations that were set up so those groups could run commercials in support of her campaign. Beyond that, liberal advocacy groups that backed her—notably the unions and the National Abortion and Reproductive Rights Action League (NARAL)—planned to run their own issue-oriented ads in the final weeks of the campaign. In 1998, for example, the teachers' union had spent $1.2 million on behalf of Chuck Schumer. A soft-money ban could cost the Clinton campaign millions of dollars.

The Lazio team was smelling a big advantage here. That same Wednesday night, campaign manager Bill Dal Col and several other Lazio aides showed up (having alerted reporters) at the Clinton campaign's door at 450 Seventh Avenue, across from Macy's, insisting that they wanted to negotiate the deal right then and there, with the press invited. DeBlasio emerged to speak with Dal Col at an elevator bank, in front of the television cameras, arguing that the media's presence would turn negotiations into a circus and that he would be happy to talk the next day.

The Clinton team spent the night in heated argument. "That was probably our most intense fighting during the entire campaign," one participant says. The question was simple: should they make a deal? "There was a good-government chorus in the campaign versus a more tactical view," says one source. Grunwald was most resistant to the idea. She thought the Lazio proposal was nothing but a publicity stunt and should be treated as such. DeBlasio was most in favor of it, because he was especially sensitive to way the New York press would play it if Hillary backed out, and because, one source says, "he just thought it was the right thing to do." Wolfson's position was closer to DeBlasio's. He argued that the Clinton campaign should unilaterally develop a soft-money ban of its own and say to the Lazio camp, "OK, this is what we're doing, you're free to do the same, or not, or whatever you want to do." Penn leaned toward Grunwald's position, although he thought it might be useful to challenge the Lazio side to some negotiations. He knew the Lazio camp was sitting on more hard money than the Clinton team. He suspected that the Lazio people wouldn't be proposing this ban if they didn't have some secret way around it, and he thought it might be useful to call their bluff. Hillary herself was "very suspicious," one source says. "She assumed they had ways around it planned. But she wanted at each step to appear reasonable."

The next morning the negotiations were due to start, in a suite at a Sheraton hotel about twenty blocks up Seventh Avenue from Clinton headquarters. The Lazio team had offered a specific written proposal about what the ban would cover. Its position was no soft money, period, from anyone, for anything—not even for mail or phone banks, although the latter in particular was traditionally financed by non-candidate money. The Clinton campaign wanted those union phone banks, at the very least. DeBlasio and Ann Lewis were dispatched to the hotel, where they met New York City Public Advocate Mark Green, the ex–Nader's Raider who had a long association with good-government initiatives. They represented, nominally, the "negotiating team," but DeBlasio and Lewis had left headquarters that Thursday morning with explicit instructions to tell the Lazio people that there would be no negotiations, and no ban.

Then, while they were in the car en route to the hotel, Hillary called. She'd changed her mind. She had concluded that not agreeing to a ban would be handing the Lazio team an issue. She told them to negotiate.

DeBlasio and Lewis weren't ready to reveal this last-minute change of plans publicly, so, at a press conference at the Sheraton, they stuck to the position that they weren't there to deal. DeBlasio called the Lazio proposal "a stunt to distract the voters" (clearly, Grunwald was winning the internal argument on the first day). Lewis remarked that she had "bought Swiss cheese that had fewer holes in it" than Lazio's proposal. From the Clinton team's perspective, the original Lazio proposal was not so clear-cut after all, containing exceptions for obscure categories of party-raised money and various escape clauses put forth by the fourteen groups. But, if DeBlasio and Lewis were saying there would be no deal, reporters on the scene wondered, why didn't they just leave the hotel after their press conference? Tish Durkin, in a blow-by-blow of the day's events in *The New York Observer*, noted that they retreated into a conference room until finally, some seven hours later, a press release emerged from the Clinton team saying "we look forward to continuing these negotiations."

For the time being, DeBlasio and Lewis had no choice but to stonewall and figure out what to do. Their marching orders had changed in midstream, but without explicit instructions about what, precisely, they should agree to. That night, DeBlasio got a letter and a written contract from Dal Col spelling out the Lazio team's proposed terms of agreement. The cover letter seemed to suggest that outside groups backing the Clinton campaign, such as the unions and the abortion-rights groups, would not be included in the ban. But the contract itself said Mrs. Clinton's outside groups would have to abide by the ban. DeBlasio, for whatever reason, emphasized the cover letter in a Thursday night conference call to his colleagues, without mentioning the language of the contract itself. And so Friday morning, Hillary told her people to accept a deal, but only with the understanding that the outside groups supporting her would not be covered by the ban.

At issue was one eighteen-word sentence in the cover letter that read: "We have dropped our precondition that you attain the signatures of the outside interest groups supporting your campaign." There was, it could be argued, a moral distinction to be made between the teachers' union and the Emergency Committee to Stop Hillary Rodham Clinton. In any case, the language clearly seemed to mean that the Clinton campaign could secure the official signed agreements from its outside groups after the deal itself was struck, not that the agreements were optional. But the Clinton campaign, in a move that reeked strongly of arguments over the definition of "is," had interpreted the phrase to its advantage. By Friday afternoon, the talks had collapsed over this question. Lazio, campaigning upstate, had announced early in the afternoon that there would be a deal. But an hour later, Hillary said there was no deal.

Who cared about all this? Not a single poll identified soft money as something of the remotest interest to voters. Even most reporters and columnists didn't care very much. For editorial writers, however, campaign finance reform is a hardy and indefatigable perennial. They love to inveigh on the evils of money in politics. They may tread with care on matters whose moral implications are ambiguous (that is, almost all matters). But where the public good is obvious—and what's more obvious than saying money in politics is bad?—editorial pages are free to unleash their full and mighty wrath.

The *Daily News* had started the day after the debate: SHE SHUDDA SIGNED IT, ran the headline. On September 19, the *News* applauded when Lazio told the paper's editorial board that he was disbanding one small political action committee and refunding its donations. On Thursday, September 21, the day after Lazio got the signed pledges, the *News* wrote that Hillary was "the Queen of Dirty Money" and that "Lazio has offered Clinton a map to the political high road. If she truly wants to clean up politics, she will take it." Three editorials in the space of a week meant that a newspaper was serious about something, perhaps serious enough to withhold its endorsement from a candidate on this ground alone.

But the bigger punch came from the *Times.* On consecutive days during the soft-money negotiations, the *Times* published two editorials that put enormous pressure on the Clinton campaign to strike a deal. The first, on Friday, September 22, concluded with the lines: "Voters are increasingly impatient with candidates who flout campaign finance laws. They may well punish the candidate who scuttles this deal." Anyone who knew how to deconstruct a *Times* editorial clearly understood that that "they" in the last sentence really meant "we," as in: We will not endorse you, Hillary, if you don't do this. It had been universally assumed that the *Times* would back Hillary. If she couldn't even get the state's flagship liberal paper, the effect on her campaign could be devastating. The *Times* was now suggesting that possibility. The next day, the *Times* published a story showing that many of Hillary's contributors had been overnight guests at the White House (specifically, the Lincoln Bedroom) or Camp David. Roughly one hundred of the four hundred overnight guests since her campaign began had been contributors. The Saturday editorial called the sleep-overs a "distasteful practice" and went on to warn again that her fund-raising practices were "the one thing that has marred her increasingly effective campaign." The language, like that of the day before, seemed to insinuate that her failure to do campaign finance their way could goad the paper into endorsing Lazio.

By Saturday night—after the second *Times* editorial, the sleep-overs story, and the chiding Hillary had taken in the papers for her campaign's interpretation of the language in the cover letter—the campaigns struck a deal. There would be no soft-money television or radio ads on either side by any outside group or committee. Other soft-money expenditures—such as those phone banks—would be all right. In the end, Hillary didn't have much of a choice. To refuse an agreement would hand Lazio an issue that he could ride straight through to election day. Polls may have indicated that most voters didn't know what soft money was, but a week's worth of intense news coverage—and, in the papers, the campaign would have been about nothing else—could change those polls. Lazio would be handed a chance to convert his worst moment, the march across the stage, into his best, taking a principled stand in favor of clean government. Whether it really was a principled stand was open to question. But Lazio would surely pitch it that way.

The editorial pages proclaimed a great triumph for the people. Time would cast doubt upon that proclamation. If the point of a soft-money ban is to eliminate the use of such lucre in politics, this ban did not accomplish that. If the point is to prevent sleazy, last-minute attacks by non-candidate committees, the ban didn't accomplish that either.

Both campaigns continued to take advantage of soft money. They simply used it for mailings (including attack pieces), get-out-the-vote operations, and other activities besides advertising. Top Clinton advisers maintain that the loss of soft money for advertising had only a minimal effect on their media plan. Grunwald says that it was always the campaign's plan to stop using soft money for advertising by October 1, because at that point television stations raise their rates for ads placed by non-candidate committees, whereas those same stations are obliged under federal election law to charge candidate committees their lowest rates. So the Clinton plan was to put the soft money to other uses anyway, and the ban cost the Clinton campaign perhaps $1 million, not the many millions some observers initially believed. And most of all, the ban certainly did not clean up the race. It would be violated—not in letter, but in spirit—by the state Republican Party in the campaign's last two weeks with a last-ditch campaign of telephone calls to voters that sent the race straight into the gutter.

Still, Lazio had finally won a round. Of course it would have been better for him if Mrs. Clinton had not agreed to the ban. That had been his campaign's secret hope; then Lazio could have pounded his "trust" issue home for the next six weeks. But the editorials had forced her to comply, and Lazio got, and deserved, the lion's share of the credit.

As much as the papers enjoyed their exercise of power, though, the deal didn't seem to be helping Lazio where it counted. A Quinnipiac poll released on September 27 gave Hillary a lead of 50 to 43 percent. She'd hit the magic 50 for the first time. A flurry of polls around the same time, with one exception, showed her with leads of 7 to 10 percentage points. Pollsters and observers also noticed that Hillary seemed to be gaining significant ground among women. The press was patting Lazio on the back for cleaning up politics. But voters, women voters especially, were less mindful of the issue itself than of the aggressive way in which he had raised it at the debate. Aggression, for this candidate who entered the race with the image of the inoffensive nice guy, would prove to be a problem as the race headed into the final lap.

CHAPTER 14

October and November 2000: The Homestretch

Never Trust an Expert

BY OCTOBER, the Clinton campaign sensed that it was making inroads in places where Democrats rarely met with success. Now, with five weeks to go, the campaign needed to make sure that progress would be converted into votes.

By the time field coordinator Gigi Georges had moved up to New York from Washington in May, a massive column of ten thousand New Yorkers had contacted the campaign to say they wanted to volunteer—calling voters, knocking on doors, stuffing envelopes. Throughout the summer and early fall, Georges and her staff made decisions on how to deploy these people and use the campaign's resources to best advantage. Those decisions were based partly on empirical evidence—voter rolls, turnout history—and partly on a hunch. "We could see when she went into a place like Watertown that something was going on," Georges says, referring to a small upstate city near Lake Ontario that normally voted Republican. "We had a feeling that there was an investment there that was paying off." If she thought the campaign had a decent chance to mine some votes in a county, Georges would place some people there, or open an office, so that citizens who had met Hillary on a rope line and raised an issue with her would have someone to follow up with.

October, Georges says, was "pull-the-trigger month": time for a disciplined effort to coordinate Hillary's appearances with follow-up from the campaign in the form of phone calls, canvassing, mailed literature, and the like, so that voters in areas that were likely to be strong for Hillary would receive a certain number of "touches" from the campaign. Voters who had a history of going to the polls and who were "touched" five or six times were far more likely to vote. The "touches" theory applied to all voters, but especially to African-Americans. Georges and Kevin Wardally put together a pull operation in the black community that Georges says used recent voting history to "target voters down to the household level."

There were many pieces of early conventional wisdom about this race that ended up being dead wrong: that Hillary was wasting her time upstate, which observers said until polls showed otherwise, or that she would never escape the shadow of scandal. But few of the expert observers' convictions were more firmly held than the belief, which developed after Giuliani dropped out of the running, that black voters would have "no motivation" to turn out. The general assessment of these experts (all of them white) was that, with Gore not campaigning in New York, and with Hillary concentrating on upstate whites and giving blacks "no reason" to vote for her, African-American voters would stay home. There was more than a whiff of condescension in this argument, as if black voters could make no sense of the stakes in an election unless a candidate whacked them over the head repeatedly with four or five well-worn buzzwords. Many of the experts who said this also never stopped to consider that they had said exactly the same thing in 1998, when black turnout was phenomenally high.

The appearance, as the race headed into its final weeks, was that Hillary was doing little to court the black vote. The reality was different. There was Georges's and Wardally's groundwork. There were the many appearances Hillary had made in black neighborhoods over the months. And there was the final push.

Every Sunday morning for the last six weeks of the campaign, Hillary spoke at anywhere from three to seven black churches. Sometimes starting as early as 7 A.M. and going until noon, Hillary worked the black churches to an extent that few white candidates in New York had in recent memory. She could not connect with black audiences in quite the way her husband could; establishing a bond that intense was beyond her oratorical capabilities. The important thing was the mere fact of her presence. Black voters understand when a white liberal is taking their support for granted. This had become an issue in the 1994 gubernatorial race. During that campaign, Calvin Butts, chief pastor of the Abyssinian Baptist Church, the most historically influential black church in New York—Adam Clayton Powell had been the pastor there—invited George Pataki to speak to his congregation. Butts was sending a signal to Mario Cuomo's campaign that it was not courting the black vote with the proper respect. Black turnout was low that year, and Cuomo lost narrowly. Hillary would not have known this anecdote, but Ickes and DeBlasio did, and they did not want their candidate to make the same mistake.

A black church was virtually the only environment in which Hillary could assume she would be almost universally adored. Upstate, she would typically be met by a small number of hecklers. If she spoke before Jewish groups or professional white women, one could always sense the unspoken disapproval of a portion of the audience. But at black churches, she was accepted without reservation, and so she managed to be far looser than usual. Her face was more animated, her smile less pasted on. She would stand next to the pastor as the choir belted out joyous numbers, swaying, clapping, losing the beat every now and again, then relocating it. When the choir finished, the pastor would step to the podium and make a few introductory remarks about "this very special lady in our presence today," as a pastor in Buffalo put it ("Yes!" parishioners would shout back, or "That's right!"), and Hillary would step to the podium.

Though she often mentioned specific issues like hate-crimes legislation and racial profiling, the real connection she sought to establish with churchgoers was emotional—a recognition that she and they were in the same army, doing battle against the same forces of darkness. She claimed that God was really on their side, no matter how often the dark forces invoked Him, by stressing the importance of prayer in her life: "You know, somebody asked me the other day"—sometimes it was "last month," other times "a couple of years ago"—"if I were a praying person. I said yes, I was. Then I said, 'But you know, even if I hadn't prayed before I got to the White House, I sure would have started praying then!' " Thunderous laughter always greeted that one. Her audience understood, without her having to say it outright, that she was talking about Newt Gingrich and Trent Lott and Ken Starr and everyone who had tried to delegitimize the administration. She invoked Harriet Tubman, who "could have stayed in the North and enjoyed her freedom, couldn't she?" ("Tell it!" "Look out!"), but who "went back down South, time after time, to free other slaves . . . And she told them, 'When you hear the dogs barking, don't turn around or look behind you . . . and when you hear the guns firing and the men shouting, don't stop, just keep going!' "

Reporters present at these speeches loved making sport of that "keep going." Indeed there was something about the way Hillary repeated the phrase and drew it out that captured the more didactic and puerile aspects of her earnestness. Hillary was always more persuasive when she tried to impress audiences with the intelligence that came far more naturally to her than displays of emotion. But black churches represented audiences so favorable to her that little persuasion was needed. (Although her first couple of audiences were shocked when, unusually for Hillary, she mixed up Harriet Tubman and the abolitionist Sojourner Truth.) One could hear ever so faintly, in that "keep going," an exhortation to her audiences to trust her to defend their interests—to forget her support for the death penalty and welfare reform, and the sacking of Lani Guinier, Hillary's old law-school friend whose nomination to head the Justice Department's civil rights division the president had withdrawn under pressure. And indeed, after the impeachment saga, all that had been forgotten and forgiven.

The experts would continue to insist, right up through the campaign's final weekend, that black voter turnout would be low. Most polls, for example, assumed that black voters would constitute about 8 or 9 percent of the statewide vote. It ended up being 11 percent—in raw numbers, at least 120,000 more black voters than anticipated. The increase was not an accident, and it was another reflection of just how well organized this once-haphazard campaign had become.

Trust Gets Fuzzier

On Sunday, October 1, as Hillary was dancing her way up the aisle at St. Luke African Methodist Episcopal Church at Amsterdam Avenue and 153rd Street, the previous month's space invaders were briefly reunited when Lazio appeared on Tim Russert's *Meet the Press.* The news accounts of the appearance led with Lazio's announcement that he supported the Food and Drug Administration's recent ruling allowing the marketing of RU-486, the abortion-inducing drug. Farther down in the stories came the following exchange apropos the first debate. "You don't think you were menacing or impolite?" Russert asked him. "I don't think so at all," he said.

Lazio was still proud of the soft-money ban, and still talking about it on the trail, taking credit for forcing the "Queen of Dirty Money" to clean up her act. He used the deal to defend his podium invasion, telling viewers of ABC's *This Week* that "if I didn't make that point as emphatically as I did, we wouldn't have an agreement right now. There's no doubt in my mind."

Reporters and other insiders did not really expect the ban to hold. Shortly after the agreement was made, Hillary announced that she would continue to raise soft money for other candidates when asked, offering one small piece of evidence that perhaps the Queen would break her pledge. The teachers' union still wanted to run television ads, and, according to one Clinton operative, had to be talked out of doing so at one point. On Lazio's side, there were the fourteen groups, although it was now looking like they'd stick to the agreement whether they'd intended to or not: Far short of the ballyhooed $32 million, thirteen of the groups had raised no money at all, and one, the Emergency Committee to Stop Hillary Rodham Clinton, had raised $1.9 million. So reporters were waiting for someone—in all probability, the distrusted Hillary—to cross the line.

But, lo and behold, it was the Lazio campaign that committed a foul. Clifford J. Levy, an investigative reporter for the *Times,* reported on Friday, October 6—not even two full weeks after the agreement—that the Lazio campaign appeared to have broken the ban. He had noticed, while watching a Lazio ad on television about the Congressman's work for disabled people, that the tag line at the end said: "Paid for by Lazio 2000/The Republican National Committee." The RNC? What was this about?

Technically, it was about a little-known provision of federal election law under which all candidates for federal office receive "coordinated contributions" from the parties' respective national committees to use however they wish. By tradition, these contributions—two cents per adult in the state or district, adjusted for inflation—are used for ads. In this race, the ceiling for such contributions amounted to about $1.85 million. The Lazio campaign had received, and spent, about $1.4 million of that. The Clinton campaign had not yet filed papers revealing whether it had received its disbursement from the Democratic National Committee, or, if it had, how the campaign had spent it.

After Levy's story broke, Lazio consultant Mike Murphy and campaign manager Bill Dal Col defended the use of the money for an ad and swore to reporters in an unusual and contentious conference call that Friday afternoon that both campaigns had agreed at the beginning of the negotiations that the "coordinateds" would not be subject to the ban. "I would sign an affidavit right now," Dal Col told the reporters, "and swear in a courtroom and take a lie detector test that we cleared it right in the beginning, and I dare Bill DeBlasio or Ann Lewis to do the same thing and say it wasn't discussed and approved." Neither DeBlasio nor Lewis answered this challenge. And there was no record to consult because the agreement was not put in writing; at the Clinton campaign's insistence, the original cover letter and contract from the Lazio team had given way to an oral agreement.

There were reasons to believe Dal Col, or at least to believe that the campaigns had innocently arrived at different understandings of how the money could be spent. After all, Murphy told reporters repeatedly during the conference call, why would our side put the tag line on television for everyone to see if we were trying to hide something? The problem was in how Dal Col had presented the ban to reporters when the agreement was reached. At the time, Dal Col said, "We've been absolutely clear about it. Nobody can spend outside dollars on this race. Period. The campaigns should raise and expend all dollars that are spent in this race." Once you tell reporters that, you don't sound very persuasive if twelve days later you say, oh, yes, there was this one exception that we forgot to mention. It also didn't help that the copy of the ad provided to the press, as is customary, did not mention the RNC in its tag line, because that earlier version of the ad had been paid for by Lazio 2000 alone.

Here, then, was an unusual circumstance: the press was giving Hillary the benefit of the doubt on a story having to do with campaign finance reform—a topic on which the Clinton White House had hardly been a role model. Lazio, at a campaign stop on Long Island at Hofstra University, defended the ad, as did John McCain and Governor Pataki, who were there with him. (Another, ultimately more pressing Lazio problem made itself apparent at that press conference, which took place in the parking lot outside the hall where the trio had just held a rally: reporters bombarded McCain with questions, while Lazio received just two queries.) Nevertheless, he returned the money to the RNC. The *Times* ran an editorial criticizing the appearance of the ad as a "boneheaded political play." The *Daily News,* interestingly, which had done more than any paper to push the ban, did not. The *Post* had not written a single editorial on the topic and did not jump in now. Apparently, the utility of soft money in politics was one subject on which Hillary Clinton and Rupert Murdoch agreed.

Lazio had handed Hillary a string of gifts, from his directionless summer to his behavior at the debate. But few presents were more welcome than this one. The congressman would find it hard now to make trust his central issue. His options were narrowing. But that very weekend, he had one more opportunity to define himself to a wider audience.

The Moment of Arrival

The second debate was scheduled for the following Sunday, October 8, at the studios of WCBS-TV in Manhattan. Lazio had come out of the first debate with two problems: First, many Republicans felt he had hurt himself terribly with upstaters by saying the economic picture there was improving, and second, as polls had begun to register, he had damaged his standing among women with the march across the stage. Heading into round two, he faced the challenge, his comment to Russert notwithstanding, of not coming across so harshly.

Hillary, paradoxically, faced an even bigger challenge. She had won the first debate largely because her opponent had looked so bad. The truth was that her performance had been fine, and nothing more, and that Lazio had acquitted himself well during the debate's calmer moments. So, if Lazio pulled no cheap stunts, and could keep himself from calling her a national embarrassment, she would have to win it without the benefit of his mistakes.

The moderator was WCBS correspondent Marcia Kramer, who in 1992 had asked Hillary's husband the question about his past marijuana use that produced the famous quote, "I didn't inhale." Lars-Erik Nelson of the *Daily News* was a panelist, as were CNN's Jeff Greenfield, the *Times*'s Joyce Purnick, and the *Post*'s Gregg Birnbaum. It was a Sunday morning, which meant the audience would be smaller than it had been for the first debate. Even so, the array of strong-willed and experienced panelists, and the mere fact that the debate was taking place in New York City, held out the promise of a few fireworks.

But there were no histrionics, and nothing dramatic happened. Kramer did ask Hillary about her marriage. She seemed annoyed, but almost bored, as she answered. "The choices that I've made in my life are right for me," she said. "I can't talk about anybody else's choices, I can only say that mine are rooted in my religious faith, in my strong sense of family, and in what I believe is right and important." Lazio, given a rebuttal opportunity, had the good sense to opine that "this was Mrs. Clinton's choice, and I respect whatever choice that she makes."

And she faced one discomfiting moment, when Birnbaum asked her about a resolution the United Nations Security Council had passed the previous night condemning Israel's use of force against Palestinians. The United States—the Clinton administration—had abstained, arguing that taking sides would weaken its status as the broker of the peace. Lazio had immediately released a statement condemning the abstention and proclaiming his loyalty to Israel. Hillary's campaign had not issued a statement yet. She said in the debate, some twelve hours after the resolution passed, that she opposed the abstention. It was pandering, but pandering of the sort that anyone who wants to be taken seriously as a candidate in New York has to do.

Outside of that, the debate was her moment of arrival as a fluent politician. It wasn't any position she took; they were the same as always. It was that she had metamorphosed—so gradually, it seemed, that until now we hadn't noticed—from someone who was trying really hard to do this right to someone who was just casually doing it right. In the first debate, she had been tight, and some of her rehearsed lines were contrived. She had used the word "chutzpah," which is not a word a Midwestern Methodist should be tossing around, even in Buffalo. This time, her set pieces were well delivered. Early on, she turned calmly to Lazio and said, "And I do want, Mr. Lazio, to put your mind at ease, in case you've been worrying. I won't be coming to your podium today." When Marcia Kramer asked her to define a New Yorker—a terrific question, and one that would have made her freeze a few months ago—she smiled, invoking *New Yorker* writer E. B. White and talking about New York's history of welcoming immigrants, "including immigrants from Washington, D.C." In her closing statement, she made an effective parry against Hillary-hating that steered clear of solipsism or self-pity and framed the race—with the kind of sound bite that had largely eluded her—exactly the way she wanted it to be framed. Invoking a Lazio fund-raising letter that urged people to donate to him on the basis of only "six words: I'm running against Hillary Rodham Clinton," she said that "New Yorkers deserve more than that. How about seven words? How about jobs, education, health, Social Security, environment, choice?" This language, scripted by Penn and Wolfson during one of the prep sessions (fewer in number and less pressure-packed this time), entered her lexicon that day and never left.

From a press perspective, the debate was a draw—no "knockout punches," or any of those other debate clichés. But by the more subtle and subjective criteria that newspapers are poorly outfitted to describe, she was the one who looked more like a senator. Lazio had not berated her, but this time she did not need the sympathy of women. She had even given, at least for the more bookish viewers, a better definition than Lazio did of what a New Yorker was. In the spin room afterwards, the governor mocked her invocation of E. B. White. "Rick Lazio looks, sounds, and talks like a New Yorker," Pataki said. "Mrs. Clinton quoted some guy, Wyatt or somebody—I don't think he was from Brooklyn—with some definition of a New Yorker somewhere. I don't know who that guy was. I don't know where he was from. But it sure doesn't sound to me like that guy was a New Yorker or understood New York the way we do." Pataki was clearly quite pleased with himself, thinking he was scoring easy points against the egghead liberal, as if she had mentioned a post-structuralist philosopher or some exotic bird. Reporters did not bother to contain their laughter. When Lazio approached the podium a few moments later, Rachel Donadio of *The Forward* asked the congressman if he knew who E. B. White was. He looked puzzled for a moment and then identified him as the author of *Charlotte's Web*.

E. B. White did indeed write that children's classic, but more than that, he is among the most revered of *The New Yorker*'s legendary writers. His classic essay, "Here Is New York," published in 1948, is one of the seminal texts on New Yorker-ness. That only the outlander knew him as such, and knew his famous essay, stood as an amusing symbol of the direction in which things were heading as Hillary prepared for the final run against her second-string opponent. As White put it in the essay in question, "No one should come to New York to live unless he is willing to be lucky."

But What Happened to the Billing Records?

There was still too much anti-Hillary sentiment for anyone to conclude that she was pulling away. Nevertheless both the polls and one's nose suggested that Hillary had built a small but solid lead. All the city dailies, at different points in October, ran stories with blind quotes from Republicans fretting over the state of the Lazio campaign. The most conspicuous appeared in the *Times* on Monday, October 16. The article quoted Republicans on a point that nearly everyone, finally, had come to accept: Lazio had squandered his summer, failing to use it to bolster his campaign's ties to the upstate local Republican organizations, and failing to define himself positively to voters. It also quoted other Republicans as saying that it was too late for Lazio to do either of those things now, and that his only choice at this point was to attack Hillary with even more vitriol. Mike Murphy was having none of the second-guessing: "There's only one Republican Senate candidate in America who's gained thirty points in the last hundred days, and that is Rick Lazio. These mystery whiners should help Rick Lazio instead of carping from their armchairs."

Lazio had tried to drive up her negatives with the trust issue, and in the campaign's final weeks, he would turn to other issues as well. But there was one issue that Lazio did not try directly to exploit. Neither had Rudy Giuliani, when he was the candidate. It seemed strange, but it was a fact: Scarcely a word had been uttered—not even, except during the race's very early days, by her opponents in the press—about all the scandals that had surrounded Hillary during her time in Washington. Where were the billing records? Where was Whitewater? Where was the White House travel office scandal? And where was the commodities investment? Before the Listening Tour began, Jack Newfield had been quoted in the *Times* as saying that "she's going to be sitting in Katz's delicatessen with her mouth full of knish, and thirty guys are going to be yelling at her to explain the $100,000 profit she made in the commodity trade in Arkansas." That hadn't been an unreasonable guess at the time. But excepting a few scattered mentions in the papers, the words "commodity futures" were barely spoken, and even Whitewater made only spotty appearances. Monica and the marriage at least hovered in the corner of the room. These other arguably more substantive matters hadn't even shown up for the party.

As with the Lewinsky scandal, the Hillary-corruption story was of greater concern to the Washington media than to the New York press, which felt generally that the scandals were old news, unless of course their Washington bureaus turned up a smoking gun, at which point the New York reporters would have pursued the matter. Instead the New York press sought to develop new variations on the theme. The sleepover story had been one such variation. Even though the *Times* had broken it, the *Daily News* was most obsessed with the story, continuing to press Hillary to release the dates on which the various guests had stayed at the White House, which she refused to do—presumably knowing that the paper would then match the dates of their stays to the dates of their contributions. Another variation arrived on October 13, again in the *Times*. Cliff Levy reported that Hillary's campaign had sent solicitations for contributions to some 1,400 people whose names had been pulled off White House visitor lists. White House invitation lists are considered government property and are not to be put to political purposes. Here were the Clintons once again using the public's property for their own political ends.

A few months before, the story might have exploded. But now, with the war room in place, the Clinton campaign was dealing with such crises far more efficiently and directly. Wolfson said initially that

Hillary had been going over two lists at the same time, the official visitors list and a separate list of contributors, and had inadvertently mixed the two up. Fearful that this first-day response sounded like more Clintonian excuse-making, he and other top advisers got together and urged Hillary to act immediately to stop the story's momentum. This time, instead of saying little and giving the appearance that she was hiding something, Hillary, while campaigning in Buffalo, said a lot. The solicitation letter, which was signed by the president, had gone out by mistake. There were journalists on the list; if she'd been trying to do something sneaky, she said, why would she have sent the letter to reporters? At any rate, the campaign took in only $225 from the letter, and all the money was being returned. "I take full responsibility for it," she added, which was a sentence reporters were not accustomed to hearing Hillary Clinton say. Lazio, going a little over the top for one trained in the law, called it "illegal" and suggested that Hillary should be prosecuted.

The new variations were causing only minor stirs. But in Washington, the original theme was still being developed by independent counsel Robert Ray. Every so often over the spring and summer, Ray would put out a press release saying he expected to finalize his findings on one scandal or the other in the coming months, hinting with a word or phrase at the rottenness that he would soon expose. Each of these blasts would set off a quick spurt of punditizing about the trouble lurking ahead, after which the scandal-ridden Washington Hillary would go back into hibernation. Then, in late September, there was one piece of actual news. On September 20—the same day Lazio announced that he had secured no-soft-money agreements from the fourteen groups—Ray announced the end of his Whitewater investigation, saying that his "evidence was insufficient to prove" that either Clinton had committed a crime. Some Republicans seized on the language, saying that it really meant Hillary was guilty, even though Ray couldn't prove it. Democrats declared the matter at rest. (The political world universally assumed that Ray couldn't possibly be as partisan as his predecessor, Kenneth Starr. But Ray had a history in New York that raised flags in the minds of those few who knew about it. In the early 1980s, Giuliani had hired him as an assistant United States attorney, and in the early 1990s, when he lived in Brooklyn, he had run for a seat on a school board on a slate of candidates endorsed by the Christian Coalition.)

What with the soft-money ban and the question of the White House sleepovers, Ray's exculpatory conclusion on Whitewater had trouble elbowing its way into the news cycle. On October 18, though, he landed a bigger punch, on the White House travel office firings. The travel office represented the last, best hope of the Clinton haters. They had watched, by this time, as Ray had concluded that the Filegate story was exactly what the White House maintained it was, a bureaucratic mix-up that had occurred at the lower staff levels. They had watched as the Whitewater story dissolved into the murk of the unprovable. But here, surely, was the opponent's Achilles heel. David Watkins, a White House aide at the time, had written in a 1993 memorandum that Hillary had complained extensively about the seven travel-office employees the administration inherited and had told him, "We need our people in there." Hillary had denied, during sworn testimony, that she explicitly directed Watkins to fire anyone. Maybe, finally, the cork would pop off the bottle of Hillary scandal.

Ray's 243-page report affirmed the preliminary conclusion that he had announced in June: Though he believed that Mrs. Clinton had played a more extensive role in the firings than she'd acknowledged, his evidence against her was insufficient to warrant prosecution. The report did, however, add a few new layers of detail to the story. He noted that Hillary had given "factually false" statements to a grand jury. Those statements did not rise to the level of a prosecutable offense, but the words "factually false" were new, as were some details of her testimony. In accordance with provisions of the independent-counsel statute, Hillary, as a subject of the probe, had had an opportunity to review the report before its release, so she knew what the gist of its conclusions would be. Nevertheless, a source says, she had been "very worried" about when in the election cycle the report might appear and how the papers would play it. When it hit, she held a news conference in Syracuse, where she delivered one of those clipped and baleful one-sentence answers that she always gave when confronted with a topic she preferred not to face: She had said back in June that she was "glad it was over after all these years and millions of dollars. I really have nothing to add to that."

The saga of the Clinton scandals had exposed sharp divides in the culture—among political leaders, who generally attacked or defended the Clintons along partisan lines, and among ordinary citizens, who communicated with their like-minded brethren through partisan Web sites and chat rooms. But it had also exposed a divide among the nation's leading journalists. There were those who tended to accept Ken Starr's view of the world: Susan Schmidt of *The Washington Post;* Stuart Taylor, Jr., who had written the sympathetic reexamination of the Paula Jones case in *The American Lawyer;* Michael Isikoff of *Newsweek,* who had been the first to make contact with Lucianne Goldberg and Linda Tripp, and most of the talking heads. And there were those who argued that the scandals were largely trumped up or that Starr's prosecution of them had violated basic tenets of American jurisprudence—Joe Conason of *The New York Observer,* Gene Lyons of *The Arkansas Democrat-Gazette,* Anthony Lewis of *The New York Times.* In Washington, those in the latter category were vastly outnumbered (indeed, none of the three journalists I just cited is based there).

The play of the story in the October 19 papers provided a fascinating glimpse into this journalistic divide. The *Daily News* gave the story to Joel Siegel and William Goldschlag, its two New York–based correspondents on the race. The paper gave the story semiprominent play, on page 6. The story led with Ray's "factually false" construction, but it quickly moved on to say that Ray conceded that "she might have been unaware that" her conversations with staffers had "played a role in the firings." The story then shifted gears entirely, its second half taken up by a discussion of whether Hillary would attend a World Series game. The *Post* story was handled by one of its Washington reporters, Brian Blomquist. Still, the *Post* found nothing new of interest in the report and veritably yawned at it. The paper ran the story on page 10, and, after quickly summarizing Ray's findings, said, "That much was known four months ago, when Ray wrapped up the probe." Other papers around the state gave the story similar play—a few new details, but a foregone conclusion.

At the *Times,* the story was handled by Neil A. Lewis, who was in the paper's Washington bureau and had been one of its chief reporters on the Whitewater matter. The tone of Lewis's story was far more excited than that of the other New York papers. It said the report "added several details" to what had been known, and noted that the report had demonstrated "for the first time" that some of Mrs. Clinton's statements were "demonstrably false." The *Times* put the story on its front page, a decision that guaranteed it would get extensive television and radio pickup in a way that would not have happened if the story had been relegated to an inside page. Lewis's was the first of three front-page stories generated out of the paper's Washington bureau that affected the race over the next week. The second, by Robert Pear, covered the well-worn ground of the failed health-care plan without adding new detail. (It appeared the same day the Lazio camp leaked word that Lazio was about to launch a major offensive against Mrs. Clinton over her 1994 plan.) The third, also by Pear, told the story of how President Clinton had signed a breast-cancer bill privately rather than publicly, because Lazio had been a sponsor of the legislation. The *Times*'s Washington bureau seemed to be making some kind of statement on the race, and on the candidate who had managed to get out of town before the bailiffs got her scent.

Still, the collective impact of the stories was not dramatic. In New York there were other things to worry about. The aforementioned World Series, which for the first time in forty-four years would be contested by two New York teams, was chief among them. There was at least a semiserious debate within Hillary's camp about whether she should attend a game. She had even turned uncharacteristically gutsy as the Subway Series approached, declaring herself, "as you all know," a Yankees fan—by now, the declaration elicited no mad torrent of editorial broadsides against her—and coyly challenging Mets fan Lazio to a bet. In the end, her advisers decided the inevitable boos were not worth the price of trying to show that she had some moxie.

Not Whitewater, and Not Even Health Care

Lazio's offensive on health care promised more trouble for Hillary than Robert Ray had delivered. On Sunday, October 22, Mike Murphy unveiled a series of strong radio spots that ran in some twenty different cities and towns all over upstate New York. The ads followed the same script, saying that Hillary's 1994 plan would have cut 72,000 jobs in New York. Each one mentioned the local teaching hospital that would have been hurt by her plan.

Throughout the campaign, Hillary had never truly been called to account on the aspect of the plan that would have hurt New York's teaching hospitals. She danced around it when Russert asked the question during the first debate, and, when asked about it on the campaign trail, she said reflexively and curtly that she had learned her lesson and was now a believer in "the school of smaller steps." Lazio and Murphy were trying to force her, finally, to answer the question. But they had left her an escape hatch. Lazio had never proposed a health-care plan of his own during the campaign, so Hillary was able to say that her opponent may have wanted to talk about the past, "but I want to talk about the future," at which point she would retail her prescription-drug plan and her proposal for expanding health care to poor children. And the Clinton campaign responded to the radio ad campaign quickly—within a day, Grunwald had answering radio ads up in every market arguing that Gingrich budget cuts that Lazio supported had cost the hospitals untold millions.

Again, Lazio's lack of specific proposals hurt him. If he'd had such a plan, Hillary's tit-for-tat answer would not have sufficed. The problem was captured nicely by an upstate Republican county leader. Murphy had just unveiled an ad in which an interviewer went around to tailgating Buffalo Bills fans and asked them to name three things Hillary had done for New York. It was effective since, naturally, no one could name a single thing. Several Republican leaders, one operative says, were discussing the ad in a conference call. One chuckled and said what a great ad it was. "Then there was kind of an awkward pause," this source says, "and finally, one of them says, 'Gee, I hope nobody asks me to name three things Rick has done.'" Hillary never did have to answer the health-care question.

One would have thought, then, that Lazio might unveil a health-care plan during health-care attack week. That Wednesday, he *did* give a major policy address, only his third of the campaign, in Syracuse, on the subject of . . . foreign relations. Mostly a swipe at the Clinton administration's "eight years of foreign policy by spin control," it suffered by comparison to an appearance Hillary had made on October 17 in Manhattan before the Council on Foreign Relations, at which she laid out her ideas about a foreign policy that was more interventionist and human-rights oriented, and spoke with casual expertise about which language in which specific clauses of the land-mine treaty gave her pause. Lazio did not lend himself much gravitas, in his speech, when he looked down at his notes and, seeing the name of North Korean leader Kim Jong Il, spoke of "Kim Jong the Second."

So things stood, two weeks before election day. Inside the Clinton campaign, the feeling was one of cautious optimism, tempered by the knowledge that much can happen in a campaign's final fortnight. Hillary had a seven- or eight-point lead in the polls. Women had rallied to her. Her upstate numbers were strong, her suburban numbers respectable. The *Times,* its enthusiasm for Robert Ray notwithstanding, endorsed her on Sunday, October 22. The editorial was not exactly unstinting in its praise, and its compliments were delivered very much with the back of its hand ("We believe . . . Mrs. Clinton is capable of growing beyond the ethical legacies of Arkansas and White House years"). Lazio's health-care assault had not amounted to much, and it was even clear by now that Whitewater and the various scandals, large and small, of her career would not be the fulcrum on which her New York fortunes would turn.

One issue, however, would be. It was the issue that sat at the epicenter of New York politics. It was the issue on which, from a New York point of view, her baggage was heaviest and most cumbersome. In retrospect, it should have been easy to predict that everything else— carpetbaggerism, scandal, the marriage—would be tossed aside, and it would all come down to this.

Finally, Israel

In the 1988 presidential primary season, Al Gore had literally not even set foot in New York—he was flying to the state later that day to begin his New York campaigning—before he announced that America should move its embassy in Israel to Jerusalem. Also that year, Ed Koch declared that Jews "would have to be crazy" to vote for Jesse Jackson. In 1993, when he wrested the mayoralty from David Dinkins, Rudy Giuliani spent days on end in the Orthodox Jewish communities of

Brooklyn, assuring this crucial constituency—which tended to vote *en bloc* as per the rebbe's instructions—that no rampaging black youths would be killing any Hasidic scholars when he was mayor, a reference to the murder of Yankel Rosenbaum in Crown Heights in 1991. In 1998, when Al D'Amato faced Chuck Schumer, he pointed to a vote on Holocaust commemoration that Schumer had missed as evidence that Schumer was soft on Israel. So New York elections go.

That Hillary would face special trouble on this front was always clear. Candidates who want to win elections in New York do not normally urge the creation of a Palestinian state, as Hillary had in 1998. Many, if not most, New York Jews support the peace process and, in logical progression, an eventual Palestinian state. But that's hardly what matters. Liberal, peacenik Jews do not control the debate on the question. The *Post* and the more vocal Orthodox communities do. Little room is left for nuance. A New York senator is not supposed to offer calibrated exegeses on the tangled history of competing Middle East land claims, or allow that maybe the Arabs have a point about the 1982 bombing of Sabra and Shatila. A New York senator is supposed to say one thing: Israel first, Israel always.

Ever since the "Jew bastard" flap, Hillary seemed to have begun to get this. Starting in late September, her campaign took care to place her alongside prominent Jewish leaders. She finally had a joint appearance with Joe Lieberman at a public school in Coney Island on September 15, where he praised her character and vouched for her on Israel. (The Clinton team was filming as Lieberman spoke, but the Board of Education maintains a strict rule that nothing that happens in a school can be used for political purposes, so the footage remained in the vaults.) Elie Wiesel, the Nobel Prize-winning author, had endorsed her on September 25 at Hunter College on the Upper East Side, where they jointly denounced Palestinian textbooks. Former treasury secretary Robert Rubin appeared at her side shortly thereafter. On Thursday, October 6, she appeared at a forum sponsored by the *Jewish Week* newspaper and held at an East Side synagogue, where she acknowledged for the first time that visiting Suha Arafat was a mistake in the first place. The night before that event, one source told me, Hillary and several advisers were on a conference call preparing for the event. When the conversation turned to how to handle the Suha question, it was Hillary who said, "I think I'll just say I was wrong."

It seemed, for a while, that Hillary just might skate through to election day without having to face another Jewish crisis. Her poll numbers among Jews were going up as the temperature went down. Hillary and key staff people were meeting quietly with individual Jewish leaders of all denominations—Reform, Conservative, and Orthodox. Ann Lewis, Bill DeBlasio, and Matthew Hiltzik met privately with Dov Hikind twice during the fall. Hillary met him privately, one last time, on Monday night, October 30. It was just the two of them in a room, with no aides. Hillary emerged from the room saying to aides waiting outside that Hikind had asked her for a commitment she couldn't make. She didn't say what it was, but surely it was that she press for Jonathan Pollard's release. She would not get Hikind's endorsement, but neither would Lazio. Coordinating their efforts with Lewis and Hiltzik, leading Jewish Democratic politicians—most notably Assembly Speaker Sheldon Silver, but also connected party operatives like George Arzt—had successfully intervened with other Jewish elected officials and prominent rabbis, urging them at least to stay neutral, even if they could not bring themselves to endorse her.

More generally, the race, in mid-October, again hit one of its periodic walls. Things were fairly quiet. Robert Ray was not going to get New Yorkers' juices flowing, and Lazio, try as he might, could do nothing to shrink the small but by now very steady lead that Hillary had held for weeks. Mark Penn and Bill Clinton had a conversation around this time, in which the president asked Penn not whether Hillary would win, but by how much. Penn said five points. The president said it looked to him more like eight or nine. (After the election, the president relayed this conversation to his cabinet, declaring the numerical impasse "the only time I've ever disagreed with Mark.") Hillary just needed, for the final two weeks, to play ball control.

Then, on Wednesday, October 25, thirteen days out: fumble.

Under the headline ISRAEL FOES GIVE HIL 50G, the *Daily News* reported that Hillary had raised $50,000 at a fund-raiser in Boston in June sponsored by a group called the American Muslim Alliance. The AMA's leader, the *News* said, "backs the Palestinians' right to use 'armed force' against Israel." It also said that another Arab-American, Abdurahman Alamoudi, who was affiliated with a group called the American Muslim Council, had made a $1,000 contribution to the Clinton campaign in May. Alamoudi had been invited to White House receptions honoring Muslim holidays, and had boasted, the article charged, that "we are the ones who went to the White House and defended what is called Hamas." Finally, the article—most unfortunately, from the Clinton team's perspective—quoted Tahir Ali, the chairman of the Massachusetts chapter of the AMA, as saying the following apropos Hillary's newly buffed fealty to Israel: "The idea is to win the election. She must change her tune. But that doesn't mean anything. It's just at the spur of the moment that she must say these things, and we understand that."

It would emerge over the next couple of days, mostly through the reporting of the *Times*'s Dean E. Murphy, who had replaced Adam Nagourney on the Hillary trail, that these men hardly spent their lives marching through the streets waving scimitars and praising Allah. Tahir Ali was a software engineer. Yahya Mossa-Basha, the Michigan-based president of the American Muslim Council, was a radiologist. Agha Saeed, the president of the American Muslim Alliance, was a political-science professor at the University of California, Berkeley. Faroque Khan, the chairman of the American Muslim Alliance's New York chapter, was a Lexus-driving doctor who lived in Rick Lazio's congressional district and had contributed to his campaigns. But none of this mattered as much as their surnames. And the fact that some of them had made statements that stated the Palestinian case forcefully, sometimes suggesting that armed struggle against Israel was appropriate. Alamoudi in particular would become the focus of much controversy, and the star of one of Mike Murphy's last commercials.

The New York political establishment can be slow to evolve, like one of those creatures that roam the sea bed and have undergone no genetic change in six thousand years. The three I's—Israel, Italy, and Ireland—have long made up the New York establishment's core DNA. Slowly the establishment admitted blacks, and then Latinos. But for Arab-Americans, New York was a uniquely hostile environment. The idea that they might be trying to exercise legitimate political influence was one that most people could not—or would not—grasp. Least of all in support of Hillary Clinton.

The same day the *Daily News* story hit, Hillary was scheduled to hold a press availability on a nondescript street corner in Queens. She was to appear with officials of the building-trades unions to argue that Lazio's contributions from home builders' groups had compromised his integrity on housing issues. Some of Hillary's advisers hoped that the story could blunt the impact of what came to be called in shorthand "the AMA thing." Wolfson informed them otherwise. "Uh, I hate to tell you, but I kind of doubt housing will be the issue of the day," he told his colleagues. Wolfson was impervious to crisis; it was a quality Hillary evidently admired, since Wolfson's influence with her grew and grew over the course of the campaign, and it was a quality she shared. "It was never panic with her," says one aide. "It was always, 'Okay, let's figure out how to deal with this one.' " This aide remembers that on the morning of that press conference the Clinton motorcade was on its way to Queens from her endorsement interview with *Newsday*'s editorial board on Long Island. The motorcade neared the site, but the aide got a call from someone saying that the podium had not yet arrived. The motorcade had to pull over a few blocks away and wait for fifteen minutes. As she faced what promised to be the most important press conference of her campaign, Hillary "just sat there and read the paper."

The press conference was beyond strange. She said, right off the bat, that she was returning the entire $50,000 she had raised in Boston, and the $1,000 from Alamoudi. (The day before, Wolfson and other aides had urged her to do this.) She then, under questioning, went into a lengthy and somewhat convoluted discussion of the Boston fundraiser itself. As far as her campaign knew, she said, the event had been sponsored by two Arab-American businessmen. She'd never heard of the American Muslim Alliance. The group was now claiming that it had taken over sponsorship of the event a week before it took place. Hillary claimed her campaign never knew that. But, reporters interjected, you received a plaque at the event inscribed "American Muslim Alliance." And you posed for a picture with your hosts, holding the plaque up (the picture had appeared in the *News*). "You know, I get handed thousands of plaques," she said; she confessed that she'd long since quit looking at them.

Present at the press conference was one Steve Emerson, a conservative freelance journalist who specialized in the study of terrorist organizations, and who had fed the *Daily News* most of its information. Here, on a street corner with eyesore-ish aluminum-sided single-family homes and attached houses, which recalled the opening credits of *All in the Family,* with a few confused and eavesdropping local residents sprinkled in, Emerson passed out what he called firm documentation of terrorist sympathizers who had been invited to the White House during the Clinton years. He held his own counter-press conference after Hillary finished.

And most bizarrely: the international press was a constant on Hillary's campaign. Always, wherever she went, even in the humblest upstate burg, there was one British or French journalist, or one Japanese television crew. This day it was a German television crew. With New York reporters heatedly pressing her about the donations, and about why she didn't look at her plaques, and how *that* should make all those plaque-givers feel, the German correspondent got his question in. Mrs. Clinton, for zuh German television, can you say, campaigning with the president, has it brought you closer together? Her press aides generally turned up their noses at the foreign press. If your readers or viewers or listeners weren't in New York, the Clinton people had less than no use for you. This one day, at least, they must have appreciated it.

Lazio, meanwhile, was in Westchester County and the Bronx, and all eyes were fixed on him for his reaction. It is a rule of thumb in politics that, if your opponent is being scorched in the papers, you hang back and just let the papers do the scorching. Hillary had observed this rule religiously during Rudy's Time of Troubles. Would Lazio do the same? The night before the AMA story broke, when the Clinton people knew it was coming, Bill DeBlasio and Harold Ickes called around to local operatives like George Arzt and John LoCicero, Harold's old and close friend, for ideas about damage control. Arzt recalls his conversation with DeBlasio. "I told him, 'Hey, you got nothing to worry about,' " Arzt says. " 'Why?' 'Because they're going to overdo it, hold a press conference, and say something stupid instead of just ripping it out of the paper and mailing it to everyone in the state.' " And sure enough, Lazio, speaking in the Bronx, called the donations "blood money." This phrase, like the "blood libel" charge tossed at Hillary after she kissed Suha Arafat, has a deeply resonant and particular meaning among Jews; in Israeli politics, these are the worst things you can say about someone. Clearly, he was going to push the issue hard.

The Clinton war room quickly lined up Ed Koch, Mark Green, and Ray Harding, the Liberal Party chairman who had endorsed Hillary after Giuliani left the race by invoking the great names of Wagner and Lehman and Kennedy and Javits, to hold a press conference.

Harding had been mostly silent since that June endorsement. Now he roared back into the picture, appearing on New York 1 that night and giving as forceful a performance as he had ever given, even including those on behalf of his great friend, the mayor. "Now all of a sudden that group claims, after Hillary Clinton has been saying strong pro-Israeli things, that they were the hosts. . . . What I say is there is a conspiracy at hand by these groups to bring Hillary Clinton down!" he thundered. It may or may not have been that. But whatever it was, it was just getting started.

The Gaffe of the Campaign

By Friday, October 27, the story was dying down a little. We were into "reax" pieces—how Muslims felt being tossed about on the mad sea of New York politics. The day after Hillary was in Queens dealing with her plaque problem, she received the endorsement of the *Forward,* probably the city's leading Jewish newspaper. She also turned 53 that Thursday, an occasion commemorated by, what else, a fund-raiser, at Manhattan's Roseland Ballroom, featuring Robert De Niro, Nathan Lane, Cher, Tom Cruise, Cameron Diaz, the president, and Chelsea. The Clinton campaign released a television ad featuring Nita Lowey, the Westchester congresswoman who had bowed out when Hillary decided to seek the nomination, vouching for the first lady's record of accomplishments. A New York 1 poll showed her ahead among white women, 49 to 44 percent. As one read the papers that Friday morning, one could be forgiven for thinking that the AMA thing was floating away.

That afternoon, Lazio did his best to keep it alive, returning at several points to Hillary's supposed link to terrorists at the third and final debate, moderated by WNBC veteran Gabe Pressman and held in the studios of *Saturday Night Live.* The location was perhaps fitting, because the debate was memorable mostly as comic relief—at one point, when Pressman asked the combatants to say three nice things about each other, Hillary averred that Lazio had a nice family, worked very hard, "and, um, you know, he's an attractive young man." There was also, one source says, an amusing moment leading up to the debate,

during one of Hillary's prep sessions. The president, again, was inter-
rupting and telling her how to answer. But this time, instead of shrink-
ing, Hillary cut him off: "No, Bill, that's not the way we do it in New
York."

That Saturday morning, Hillary was beginning her last lengthy
upstate swing. She had continued to run ads heavily upstate, including
a widely praised one that used an image of an ostrich as a way of telling
voters that, when it came to upstate economic woes, Lazio had his head
in the sand. (The ad was the creation of Ellis Verdi; finally, he got his
shot of humor in the race!) Apart from the ads, though, Hillary had
been concentrating her efforts on the suburbs and the city for the previous two or three weeks. Meanwhile, Lazio, finally acceding to the demands of nervous GOPers, had devoted almost all of his time to
upstate. He had launched, in mid-October, a series of fund-raising
lunches and dinners whose gustatory rubrics—"Rigatoni with Rick,"
"Lasagna with Lazio"—conveyed both the right timbre of folksiness
sought by the man challenging a candidate who could snare the likes of
Robert De Niro on a moment's notice, and the candidate's Catholic
roots. Gigi Georges and Hillary's other top advisers decided that the
upstaters were in need of one more "touch."

She started on Saturday, October 28, in Ithaca. She flew up from
the city in the company of the actor Ben Affleck, who was to appear
with her at a rally at Cornell that afternoon. She was also armed with
copies of *The New York Times* and the *New York Post,* which were offering competing versions of a very interesting story. In the *Times,* Cliff
Levy was reporting that the state Republican committee was conducting a telephone campaign to Jewish voters in which the callers asked
questions like, "Did you know that Hillary Rodham Clinton had been
a supporter of a Palestinian state before she decided to run for Senate?"
The line of questioning rang alarm bells in the mind of a Manhattan
man Levy interviewed, who asked to speak to a supervisor, who "eventually disclosed that the call was being paid for by the Republican State
Committee." In the *Post,* Gregg Birnbaum had an even more explosive
version. Birnbaum had a script, "provided by GOP sources," saying
that Hillary had accepted money from an Arab organization that
"openly brags about its support for a Mideast terrorism group, the
same kind of terrorism that killed our sailors on the USS *Cole.*" The
Cole had been sunk on October 12 by a terrorist bomb in the Red Sea

port of Aden, Yemen, killing seventeen Americans. The script urged recipients of the calls to phone Hillary "and tell her to stop supporting terrorism and give the money back." Hillary had many "firsts" as a first lady. She was surely the first to stand accused of supporting terrorism.

The calls had started Thursday, the day after the *Daily News* story broke, and were intended to go to 500,000 voters. The Lazio camp, one source says, had sensed the race slipping away the previous week and had asked the state Republicans to do something. The calls are what they did. The state GOP was initially quite pleased with its efforts. But once the story broke, especially the part about the mention of the USS *Cole,* Lazio and the Republicans were put on the defensive, and Hillary wasted no time in playing offense. Shortly after she landed in Ithaca, in one of those side buildings common to small airports, Hillary met us in a small room at 10:48 A.M. and let go. She was quiet and controlled, and suffering from a terrible cold, but she was letting more emotion show through, and using more direct language, than was her custom. "They have stooped to a level I never thought we'd see," she said. "I just really never thought I would see this kind of tactic used. This hits a new low."

At Cornell, Hillary introduced the *Cole* calls into her speech to about fifteen hundred students scattered across a sloping lawn. She had attended the memorial service in Norfolk, Virginia, she said, and had talked with the dead sailors' families, who "represented every shade of skin color, every texture of hair"; she linked their deaths to vigilance on liberty's behalf and to the obligation of everyone to vote. Later that Saturday, at a feed store in Elmira, where mountains of pumpkins were arranged in various displays, Chuck Schumer materialized, as if rising out of the pumpkin patch. For a year or more, the political class had sniggered about Schumer's real feelings regarding Hillary's candidacy. Hillary's election would make him New York's second-best-known senator by some distance, and Chuck had never been exactly shy about publicity (once, in the 1970s, when he was a young, unknown assemblyman, he was mugged, and somehow or another it made the *Times*). But he joined her side that Saturday, ten days before the election, and never left it. He, too, denounced the *Cole* calls, saying, "No, it doesn't work, it backfires, and thank God it does."

Hillary was succeeding in making the calls, not the fund-raiser itself, the issue—most political observers agreed that the mention of the *Cole* crossed a line. But it was not yet clear, that weekend, that the calls would backfire. After all, the AMA story had begun to die down on Friday; the calls kept it alive. Hillary's constant mention of them kept Lazio on the defensive, but it also kept alive mentions in the press of Hillary and the $50,000. Republicans sensed this; far from backing down, they continued to push the issue. The same Saturday that Hillary was talking about "a new low," Lazio, while making it clear that the calls were not being made by his campaign, asserted that they were fair. And Bill Powers, the state GOP chairman, said the language about the *Cole* was absolutely in bounds. Her association with Hamas, GOP spokesman Dan Allen said, is "something Mrs. Clinton has to answer for."

In Washington, meanwhile, Mandy Grunwald was working on two commercials responding to the calls. One used footage of the *Cole* itself. Another went one step further, using footage of Hillary wiping away tears at the memorial service. Both ads tested very well, and Grunwald was inclined to go with the one featuring Hillary, clearly the more powerful of the two. But a consensus quickly developed within the campaign that the ad featuring the first lady could backfire, making it seem that she was exploiting the tragedy with an overly maudlin image. Wolfson was against using it. The president saw the ad and agreed. "No," he said. "It's too powerful." Still, the campaign was about a half-hour away from shipping copies to television stations when Hillary, traveling upstate, agreed that it was too strong and told her advisers, "Let's wait until we have editorial support."

That support came Tuesday, October 31, from *The New York Times* and from *Newsday.* By then, there had been enough pressure on Republicans that they had announced they were stopping the calls. Still, Lazio, now being pressed at every news conference to denounce the calls, refused to do so. The *Times* blasted him on this point, accusing him of trying "to be cute" about accepting responsibility for the calls. *Newsday* called them "reprehensible"—more than a little ironic, since it did so inside an editorial that endorsed Lazio as its candidate. Nevertheless, Grunwald was able to use quotes from both editorials, and she had an ad up within hours.

In the end, it was a radio ad that did the most to undo the damage the campaign had sustained over the *Cole* fracas. Speechwriter June Shi discovered an e-mail to the campaign from a man who lived in Queensbury, a town near Lake George, and who identified himself only as "Mike." He wrote: "Until today, I said nothing would make me vote for Hillary . . . And I said that all Rick Lazio had to do was show up and not be Hillary." But, he continued, his son had served on the U.S.S. *Stethem* and had trained some *Cole* crew members. He found it "totally unacceptable" for the Republicans and Lazio to "trade on the deaths" of American soldiers. "Okay, you've got my vote, and I hope you win," he concluded. Shi forwarded the e-mail to her colleagues, who decided it would make a great commercial, and Wolfson tracked down Mike from Queensbury. At first hesitant, Mike finally agreed to allow an actor to read his e-mail for use as a radio spot. That this anti-Lazio statement came from someone who was clearly a regular citizen, and who had originally been dead-set against Hillary, made it among the most powerful ads of the campaign. And the fact that Hillary's team was willing to acknowledge in an ad that there were people who had not always been Hillary fans showed that both the candidate and her campaign had come a long way from those early days when they were loath to admit that Hillary-haters even existed.

By now, the election was only a week away. And, by now, it was more than clear that the calls were backfiring, as Schumer had predicted. And Hillary was picking up steam on other fronts. Editorial endorsements were now in and, *Newsday* notwithstanding, Hillary was faring well. She had the *Times.* She got the Westchester Gannett papers, something of a surprise. Upstate, she corralled three of the major four: *The Buffalo News, The Rochester Democrat and Chronicle,* and *The Albany Times-Union.* Only the paper in Syracuse, a Republican stronghold, went for Lazio. And, finally, after all the wooing of Mort Zuckerman, and sitting at his table at the Inner Circle dinner, and getting whacked by his page over soft money, she got the *Daily News.* Obviously, she didn't get the *Post,* but the mere fact that the *Post* hadn't run its Lazio endorsement on its front page, as the paper had with its endorsements of George Pataki in 1994 and Al D'Amato in 1998, was something of a moral victory for the Clinton camp.

The *Cole*-call screw had one more turn. On Thursday night, Governor Pataki was appearing on New York 1. Pataki was, by now, making many appearances with Lazio, clearly putting his own reputation on the line. Mayor Giuliani, too, was doing whatever Lazio asked—he'd made a commercial for Lazio on Israel, and appeared with him several times in the city. But Pataki had committed himself to this race to an unusual degree. He and his people, sources said, made many calls toward the campaign's end—to newspaper publishers, to key rabbis—to try and move them toward Lazio. Now he wanted to appear on New York 1—he hadn't been to the station's studios since his reelection campaign in 1998—to make his best case for his candidate. For about ten minutes, he did so. Then host Andrew Kirtzman asked him point-blank if he thought the state party's telephone campaign was wrong. "Yes, it was wrong," he said. "I didn't know of it. Rick Lazio didn't know of it. The minute he heard of this and I heard of this, we said, 'Stop this.' It's not the right thing to do." But Lazio had said no such thing, for six days, since the story broke. If he had, the story's momentum would have slowed or even died; but until he acknowledged that calling the first lady of the United States a friend of terrorists was perhaps going over the line, the story kept bouncing.

And now the governor, his chief sponsor, had cut his knees out from under him. It seemed unintentional. He had said it innocently and offhandedly, so quickly that a typical viewer might not even have noticed. But it was the gaffe of the campaign, and any insider watching would have realized it immediately. Now Lazio was going to have to denounce the calls, shifting away from the position he had held for nearly a week. His argument about Hillary "cavorting" with terrorists, as he had put it at the third debate, was dead. And the governor had killed it. Ann Lewis followed Pataki on the show, and she wasted no time in seizing on the governor's denunciation of the calls. The Clinton campaign had e-mailed a press release quoting the governor before the show even ended at eight o'clock.

The race wasn't over. Hillary still had one more crisis to negotiate. But the governor had certainly cleared her path.

End Game

In Hillary's war room, whence the timely e-mail was launched, they were celebrating Pataki's blunder. In Mark Penn's office on Pennsylvania Avenue, however, the mood was considerably more vexed. Penn had been running nightly tracking polls for the previous few nights.

Hillary's lead was six, seven, eight. Suddenly, on Thursday night, it was three. Jeff Garin was doing tracking polls for the state Democratic committee. His polls, like Penn's, had shown Hillary ahead by six or seven. But he, too, on Thursday night, found her ahead by just three points. What was happening?

Penn and Grunwald were on the phone with Hillary until two in the morning. "What's happened?" she asked. "Is it the calls?" Penn and Garin had examined the cross-tabulated results of their polls, which break the findings down by sex and religion and region and demographic. It seemed that it wasn't the calls, and it wasn't even anything having to do with Israel. It was suburban women. Earlier in the week, Murphy had put up a shrewd ad featuring two actresses, looking very suburban-housewife-ish, talking in a yard. They complained of Hillary's sense of entitlement, wondering why she hadn't started her electoral career with the House of Representatives or the city council, until one said of Lazio, "Sure, he's a scrappy guy. But, hey, that's New York. I like that." Another ad unveiled that week showed Lazio and his wife helping their two daughters with their homework, an everyday ritual in which, fairly or not, few voters could imagine Hillary having taken part. Evidently, the ads were working.

Grunwald, Penn, and Hillary hung up that night having reached no firm conclusion about how to respond. The next morning, they spoke again. Hillary asked if they should "go back to Eshoo." Anna Eshoo, a congresswoman from California, had long ago taped an ad for the Clinton campaign about Lazio and the breast-cancer bill that President Clinton had signed privately earlier in the month. Eshoo and Lazio had been original cosponsors, and she had long complained that Lazio—once he saw that the House leadership wouldn't get behind the bill—backed off and sponsored a weaker version. Then, after the breast-cancer lobby went to work and lined up enough votes for the stronger bill, Lazio, Eshoo charged, put his name back on the original legislation and tried to take all the credit for it. At several points, the campaign was on the verge of releasing the Eshoo ad. Each time, someone thought the moment wasn't quite right, and the ad was pulled. Now maybe its time had come.

Ann Lewis was also on the Friday morning call. Lewis said she had just received an e-mail from a woman named Marie Kaplan, a breast cancer survivor who worked on the issue and, as fate would have it, lived in Lazio's district. Kaplan, a Hillary supporter, had told Lewis in the e-mail about her anger at Lazio's pirouette on the legislation. Hillary remembered meeting Kaplan not long before. "Well," Hillary asked, "why don't we just see if we can use Marie Kaplan in an ad?" That was around ten in the morning. Lewis called her. Within an hour, she was on a Long Island Rail Road train heading into the city. Two hours later, the ad was in the can. The next day, it was on the air. "I'm no actress," Kaplan said, referring to Murphy's suburban housewives. "I have friends with questions about Hillary. I tell them, 'Get over it! I know her.' "

Campaigns unfold in a kind of false time. They seem to last—this one especially—forever. At so many points, this event or that one had seemed crucial and decisive. But time asserted its power over events, and it revealed that those presumed crises were not, in fact, decisive. Something else always happened next. But by this day, Friday, November 3, there wasn't much "next" left. In the next ten hours, Hillary's fate would be decided.

At 10:20 that morning, Hillary appeared on a boardwalk in Long Beach, Long Island, with Schumer and Robert Kennedy, Jr. Kennedy gave a slightly overlong but brilliant speech detailing, among other things, a piece of 1996 legislation that Lazio had voted against that "would have cleaned the Long Island Sound." At 11:30, Hillary did a Q&A on the boardwalk. Lazio, that morning, had finally said—now having little choice in the matter—that the *Cole* calls were wrong. "I appreciate Governor Pataki yesterday saying the calls were wrong," she said. "It's taken my opponent a week to get around to the same conclusion."

At 12:45, she appeared at Hofstra University with Schumer and Alec Baldwin. The university having decided that students needed tickets to attend the event, it was strangely low-key and sparsely attended. The next stop was North Shore Towers, a seniors' housing complex on the Queens-Nassau County line where Schumer's parents lived, and where she spoke to a packed auditorium. It's one of New York's charming characteristics that politically like-minded people group themselves in such tightly packed clusters that, with only minimal tutoring, one can draw a precise ideological map of the city and its environs. North Shore Towers is old-line liberal Jewry, the sort of people for whom the old *Post,* back in its pre-Murdoch, Dolly Schiff days, was the delivered word. They may or may not have stuck with the *Post,* but they probably listened to Bill Mazer's radio show on WEVD-AM, the station whose call letters stood for Eugene Victor Debs. And they loved Hillary.

Next, at 4 P.M., Lefrak City, a housing project in Queens. A black and Latino audience had congregated in front of one of the massive complex's buildings, and tenants gathered on their small balconies, astonished that Hillary Clinton had come to their neighborhood. Harrison Lefrak, scion of the family that built the complex, welcomed her. As she worked the rope line, people grabbed at her, frantically reaching for their disposable cameras.

Back in Washington, Penn and Grunwald learned that the next day the Lazio campaign would begin running a Murphy ad that featured Abdurahman Alamoudi, the American Muslim Council member who had boasted about representing Hamas in the White House. Usually during campaigns, Friday was the cut-off date for new ads. But the television stations had told both campaigns that, for this race, they would accept ads through Saturday morning. Murphy had footage of Alamoudi in Washington's Lafayette Park, across the street from the White House, shouting into a microphone, "I wish they added that I am also a supporter of Hezbollah!" Grunwald learned of the gist of the ad and immediately asked: "Where's Ed Koch?"

Koch had done everything the Clinton campaign had ever asked of him. In July, when Hillary still faced intense skepticism from voters, he had cut an ad in which he told viewers that he was confident Hillary would be good for New York. Shortly thereafter, Lazio had requested, and been granted, a meeting with him. But when word of the meeting appeared in the *Post,* Koch was furious. It was supposed to be private. "Ed already just liked Hillary," says a source, "but from then on, Ed was resolved. He'd do anything for her." Grunwald called DeBlasio. DeBlasio got to Koch. Within two hours, Koch was in a studio, filming an ad that may have been the best of the campaign. "Rick," Koch said, "stop with the sleaze, already!" Koch then produced the photo of Lazio shaking hands with Yasir Arafat. "This means Lazio supports terrorism? Come on!" Koch said in his gleeful way. So there was a last-minute ad featuring a photo of an Arafat after all.

Back to Hillary: From Lefrak City, she headed into Manhattan. She was to speak at the Plaza Hotel to the annual conference of the

Anti-Defamation League. The commitment had been made long before the AMA story broke, and even though the *Cole* calls had moved the story in a direction more favorable to her, she still could not count on unanimous goodwill from this audience. As Hillary was on her way to the Plaza, Howard Wolfson was starting to get some press calls. Apparently a letter had surfaced, written on White House stationery, from Hillary to the American Muslim Alliance, thanking the group for the fund-raiser. But hadn't she said that she didn't know the AMA sponsored the event? The letter, which bore Hillary's signature, seemed to blow a huge hole in her story. I learned about it from a source as we arrived at the hotel. She had fought her way through Suha Arafat, and through the "Jew bastard" allegation, and, it seemed, through the AMA story, thanks to the Republicans' clumsy use of it. Did New York's Jewish community have the patience for still one more flap, and one more explanation?

Hillary had learned, before she gave her speech, that this final twist on the AMA story was on the way. She plowed ahead with her speech. It was a standard expression of her belief in tolerance and her dedication to Israel. Then she said, "If I may be permitted a personal reflection." In recent days in the campaign, she said, "terrorism has cropped up as a crass political tool." Lazio, she told her audience, had finally denounced the *Cole* calls that morning. But this afternoon, she learned, her opponent's campaign had prepared an ad that tried to tie her to Hamas. "It is disgraceful," she said, "it is beneath him, and it should be beneath anyone who wants to go to the United States Senate, who wants to replace Daniel Patrick Moynihan." Rarely had she spoken that directly and personally, not since the March event at the Harlem church where she accused Giuliani of dividing the city.

The speech was well received, but as soon as it ended she was in a back room with aides figuring out what to do about the letter. Her public schedule for the day was over, but aides told reporters to stick around. Forty minutes later, Hillary reappeared at the same podium from which she had delivered her speech. Howard Wolfson arrived on the scene—a rarity since he had locked down in the war room in August. Just before Hillary spoke, Wolfson distributed copies of the White House letter to reporters. Dated August 8, the brief missive was addressed to Tahir Ali and mentioned the American Muslim Alliance, thanking the group for the plaque and the event. Hillary said it was a form letter generated by the staff at the White House gift office and signed by an auto-pen machine.

Since the idea that Hillary Clinton personally writes thank-you notes for every plaque and coffee mug she receives is rather absurd, most reporters found this explanation plausible, once they fought past the image, so easy to mock, of Hillary blaming some nameless basement staff person and a machine. There lingered the question of whether, as she asserted, she had never known of the letter until that day. But in the absence of proof to the contrary, what was more important was the fact that the campaign released copies of the letter preemptively. Most reporters clearly hadn't even heard about the letter, so they didn't know what they were being handed, or why. Indeed the confusion was such that, after Hillary finished and Wolfson stuck around to take questions, the first few inquiries he received dwelled not on whether the letter proved Hillary knew that the AMA had hosted the event, but on the fact that it was written on White House stationery. "Folks, if the use of White House resources is tomorrow's story here," a bemused Wolfson said, "that's fine by me."

It was a gutsy, smart move to release the letter that day. Had she waited until it was in the next day's papers to respond, she would once again have been surrounded by cameras and faced intense questioning about her credibility. But the woman who six years before had ordered that Ken Starr be stonewalled and congressional Republicans be steamrolled decided, this time, to put potentially damaging information out there before she was asked about it. The letter was a story in the next day's papers, but nothing on the order of what it might have been if she'd tried to ignore it that Friday evening.

Essentially, the campaign ended then. She had handled a potential crisis in a way she would have been completely incapable of just a few months before. One also had the feeling that this was her last one. That night, she privately attended a service of the Congregation B'nai Jeshurun on the Upper West Side. Jerry Goldfeder, the chairman of the synagogue's social action committee and a West Side district leader (from Harold Ickes's old political club, no less), introduced her. Earlier in the year, when Goldfeder was out on upper Broadway asking passersby to sign petitions for Bill Bradley, he'd been astonished at the number of people—women in particular—who had said things like, "I'll sign for Bradley, but don't ask me to sign anything for that

Hillary!" But this night, Goldfeder says, she received an ovation "so warm and sustained that it surprised me, and I could tell by looking at her that it even surprised her." Also, that night, Mark Penn's and Jeff Garin's polls stabilized. Suburban women began to come back, and undecided voters—whom the conventional wisdom, again incorrectly, had pegged for Lazio—started breaking toward Hillary.

There were three more days of campaigning. Saturday, the president came to the city for three appearances. (The same day, Dick Morris, true to the bitter end, lobbed his final, sputtering grenade: "Hillary's bold bluff gets called on Tuesday," he thundered in the *Post*.) That night, with no press, Hillary paid a call on the Bobover rebbetzin, the wife of the rabbi of the Bobover Hasidic sect in Brooklyn's Borough Park, where she all but received an endorsement. Sunday, Hillary hit seven black churches. On Monday, she made the customary final lap around the state, starting in Buffalo, where Bills quarterback Doug Flutie endorsed her at a rally, and winding up, as New York Democrats traditionally do, at the West 43rd Street headquarters of Dennis Rivera's health and hospital workers' union. With Pat Moynihan on one arm and Chuck Schumer on the other, she left the stage of her final public event of this eternal and tumultuous campaign just before nine o'clock. But even then she wasn't finished: Upstairs, in a private room, she met with the parents of three Israeli soliders who had recently been kidnaped in Lebanon. It was a fitting coda for a candidate who left nothing to chance.

The next morning, Hillary, Bill, and Chelsea voted in Chappaqua. They spent most of the day in their adopted home, making phone calls to thank supporters and check up on turnout figures. The first exit polls came in around one o'clock. They showed Hillary up by ten, but no one quite believed them. The second round came at 2:30 and showed Hillary ahead only by four. Penn had to break the news to her that, against all their knowledge and expectations, the race seemed to be tightening. But by the time of the third and final wave, around five o'clock, the margin was back to eight. Hillary was on another line, so this time when Penn called, he spoke with Bill. "Thank God!" the president shouted into the phone.

The networks declared her the winner the moment the polls closed at nine o'clock. Some commentators, ever on the lookout for signs of gracelessness on Hillary's part, clucked about the fact that she began her victory speech before Lazio, in a hotel just a few blocks away, had finished his concession speech. No one thought to mention that Lazio didn't call her to concede until 10:40 (she was, at that exact moment, having her hair blow-dried); given the results, he could have phoned at 9:05. She ended up taking the stage just after eleven. It's the winner's prerogative to speak while the local newscasts are on. She'd waited long enough—two hours that night since the polls had closed; sixteen months to the day since she first set foot on Pat Moynihan's farm; or, counting all the time she'd spent playing political spouse instead of political candidate, twenty-five years. It was fairly, and finally, Hillary's turn.

Epilogue: "This Hillary"

IN THIS BITTEREST and most partisan political season in years, with a presidential election limping into December, and with elections all over America decided by mere handfuls of votes that were contested and recounted, it's ironic that it was Hillary Clinton, one of the nation's most polarizing figures, who ran a race that transcended virtually every line that divides New York voters.

The margin of victory was far greater than the experts expected. (For the record, one polling outfit, Quinnipiac University, called the margin exactly right.) At 55 to 43 percent, Hillary passed the ten-point threshold that these days constitutes a landslide and won, in raw numbers, by more than 800,000 votes. She carried ten upstate counties, including Onondaga, home to Syracuse, where Democrats never even bother to try, and three mostly Republican counties in the northern reaches of the state. (The equivalent would be Al Gore having won four states like Arizona, Nebraska, Wyoming, and Montana.) While Lazio hammered her in Long Island, she carried the other suburban bellwether, Westchester County, home of the women we met in Chapter 10 who concurred that if you crossed Hillary, she would "nail you and squash you." She won 73 percent of the city vote; a respectable 45 percent in the suburbs; and a remarkable 47 percent upstate, where most Democrats are happy to finish in the mid-to-high thirties. Those sixteen months in the HRC Speedwagon paid dividends.

The Jewish vote, Hillary's fire-walk, didn't end up being decisive at all. Exit polls showed she got between 53 and 57 percent of the Jewish vote, far less than the two-thirds that is the rule of thumb for Democrats in statewide races. But such was her sweep of other blocs that it made no difference. She won—barely, but she won—among Catholics. After all the melodrama, she carried the women's vote by more than twenty points. And, in the wake of those confident predictions that minorities had no motivation to come to the polls, they did so in huge numbers; Hillary got 85 percent of the Latino vote, and more than 90 percent of the black vote.

She pulled off a feat that one doubts any homegrown Democrat could have. It was not so much the size of her victory as its nature. The state's political balance of power has always depended on hostility between upstate and the city as a fundamental fact. Both parties have been guilty of exploiting the difference—Democrats playing the role of urban snobs sniffing at the rubes, Republicans playing the role of protectors of the hardworking simple folk against the urban interests commonly referred to as "them." Hillary refused to play this game. Most observers expected coming in that she would rely on the usual Democratic math and eke out a narrow and contentious victory that would carry no broader meaning or lessons for New York Democrats. But she ended up accomplishing considerably more than that with the strategy she chose of investing so much time upstate, and those who charge that her victory was only about her own greater glory are not taking into account the perspective of the future of politics in New York. By discarding the standard math, she cobbled together a coalition of urban minorities, Giuliani Democrats (with the mayor out of the race, they came back to the fold), and white upstaters that, in the post-Reagan age, we've been told it was impossible for a Democrat to achieve. It is too early to say that her victory, combined with Chuck Schumer's—he won 44 percent of the upstate vote—constitutes a new phase of a reborn New York liberalism. For that to happen, Hillary will have to keep her promises, to upstate residents in particular. But at the very least, Schumer and Hillary have changed historical assumptions about politics in New York State that have held sway since the New Deal.

From the perspective of New York's Democrats, their celebrity gambit could hardly have worked out more handsomely. Judith Hope and her fellow Democrats had taken a huge risk in going after Hillary. There would have been no shame in her losing to Rudy Giuliani. But if she'd lost to Lazio, not only would she have been humiliated, but the state party's leadership would have been excoriated by many of its own local officials and much of its rank and file. Hillary would have gone down in New York lore as "Hope's Folly," and New York liberalism's limits would have been revealed as being what everyone reflexively assumed they were—the Bronx-Westchester line.

The gamble paid off. It did so in part because her fellow Democrats ended up united behind Hillary to a degree that no one would have expected in the campaign's early, stumbling days. Pat Moynihan descended from his tower and did quite enough to be able to say that he helped elect his Democratic successor. In July, when a Republican group had put up the Lazio-Moynihan commercial, he sent his letter of protest. In the campaign's final weeks, he made an effective ad for Hillary in which he thanked New Yorkers for the honor of serving them and advised that Hillary would make "a splendid senator." He told me after the election that he had long since made peace with Hillary over the health-care mess and that he "approved of [Hillary's candidacy] completely." Chuck Schumer, facing the prospect of instantly being overshadowed by a colleague who was technically junior to him, put far more effort into Hillary's victory than anyone expected him to do. Ed Koch ended up being probably her best and most loyal weapon. Politicos often wondered why Koch, the most thoroughly "Noo Yawk" prominent political figure of the late twentieth century, had proved himself so willing to do the bidding of this Midwestern alien. Lazio had put Koch off by leaking the news of their meeting in July. And Koch, who has no shortage of ego, would be delighted to be able to claim for himself a prominent role in a historic candidacy. But besides all that, you could tell he just sort of liked her.

The gamble paid off also because she got good advice. Penn and Grunwald were right after all: Hillary overcame her negatives, as Penn put it, "just through hard work, through doing." And, from August on, the Clinton campaign was as focused and disciplined as any I've covered. The advisers, and their candidate, covered every base. One signal of its internal discipline: in the race's final months, there were no signs in the press of discord or internal strife. Not a single blind quote from a "campaign insider" or a "disgruntled Democrat" complaining about the campaign's minority strategy or failure to seize this or that issue. Almost always in a New York campaign, someone yaks to the press about being ignored, or second-guesses the strategy. But after the Clinton campaign reorganized itself, there was none of that.

Instead it was left to the Republicans to bicker and point fingers. The papers, in the days after Hillary's victory, were full of stories about the rancor within the GOP about their candidate's collapse. Lazio and Mike Murphy had been at loggerheads; against Lazio's advice, Murphy had placed a radio ad upstate accusing Hillary of supporting the "radical" Kyoto environmental accords, even though Lazio himself had expressed support for them. The candidate and his consultant had been divided over when or indeed whether to give policy addresses. Though he was polite about it, Lazio was upset after the election about the *Cole* calls linking Hillary to terrorism. State GOP chairman Bill Powers, under whose auspices the calls were made, was blamed for a lot of what went wrong. The man who had guided Al D'Amato's reelection in 1992 and George Pataki's 1994 victory over Mario Cuomo had now overseen consecutive Senate losses to Schumer and, of all unbearable people, Hillary. Questions about Governor Pataki's hold on power were raised anew with Hillary's avalanche. An incumbent politician usually knows how to smell a loser and keep his distance, but Pataki had allowed himself to get strangely close to his candidate. Two years being the proverbial lifetime in politics, it is too much to say, as some commentators did in the flush of Hillary's victory, that Pataki was now vulnerable heading into his 2002 reelection effort. All the same, this election made him the governor who fought Hillary and lost.

Lazio was left to ponder the what-if's. The papers decided, with the help of the governor's wife, who tore into Mayor Giuliani in an election-day radio interview, that he'd been given too little time, just five and a half months. On the other hand, the day he got into the race, he inherited 43 percent of the vote. Most politicians would gladly trade an abbreviated campaign schedule for an automatic 43 percent, a figure they typically spend months (and millions) trying to reach. To be sure, the late entry gave his campaign little time to work through its growing pains, but it was not his fundamental problem. His problem was that he came into the race at 43 percent, and, after five months of work and $40 million, he left it at 43 percent.

The man who had told me back in June 1999 at a Long Island waterfront restaurant that the most important thing about running for the Senate was to "be true to yourself" had been, finally, as untrue to himself as he could possibly have been. There was a poignant moment the weekend before the election, when Lazio was speaking, yet again, about Hillary and the Muslims. His words were the same; he denounced her and urged her to come clean. But he spoke with no conviction whatsoever. His face was downcast, staring at a random spot in the air about two feet in front of him. His voice was disembodied, and his wife, standing next to him, seemed on the verge of tears. It appeared as though he was thinking, even while the words were coming out of his mouth: "What has happened to me? I've been planning a Senate run for years, and here I stand, just hours away from the fateful day, talking about this thing that has nothing to do with who I am." He is scarcely an intellectual; he has always been overly concerned about the question of his future political viability; he has played hardball in his political career; but at bottom, he *is* a nice guy. With a more positive campaign that emphasized his better nature, that told people, "Don't vote for me because you hate Hillary Clinton; vote for me because I am the better candidate and will be the better senator, and I will show you why," he might have written a very different ending for himself.

And finally, back at Gracie Mansion, where his estranged wife still lived in a top-floor apartment, Rudy Giuliani went about the business he loved best—celebrating the Yankees' World Series victory over the Mets, and announcing, the week after the election, yet another new crackdown on quality-of-life offenders. As resistant as ever to popular sentiment, he refused to break the 1 A.M. curfew in Central Park for the mourners who congregate there annually on December 8 to recall John Lennon's death. He, like Schumer, had done more for his party's candidate than one might have expected, though such is the mayor's reputation for pertinacious independence that Lazio's humiliation was not transferred to him in any way. Instead, he came out of all this with his image somehow burnished. The mood in New York City toward the mayor changed dramatically after his cancer diagnosis, and after he quit the race. He became a less threatening figure; the city seemed to have decided collectively that a man who both suffered from cancer and laid the most private aspects of his life before his constituents for judgment deserved a period of sympathetic reassessment. No one, any more, called him "fascist." They would have, of course, if he'd stayed in the race. But, given his talents as a campaigner, and his ability—far beyond Lazio's—to control the tone of the argument during an election season, chances are better than sporting that they would also be calling him "Senator." Fate had other plans for him, and no doubt has still more.

And the junior senator? Impressive as her win was, it cannot be said that *tout* New York succumbed to her charms. In fact, for all the disparate voting blocs she managed to pull together, there was one constituency, oddly enough, that she did little to inspire: Sophisticated white liberals, the cultural elite, never got very excited about her. I don't mean celebrities, who backed her fulsomely, but the rank-and-file cultural elite—intellectuals, writers, activists, and so on. Most ended up voting for her, but they continued to feel conflicted about her. Right after Hillary won, journalist Marjorie Williams expressed this ambivalence in *Slate,* writing that she wondered "when I will stop being weary of everything having to do with Hillary . . . and start being mildly curious about what swath she might cut through the United States Senate."

The reason the liberal intelligentsia never warmed to her is that Hillary never aimed to win their hearts. This was, to a considerable extent, a matter of strategy. Hillary knew she could rely on the bulk of the white liberal vote, and so she didn't have to do much to woo it. In addition, she clearly did not want to come across as a liberal firecracker. If she'd tried to run a race like Democrat Jon Corzine, the Wall Street millionaire who won the New Jersey senate race and who was in favor of universal everything and damn the cost, she would have played into all the worst stereotypes of herself and lost. So there was political calculation in the way she presented herself.

But it wasn't all calculation. It was pretty clear to anyone who watched this race closely, and who was open-minded enough not to assign a malevolent motive to every move she made, that this was just Hillary being Hillary. She *is* interested in why New York's utility rates are higher than Pennsylvania's, and she wants to know what the federal government can do about it. That's where the liberalism creeps in, but it's a liberalism that is far more oriented toward fixing a problem than changing the world.

Everyone—those who love her, those who hate her—has thought of Hillary as one who believed in making vast change through bold strokes. And through much of her life, she has done just that, both with good results (her speech on women's rights in Beijing) and bad (overhauling health care). But the New York Hillary was no dreamer. She was a problem-solver—one could almost say a caseworker. It was an approach that left the intelligentsia rather cold, and the press suspicious about her real motives and passions. But the people who decide elections took her at her word.

If there's any larger lesson in her victory, it may repose in exactly that fact: she succeeded by ignoring the demands of the intelligentsia and the clamor of the media. This was an election year in which the Democratic presidential candidate responded to the shifting conventional wisdom on him by changing to earth tones, then changing back; by moving to populist themes, then moving away from them; by caving in to a censorious punditry about his little embellishments instead of standing his ground; by being so spooked by Bill Clinton's shadow that he couldn't even find a compelling way to take credit for the prosperity of the last eight years. Al Gore's campaign often seemed as though it was mostly about his efforts to reinvent himself in relation to the chatter of the experts. As a result, his reinventions always seemed inauthentic. Hillary paid no attention to the experts at all, and so managed to remake herself in a more authentic way. Of course there were moments when she did damage control ("Jew bastard") or responded to editorial pressure (soft money). But her general attitude toward the sixteen-month hurricane through which she strolled was: ignore it.

People wrote and said enough vicious things about her to have sent most candidates into isolation.* She just kept about her work. Reporters complained that she didn't answer their questions. She carried

---

* One amusing media footnote: A research assistant and I did a count of all three New York City papers' editorial assessments (not counting regular news coverage) of Hillary from January 1999 until election day. We toted up both unsigned editorials and pieces written by the papers' regular columnists that were about Hillary and assigned them to three categories—positive, negative, and neutral. The *Times* had twenty-four positive pieces, twenty-six negative, and twenty-five neutral. The *Daily News* ran nineteen positive pieces, twenty-three negative, and nine neutral. And in the *Post*, there were seven positive pieces, seventeen neutral ones—and 212 negative ones.

right on not answering if the question didn't suit her. Baby Boomer women wanted her to take Bill to task. That's your problem, not mine, was her implicit response. It was infuriating. It took a lot of gall. And in the end it was kind of brilliant. In refusing to acknowledge the elites' expectations about who she was and the media's ideas about how a candidate should accede to their demands, she made each seem sort of irrelevant, and she discarded a fair amount of her famous baggage. And if some people found this new Hillary less fascinating and controversial than they wanted her to be, that was fine by her. She didn't need to be fascinating, and she didn't want to be controversial.

And now she turns around and starts all over again, returning to the city that has always been more hostile to her than New York was and that did not witness her transformation firsthand. Whatever baggage she jettisoned in New York will be waiting for her in Washington. She will probably be the most scrutinized senator ever. She'll make mistakes. Any sign of overreach, such as her terribly ill-considered remark three days after her victory, during the heat of the controversies unfolding in Florida, that she would support abolishing the Electoral College, will be pounced upon as evidence that she's just there to grab attention. The sight of Secret Service agents walking with her as she goes to vote will send Capitol Hill staffers and the Washington media into apoplectic seizures. And of course the soap opera of her life will not end any time soon. After she won, with all political eyes fixed on Florida, I got only one call from a national television show asking for my comments about her victory. But the show wasn't interested in her formidable upstate performance or what sort of senator she might be. It was preparing a piece on the fact that Hillary seemed to dance away from Bill's embrace on stage the night she won. (I didn't do the show.)

Trent Lott signaled the sort of attitude she will find in Washington the day after her victory. If "this Hillary," as he called her, comes to the Senate thinking she will be some sort of star ("and maybe lightning will strike and she won't," he interjected), Lott wanted it known that she will be only one of one hundred and will be reminded of the fact. The comment was vile by any measure, but it didn't even inspire much protest. That was partly because people had turned their attention to Palm Beach County. Still, he got away with it because people can talk like that about Hillary. She knows this. In New York, she dealt with people like Lott by pretending their hostility didn't exist. In Washington, I suspect, she will deal with the likes of him by sticking to her work, and it wouldn't be too surprising, two or three years from now, in a magazine article proclaiming her Washington rehabilitation, if Lott is quoted as saying something like, "You know, we have our differences, but I guess she's not all that bad."

That scenario hinges on whether the transformation will hold. If it does, she will again defy people's expectations. And if it doesn't—if being in Washington sucks her back into the old habits—her legislative career could be a disaster. I would like to be able to say with confidence that the former is the case—she is, without even trying, one of the most intelligent people in the Senate, and if she can wear down others' resistance to her as she did in New York, she has the potential to become, like Teddy Kennedy, a great legislator. But there have already been small signs to the contrary. The day after she won, she held a press conference at which she was relaxed, expansive—even, for her, playful—asking reporters to join in a round of applause for her beleaguered press officers. Except for one moment—when she was asked if she was now entertaining thoughts about the presidency. "No," she said. "I'm going to serve my six years as the junior senator from New York."

She said the right words, but she did not elaborate, as she had in response to the day's other questions, and her tone changed from casual to serious. She tightened up visibly; suddenly I was seeing not the Hillary who had spoken openly and forcefully in the campaign's final weeks, but the Hillary of the previous February, in that hotel mezzanine in Rochester, when she couldn't bring herself to elaborate on her religious beliefs in response to Mayor Giuliani's attack letter. It may simply have been that she resented being asked the question yet again. Whatever the reason, it made her very uncomfortable.

The $8 million book deal with Simon & Schuster that she announced in mid-December also opened the door to questions about what the campaign had, and had not, taught Hillary. Some of the criticism of the deal was unfair and showed that, about Hillary, people feel free to invent things: she apparently did not ask to be paid an extravagant percentage up front, as initial reports had it, and she settled on a $2 million first installment, which is consistent with the way large advances are normally paid out. But striking the deal before she even took office showed a cavalier disregard for how this might look to her new constituents, to say nothing of her new colleagues, the vast majority of whom couldn't get $8,000 for a book, let alone $8 million. And that she did not clear the deal with the Senate ethics panel before she consummated it calls to mind the old Washington Hillary, who stone-walled Ken Starr and who was suspicious of those who questioned her. If she cannot see the difference between an in-house panel that basi-cally exists to say yes and the independent counsel's office, her Wash-ington tenure will not be an easy one.

We haven't heard the last of the book deal, and the talking heads will undoubtedly devote an inordinate amount of time to the topic of her presidential aspirations. It's understandable; it's a made-for-punditry topic, in that it depends on conjecture and no particular expertise, and she can probably do nothing to put a stop to it even if she wants to. But if this campaign should have taught people anything about her, it's that they should watch what she actually does instead of making assumptions about what they think she'll do. What she did, if one watched closely, was often very different from those assumptions, and usually more interesting. Hillary in the Senate, trying to establish her *bona fides,* not to mention cordial relations with fifty or so men who wanted to throw her husband—and her—out of town, should provide enough drama on its own.

Sources

THIS BOOK is based primarily on four categories of research. The first and most important was my close observation of the candidate herself. Over the course of sixteen months, I must have seen her give more than one hundred speeches, and many press conferences. When I was present, I have tried to make it clear by the writing that I was there and observed what she said firsthand. When I was not present, I have tried to be honest about that, too, by relying on other press accounts or my subsequent conversations with those who were present, crediting them whenever possible.

Second, I did extensive interviews with most of the major players in Hillary's campaign and with leading New York Democrats associated with the campaign. Some I spoke to two or three times. Others I spoke with dozens of times over the course of the campaign. The verb "says," or the occasional phrase such as "recalled to me later," indicates that the quote was given to me directly by the person quoted.

Third, I had literally hundreds of conversations over the sixteen-month period of Hillary's candidacy with the many sources I have developed over my years of covering politics in New York—Democratic and Republican operatives, various elected officials, political consultants, activists, public-relations people, and other insiders. While I was writing this book, I was also covering the race for *New York* magazine—

from July 1999 to November 2000, I wrote exactly one column on a topic other than Hillary and this race. Every week during that time, I spoke daily with these sources about the many different aspects of the race. The vast majority of them did not end up being quoted in the book, but the narrative often reflects their insights.

And fourth, I relied on other press reports. The first thing I did every morning during this election was to race to a Web site, the Empire Page (www.empirepage.com), that brought the coverage of this campaign in all the state's newspapers (and some other media outlets) under one convenient roof. I collected all the pieces I considered especially relevant. In the text, I've done my best to give credit to other reporters either when I relied heavily on their work or when they broke major stories. Just as "says" indicates the person spoke to me directly, "said" or "told reporters" indicates that I'm quoting other published material. I have also included the dates of the articles I consider especially important, so that curious readers can look them up if they desire.

Acknowledgments

THIS BOOK is my responsibility, but it was not my idea. For that I thank Paul Golob, the editor at the Free Press who called me in the spring of 1999 and suggested to me that, if Hillary did in fact run, he'd like me to write a book about the race. He left the Free Press before we had much of a chance to work together on the text, but this project would never have begun without him.

The editor I *did* work with, Rachel Klayman, was amazing. Sixteen times, I turned in a chapter thinking, "Hey, that's pretty good." And, sixteen times, I received back from Rachel heavily marked-up manuscripts that showed me just how much better it could be. Our lengthy considerations of the big questions—whether I was really conveying the ideas I wanted to get across in the most effective way—and the small ones could sometimes be draining, I'm sure for her as well as for me. But each conversation was well worth the time, and I can't thank her enough. Brian Selfon at the Free Press made many valuable catches, and at one point had me stopping to ponder, for a good ten minutes, whether "1970s rock monsters" was the very best way to refer to Z.Z. Top. Carol de Onís and Camilla Hewitt also gave incredibly minute attention to the manuscript.

I benefited greatly from one other keen set of eyes. Sarah Kerr, my wife, is a wonderful writer, and she had plenty of her own work to do while I was writing this book. But she always took time out to read what I'd produced, and her suggestions always, always made it stronger—to say nothing of the time out she took to provide a much more profound support and comfort.

My sister, Susan Tomasky, was there whenever I asked to provide her insights—as a woman who, like Hillary, beat down the doors of male preserves in the 1970s, as an experienced Washington hand, and as a generally wise human being.

At *New York* magazine, Caroline Miller, Jeremy Gerard, John Homans, and Sarah Jewler all encouraged me and were patient with me as I tried my best to devote time both to my magazine columns and this book. I thank them all. Boris Kaschka and Mary Kate Frank provided valuable research assistance.

My agent, Chris Calhoun, of Sterling Lord Literistic, poured himself into this project with an extraordinary enthusiasm and élan. The many people in the New York literary world who know Chris know that he leaves a little cheer wherever he goes. He sprinkled some over this project, talking me through difficult stretches, and he, too, contributed numerous ideas that helped shape my thinking, and the book.

There's something about spending days on a bus with people that lets you see their unvarnished selves (as they, of course, see yours). My friendships with a number of colleagues in the press grew deeper as a result of this bizarre experience. Many of them shared their insights and anecdotes with me. I am grateful to them, and I have a feeling that, after we've gone our various ways and we run into one another twenty years from now, I know what the first topic of conversation will be.

Finally, a word about one man who had nothing to do with the book at all. Just before Thanksgiving, as I was rushing toward completion, word came that Lars-Erik Nelson, the *Daily News* columnist and *New York Review of Books* contributor, had died at age fifty-nine. Lars knew I was working on the book, and he had offered his encouragement and support. I'm very sorry he's not here to read it, but the impact of his loss on me and on a legion of journalists and readers—virtually every serious person I know held him in singular esteem—is far, far greater than that. He was a voice of moral clarity, and a beacon for all those fortunate enough to have known or simply read him.

Index

About the Author

MICHAEL TOMASKY is a columnist at *New York* magazine, where he has written "The City Politic" column since 1995. His work has appeared in many publications, including *The New York Times Book Review, The Washington Post, Harper's, The Nation, The Village Voice, Dissent, Lingua Franca, George,* and *GQ.* He is the author of *Left for Dead,* a study of the intellectual collapse of the American Left. Born and raised in Morgantown, West Virginia, he lives with his wife in Brooklyn.